北语对外汉语精版教材

初级汉语课本

CHINESE FOR BEGINNERS

听力练习

LISTENING

主　编　鲁健骥

编　写　李世之　李继禹

北京语言大学出版社
BEIJING LANGUAGE AND CULTURE
UNIVERSITY PRESS

图书在版编目（CIP）数据

初级汉语课本·听力练习/鲁健骥主编；李世之，李继禹编．
－北京：北京语言大学出版社，2011 重印
北语对外汉语精版教材
ISBN 978-7-5619-1138-9

Ⅰ.初…
Ⅱ.①鲁…　②李…　③李…
Ⅲ.汉语－听说教学－对外汉语教学－教学参考资料
Ⅳ.H195.4

中国版本图书馆 CIP 数据核字（2002）第 098072 号

书　　　名：初级汉语课本·听力练习
责任印制：汪学发

出版发行：**北京语言大学出版社**
社　　　址：北京市海淀区学院路 15 号　　邮政编码：100083
网　　　址：www.blcup.com
电　　　话：发行部　82303650/3591/3651
　　　　　　编辑部　82303647
　　　　　　读者服务部　82303653/3908
　　　　　　网上订购电话　82303668
　　　　　　客户服务信箱　service@blcup.net
印　　　刷：北京画中画印刷有限公司
经　　　销：全国新华书店

版　　　次：2003 年 3 月第 1 版　2011 年 3 月第 5 次印刷
开　　　本：787 毫米 × 1092 毫米 1/16 印张：19.75
字　　　数：230 千字　印数：13001－14000 册
书　　　号：ISBN 978－7－5619－1138－9/H·02131
定　　　价：40.00 元

凡有印装质量问题，本社负责调换。电话：82303590

说　　明

　　1．本教材是为配合《初级汉语课本》，对初学汉语的人进行听力训练而编写的。第一部分是练习，供学生听录音做笔头练习时使用，口头练习部分均未编入。第二部分是录音文本，可作为教师用书，一些练习的参考答案也在其中。

　　2．本教材每课大致包括发音练习、语调练习、词重音练习、句重音练习、听后选择正确答案和听后回答问题等几种练习形式。有些练习难度较大，教师可根据学生的情况加以取舍。

　　3．练习中"听写"一项，目的是对学生进行辨音和辨调的训练，并为今后对学生进行汉语记录能力的培养打下基础。

编　者

Compilers' Note

1. This book is a companion to *Chinese for Beginners* to train beginners of Chinese in listening comprehension. It consists of two parts: Part I is exercises which include the written work to be done by the learner while listening but not the oral work. Part II is the Tapescript that can be used as an instructor's guide and, in part, as the key to exercises.

2. Each lesson is composed of the following sections: pronunciation drills, intonation drills, word stress drills, sentence stress drills, multiple choice exercises and question and answer exercises. Some items are comparatively difficult and are left to the instructor to choose whatever he or she thinks suitable for his/her students.

3. The dictation in the exercises aims at training the learner to discriminate confusing sounds and tones and in the later part, at getting the learner competent in taking notes in class.

Compillers

目　　录
CONTENTS

练　习　Exercises

第一课　Lesson 1

一、听韵母。第一遍听，第二遍、第三遍跟读。

Listen to the finals. Each final will be read three times. The first time is for you to listen and the second and third times are for you to follow.

二、听声母。第一遍听，第二遍、第三遍跟读。

Listen to the initials. Each initial will be read three times. The first time is for you to listen and the second and third times are for you to follow.

三、音节。第一遍听，第二遍、第三遍跟读。

Listen to the syllables. Each syllable will be read three times. The first time is for you to listen and the second and third times are for you to follow.

四、听声调。第一遍听，第二遍、第三遍跟读。

Listen to the tonal syllables. Each tonal syllable will be read three times. The first time is for you to listen and the second and third times are for you to follow.

五、听后画出声母　**Circle out the initials in the syllables you hear:**

(1)	na	la	(2)	san	lan
	nao	lao		sa	la
	nu	lu		sai	lai
(3)	dan	tan	(4)	gao	kao
	dai	tai		gu	ku
	dian	tian		gua	kua

六、听后画出韵母　**Circle out the finals in the syllables you hear:**

(1) b { a / ao / u }

(2) t { ao / u / i }

(3) h { a / an / ao }

(4)   l $\begin{cases} \text{iu} \\ \text{in} \\ \text{i} \end{cases}$ (5)   y $\begin{cases} \text{a} \\ \text{ao} \\ \text{o} \end{cases}$ (6)   w $\begin{cases} \text{a} \\ \text{u} \\ \text{o} \end{cases}$

七、画出你听到的音节　Underline the syllables you hear:

(1)	tā	tǎ		(2)	dá	dà
	bái	bǎi			bù	bú
	hú	hǔ			huā	huà
	tāo	táo			gǎo	gào
	liú	liǔ			lù	lú
	hǎi	hái			wāi	wài
	sān	sǎn			ér	èr

八、听后标出调号　Give the tone-marks:

(1) la   (2) nu   (3) da   (4) san

(5) yao   (6) bai   (7) hua   (8) lian

(9) liu   (10) bao   (11) ti   (12) yi

九、练习对话　Act the following dialogues.

(1) 情景:两个老朋友又见面了。

Situation: Two old friends meet each other again.

(2) 情景:在路上学生见到了老师。

Situation: A student meets his teacher on the way.

(3) 情景:两个人第一次认识。

Situation: Two people meet each other for the first time.

第二课　Lesson 2

一、听韵母。第一遍听,第二遍、第三遍跟读。

Listen to the finals. Each final will be read three times. The first time is for you to listen and the second and third times are for you to follow.

二、听声母。第一遍听,第二遍、第三遍跟读。

Listen to the initials. Each initial will be read three times. The first time is for you to listen and the second and third times are for you to follow.

三、听音节。第一遍听,第二遍、第三遍跟读。

Listen to the syllables. Each syllable will be read three times. The first time is for you to listen and the second and third times are for you to follow.

四、听声调。第一遍听,第二遍、第三遍跟读。

Listen to the tonal syllables or tones of words. Each tonal syllable or word will be read three times. The first time is for you to listen and the second and third times are for you to follow.

五、听后画出声母　Circle out the initials in the syllables you hear:

(1)			(2)		
da	ta		gu	ku	hu
dai	tai		gen	ken	hen
di	ti		gao	kao	hao
dao	tao		gua	kua	hua
dan	tan		gan	kan	han

六、听后画出韵母　Circle out the finals in the syllables you hear:

(1)		(2)	
ben	ban	lin	lian
sen	san	diu	dian
men	man	niu	nian
nen	nan	miu	mian
wen	wan		

七、听后把每个音节的声韵母连在一起：

Link each initial to a proper final as you hear in the recording:

h	ao
l	ua
w	ai
d	in
y	an
m	u
t	en
g	e

八、听后标出调号　**Give the tone-marks:**

（1）mu　men　ge　bei　wan　dai　tian　ke

（2）bayi　maoyi　guke　yanse　ditu

（3）meimei　baba　tamen　wode　yeye

九、练习对话　**Act the following dialogues.**

（1）情景：孩子给爸爸打电话。

Situation：A child telephones his father.

（2）情景：孩子给妈妈打电话。

Situation：A child telephones his mother.

（3）情景：上课了，老师走进教室，师生互相问候。

Situation：The teacher enters the classroom when the bell is ringing. He and his students exchange greetings.

第三课　Lesson 3

一、听韵母。第一遍听，第二遍、第三遍跟读。

Listen to the finals. Each final will be read three times. The first time is for you to listen and the second and third times are for you to follow.

二、听声母。第一遍听，第二遍、第三遍跟读。

Listen to the initials. Each initial will be read three times. The first time is for you to listen and the second and third times are for you to follow.

三、听音节。第一遍听，第二遍、第三遍跟读。

Listen to the syllables. Each syllable will be read three times. The first time is for you to listen and the second and third times are for you to follow.

四、听声调。第一遍听，第二遍、第三遍跟读。

Listen to the tonal syllables or tones of words. Each tonal syllable or word will be read three times. The first time is for you to listen and the second and third times are for you to follow.

五、辨韵母。画出你听到的音节：

Discriminate confusing finals. Underline the syllables you hear:

（1） gai　gei　　　　　　　（2） ben　beng
　　　shai　shei　　　　　　　　pen　peng
　　　pai　pei　　　　　　　　　fen　feng
　　　mai　mei　　　　　　　　　shen　sheng
　　　nai　nei　　　　　　　　　ren　reng

（3） man　men　　　　　　　（4） gao　gou　gong
　　　nan　nen　　　　　　　　　dao　dou　dong
　　　shan　shen　　　　　　　　rao　rou　rong
　　　ran　ren　　　　　　　　　yao　you　yong
　　　han　hen　　　　　　　　　lao　lou　long

六、辨声母。画出你听到的音节：

Discriminate confusing initials．Underline the syllables you hear：

beng	peng		shan	san
tong	dong		long	rong
gu	ku		fu	mu

七、听后标出调号　**Give the tone-marks：**

（1）gongtong　　（2）gaige　　（3）heshi　　（4）baogui

（5）dahai　　（6）meili　　（7）shidai　　（8）putao

（9）neirong　　（10）pengpai　　（11）shoutao　　（12）gudai

八、听后填空　**Listen to the dialogues and fill in the blanks：**

（1）情景：A 向朋友介绍他的弟弟。

Situation：A introduces his brother to his friend．

填空：他弟弟是＿＿＿＿＿＿。

（2）情景：A 在 B 家看 B 的全家福照片。

Situation：A is at B's, looking at a picture of B's family．

填空：他妈妈是＿＿＿＿＿，妹妹是＿＿＿＿＿，哥哥是＿＿＿＿＿。

第四课　Lesson 4

一、听韵母。第一遍听,第二遍、第三遍跟读。

Listen to the finals. Each final will be read three times. The first time is for you to listen and the second and third times are for you to follow.

二、听声母。第一遍听,第二遍、第三遍跟读。

Listen to the initials. Each initial will be read three times. The first time is for you to listen and the second and third times are for you to follow.

三、听音节。第一遍听,第二遍、第三遍跟读。

Listen to the syllables. Each syllable will be read three times. The first time is for you to listen and the second and third times are for you to follow.

四、听声调。第一遍听,第二遍、第三遍跟读。

Listen to the tonal syllables or tones of words. Each tonal syllable or word will be read three times. The first time is for you to listen and the second and third times are for you to follow.

五、辨声母。画出你听到的音节:

Discriminate confusing initials. Under line the syllables you hear:

（1）

zhi	chi		zhen	chen
zhu	shu		shui	zhui
zhai	chai		zhou	shou
shang	chang		shua	zhua

（2）

gua	kua		guan	kuan
huo	guo		huo	kuo
gai	hai		gong	kong
kang	gang		gou	hou

六、辨韵母。画出你听到的音节：

Discriminate confusing finals. Underline the syllables you hear:

rou ruo rong

zhao zhuo zhong

shan shang sheng

chou chong chao

七、听后标出调号 **Give the tone-marks:**

（1）senlin （2）zhenli （3）shenru （4）songshu

（5）huanteng （6）shichang （7）fangfa （8）hongse

（9）yanchu （10）beifeng （11）duanlian （12）gongchang

八、听后填"-r" **Indicate the retroflexed syllable in each:**

（1）Yí dà dá.

（2）Zhēn méi fǎ.

（3）Tā shàng nǎ?

（4）Wǒ shàng nà.

（5）Zhè ge wǎn hěn hǎo.

九、听后选择正确答案：

Listen to the dialogues and circle the correct answers to the questions:

（1）情景:学生们在楼前遇见了张老师。

  Situation：The students meet their teacher in front of a building.

  答案:a b c

（2）情景:两个老人在路上相遇。

  Situation：Two old men meet on the way.

  答案:a b

十、听录音,口头回答问题 **Answer the following questions.**

第五课　Lesson 5

一、听韵母。第一遍听，第二遍、第三遍跟读。

Listen to the finals. Each final will be read three times. The first time is for you to listen and the second and third times are for you to follow.

二、听声母。第一遍听，第二遍、第三遍跟读。

Listen to the initials. Each initial will be read three times. The first time is for you to listen and the second and third times are for you to follow.

三、听音节。第一遍听，第二遍、第三遍跟读。

Listen to the syllables. Each syllable will be read three times. The first time is for you to listen and the second and third times are for you to follow.

四、听声调。第一遍听，第二遍、第三遍跟读。

Listen to the tonal syllables or tones of words. Each tonal syllable or word will be read three times. The first time is for you to listen and the second and third times are for you to follow.

五、听后把每个音节的声韵母连在一起：

Link each initial to a proper final as you hear in the recording:

zh	ai
ch	an
sh	ao
s	en
r	ei
h	ong
g	uo
f	ou

六、听后填上声母　**Fill in the blanks with the initials you hear:**

_____ āshi　　　zhī _____ í　　　_____ ēnshí　　　_____ òngyào

____ āisàn   ____ óngféng   ____ ēnchéng   péi ____ èn

七、听后填上韵母　**Fill in the blanks with the finals you hear**:

zh ____ zh ____   sh ____ sh ____   f ____ w ____

ch ____ l ____   ch ____ g ____   w ____ sh ____

zh ____ ch ____   sh ____ sh ____

八、听后标出调号　**Give the tone-marks**:

tongzhi   suishi   dianshi   youlan

zhuanwanr   huabao   huochai   haoshi

九、听后选择正确答案:

Listen to the dialogues and circle the correct answers to the questions:

（1）情景:A 和 B 在食堂买饭。

Situation：A and B are buying their dinner at the dining-hall.

答案:a　　　b

（2）情景:李大年和刘天华在路上相遇。

Situation：Li Danian and Liu Tianhua meet on the way.

答案:a　　　b　　　c

（3）情景:A 向 B 询问银行在哪儿。

Situation：A asks B where the bank is.

答案:a　　　b

十、听录音,口头回答问题　**Answer the following question**.

<h1 style="text-align:center">第六课　Lesson 6</h1>

一、听韵母。第一遍听,第二遍、第三遍跟读。

Listen to the finals. Each final will be read three times. The first time is for you to listen and the second and third times are for you to follow.

二、听声母。第一遍听,第二遍、第三遍跟读。

Listen to the initials. Each initial will be read three times. The first time is for you to listen and the second and third times are for you to follow.

三、听音节。第一遍听,第二遍、第三遍跟读。

Listen to the syllables. Each syllable will be read three times. The first time is for you to listen and the second and third times are for you to follow.

四、听声调。第一遍听,第二遍、第三遍跟读。

Listen to the tonal syllables or tones of words. Each tonal syllable or word will be read three times. The first time is for you to listen and the second and third times are for you to follow.

五、画出你听到的音节　**Underline one from each pair of syllables you hear:**

(1) ji	qi	jian	qian	(2) bin	bing	nin	ning
jie	qie	jin	qin	pin	ping	lin	ling
jiu	qiu	jing	qing	min	ming	xin	xing

六、听后填上声母　**Fill in the blanks with the initials you hear:**

_____ ītǐ　　　_____ ìchē　　　_____ iūtiān　　　_____ iēshòu

_____ iántú　　_____ iànmiàn　　_____ ǐnjí　　　_____ ínglǎng

七、听后填上韵母　**Fill in the blanks with the finals you hear:**

x _____ qī　　　j _____ bù　　　p _____ pāng　　　y _____ shè

j ＿＿ shén　　niánq ＿＿　　　rèl ＿＿　　　　p ＿＿ kāi

八、学说绕口令　Practice the tongue twister.

九、听后选择正确答案：

Listen to the dialogues and circle the correct answers to the questions:

（1）情景：A 在教室的窗台上看到一本画报，不知道是谁的。

Situation: A sees a pictorial on the windowsill of the classroom and he doesn't know whose it is.

答案：a　　　b

（2）情景：阿里在路上遇见了李大年和他的姐姐。

Situation: Ali meets Li Danian and his sister on the way.

答案：a　　　b　　　c

十、听录音，口头回答问题　Answer the following questions.

第七课　Lesson 7

一、听韵母。第一遍听,第二遍、第三遍跟读。

Listen to the finals. Each final will be read three times. The first time is for you to listen and the second and third times are for you to follow.

二、听声母。第一遍听,第二遍、第三遍跟读。

Listen to the initials. Each initial will be read three times. The first time is for you to listen and the second and third times are for you to follow.

三、听音节。第一遍听,第二遍、第三遍跟读。

Listen to the syllables. Each syllable will be read three times. The first time is for you to listen and the second and third times are for you to follow.

四、听声调。第一遍听,第二遍、第三遍跟读。

Listen to the tonal syllables or tones of words. Each tonal syllable or word will be read three times. The first time is for you to listen and the second and third times are for you to follow.

五、听后填上声母　**Fill in the blanks with the initials you hear:**

_____ i	_____ ie	_____ iang	_____ ai
_____ iu	_____ ou	_____ ian	_____ u

六、画出你听到的音节　**Underline one from each pair of syllables you hear:**

（1）
jiang	zhang
qian	jian
xiu	jiu
jie	qie
gong	kong
shan	xian

（2）
jian	jiang
xian	xiang
zhan	zhang
chan	chang
xie	xiu
shan	shang

七、听后标出调号　**Give the tone-marks：**

　　（1）jiandan　（2）wushi　（3）nuli　（4）nuanhuo

　　（5）erduo　（6）Faguo　（7）yixie　（8）kaishui

八、听后选择正确答案：

Listen to the dialogues and circle the correct answers to the questions：

（1）情景:阿里想借摩托车用。

　　Situation：Ali wants to borrow a motorbike.

　　生词:用　　yòng　use

　　答案:a　　b　　c

（2）情景:A 想借日文画报看。

　　Situation：A wants to borrow a Japanese pictorial.

　　答案:a　　b　　c

九、听录音,口头回答问题　**Answer the following questions.**

第八课　Lesson 8

一、听韵母。第一遍听，第二遍、第三遍跟读。

Listen to the finals. Each final will be read three times. The first time is for you to listen and the second and third times are for you to follow.

二、听声母。第一遍听，第二遍、第三遍跟读。

Listen to the initials. Each initial will be read three times. The first time is for you to listen and the second and third times are for you to follow.

三、听音节。第一遍听，第二遍、第三遍跟读。

Listen to the syllables. Each syllable will be read three times. The first time is for you to listen and the second and third times are for you to follow.

四、听声调。第一遍听，第二遍、第三遍跟读。

Listen to the tonal syllables or tones of words. Each tonal syllable or word will be read three times. The first time is for you to listen and the second and third times are for you to follow.

五、听后填上声母　**Fill in the blanks with the initials you hear：**

(1) ＿＿ì＿＿ào　　(2) ＿＿ēng＿＿àn　(3) ＿＿áng＿＿u

(4) ＿＿īn＿＿àng　(5) ＿＿āo＿＿ǎng　(6) ＿＿ù＿＿ǐ

(7) ＿＿ǒng＿＿ì　(8) ＿＿ǎo＿＿āo

六、画出你听到的音节　**Underline one from each group of syllables you hear：**

(1)　zhuan　　　zhuang　　　zhong

　　 chuan　　　chuang　　　chong

　　 shuan　　　shuang

(2)　guan　　　guang　　　gong

　　 kuan　　　kuang　　　kong

　　 huan　　　huang　　　hong

七、听后画出第四声和第二声连续的词语(在序号后画√):

Mark out the words of "4th + 2nd" tone sequence with a (√):

（1）　　　　（2）　　　　（3）　　　　（4）　　　　（5）

（6）　　　　（7）　　　　（8）　　　　（9）　　　　（10）

八、听后回答问题　**Listen to the dialogues and answer the questions:**

（1）情景：一个学生和宿舍的管理人员谈话。

Situation：A student is talking with the dormitory janitor.

生词：明天　　míngtiān　　tomorrow

（2）情景：A 想借阿里的辞典。

Situation：A wants to borrow a dictionary from Ali.

生词：在　　zài　　in, on, at

（3）情景：阿里在商店买练习本。

Situation：Ali is buying some exercise books in a shop.

九、听录音,我说一个名词,请你在前边加上数词"一"和量词。

Add the numeral 一 and a proper measure word to each of the following nouns.

第九课　Lesson 9

一、听韵母。第一遍听,第二遍、第三遍跟读。

Listen to the finals. Each final will be read three times. The first time is for you to listen and the second and third times are for you to follow.

二、听声母。第一遍听,第二遍、第三遍跟读。

Listen to the initials. Each initial will be read three times. The first time is for you to listen and the second and third times are for you to follow.

三、听音节。第一遍听,第二遍、第三遍跟读。

Listen to the syllables. Each syllable will be read three times. The first time is for you to listen and the second and third times are for you to follow.

四、听声调。第一遍听,第二遍、第三遍跟读。

Listen to the tones of the following words. Each word will be read three times. The first time is for you to listen and the second and third times are for you to follow.

五、听后填上声母　**Fill in the blanks with the initials you hear:**

　　___´ ū ___ ā　　___ uò ___ ǔ　　___ uē ___ iàn ___ ǔ ___ óu

　　___ ī ___ í　　___ uò ___ è　　___ uó ___ uè ___ ù ___ ǐ

　　___ éng ___ īng ___ ué ___ īn

六、听后填上韵母　**Fill in the blanks with the finals you hear:**

　　j ___ dìng　　q ___ bié　　x ___ zé　　shàngx ___

　　n ___ 'ér　　j ___ shì　　x ___ chuán　　m ___ máng

七、画出你听到的词语　**Underline one from each pair of words you hear:**

　　⌜ qūtǐ　　⌜ xuéyuàn　　⌜ lüèduó　　⌜ liú xuè
　　⌞ jùtǐ　　⌞ juéyuán　　⌞ nüèdài　　⌞ liù juàn

$$\left\{\begin{array}{l}\text{xuǎnzé}\\ \text{juézé}\end{array}\right.\quad \left\{\begin{array}{l}\text{yīyuàn}\\ \text{yǔyán}\end{array}\right.\quad \left\{\begin{array}{l}\text{cǎisè}\\ \text{cāicè}\end{array}\right.\quad \left\{\begin{array}{l}\text{xuānbù}\\ \text{shuānzhù}\end{array}\right.$$

八、听后选择正确答案：

Listen to the dialogues and circle the correct answers to the questions：

（1）情景：三个人在楼前相遇,谈去看什么。

Situation：Three people meet in front of a building, talking about what to see.

答案:a   b   c

（2）情景：阿里和朋友谈看什么节目。

Situation：Ali and his friend are talking about what program they are going to watch.

答案：a   b   c

（3）情景：一个人询问北京音乐厅在哪儿。

Situation：A man is asking where the Beijing Concert Hall is.

答案:a   b

九、听录音,口头回答问题 Answer the following questions.

第十课　Lesson 10

一、听韵母。第一遍听，第二遍、第三遍跟读。

Listen to the finals. Each final will be read three times. The first time is for you to listen and the second and third times are for you to follow.

二、听音节。第一遍听，第二遍、第三遍跟读。

Listen to the syllables. Each syllable will be read three times. The first time is for you to listen and the second and third times are for you to follow.

三、听声调。第一遍听，第二遍、第三遍跟读。

Listen to the tones of the following words. Each word will be read three times. The first time is for you to listen and the second and third times are for you to follow.

四、学说绕口令　**Practice the tongue twister.**

五、画出你听到的词语　**Underline one from each pair of words you hear:**

jīchǎng	jūnqū	jūnrén	jīnyú
jùchǎng	juānqū	qióngrén	jīngyú
qūxiàn	chūnfēng	chéngqīng	píqiú
qīxiàn	chōngfēng	céngjīng	píjiǔ
shìjuàn	yīngxióng		
shìjiàn	yīngyǒng		

六、画出你听到的词语　**Underline one from each pair of words you hear:**

十一	七号楼	十号楼	311
十七	一号楼	四号楼	331
5030	6060		
5300	6006		

七、听后选择正确答案:

Listen to the dialogues and circle the correct answers to the questions:

（1）情景:学生和老师互问地址。

　　　Situation：A student and his teacher ask about each other's addresses.

　　　生词:晚上　　wǎnshang　　evening

　　　答案:a　　　b　　　c

（2）情景:贾红春接到了李大年的电话。

　　　Situation：Jia Hongchun is talking with Li Danian on the phone.

　　　生词:很　　hěn　　very

　　　答案:a　　　b　　　c

八、听录音,口头回答问题　　**Answer the following questions.**

第十一课　Lesson 11

一、听音节。第一遍听，第二遍跟读。

Listen to the syllables. Each syllable will be read twice. The first time is for you to listen and the second time is for you to follow.

二、听声调。第一遍听，第二跟读。

Listen to the tones of the words. Each word will be read twice. The first time is for you to listen and the second time is for you to follow.

三、画出你听到的音节　**Underline one from each pair of syllables you hear:**

（1）zhuai　zhuan　　　　　（2）mao　miao

　　　chuai　chuan　　　　　　　dao　diao. ..

　　　shuai　shuan　　　　　　　nao　niao

　　　guai　guan　　　　　　　　lao　liao

　　　kuai　kuan　　　　　　　　tao　tiao

　　　huai　huan　　　　　　　　pao　piao

四、听后填上声母　**Fill in the blanks with the initials you hear:**

（1）＿＿ uài ＿＿ i　　（2）＿＿ í ＿＿ uài　　（3）＿＿ uī ＿＿ è

（4）＿＿ uì ＿＿ i　　（5）＿＿ òng ＿＿ uai　　（6）＿＿ uāi ＿＿ a

（7）＿＿ uái ＿＿ iàn　　（8）＿＿ uī ＿＿ án　　（9）＿＿ uài ＿＿ ǐng

（10）＿＿ uǎi ＿＿ è　　（11）＿＿ uā ＿＿ ēng　（12）＿＿ uǎ ＿＿ ái

五、听后标出调号　**Give the tone-marks:**

（1）Chi xican zuo zuoce.

　　　Chi zhongcan zuo youce.

　　　Ta zuo zuoce chi xican.

　　　Wo chi zhongcan zuo youce.

（2）Ta you shi zhang chuang.

Ni you shi zhang chuang.

Women dajia quan you shi zhang chuang.

六、听后填空　Listen to the statements and the dialogue and fill in the blanks：

（1）这是________________________电影。

（2）他听________________________音乐。

（3）这是________________________银行。

（4）他看________________________画报。

七、听后选择正确答案：

Listen to the dialogues and circle the correct answers to the questions：

（1）情景：三个人在路上相遇。

　　　Situation：Three people meet on the way．

　　　生词：和　hé　and

　　　① a　　　b　　　c

　　　② a　　　b

（2）情景：A 在路上问书店在哪儿。

　　　Situation：A asks where the bookshop is on his way．

　　　① a　　　b

　　　② a　　　b

八、听后回答问题　Listen to the dialogue and answer the questions：

情景：一个学生去张老师家。

Situation：A student is at the doorway of his teacher's home．

（1）

（2）

九、听录音，口头回答问题　Answer the following questions．

24

第十二课　Lesson 12

一、听音节，边听边说。

Listen the following syllables and read after the recording.

二、听声调，边听边说。

Listen to the tones of the following words and phrases and read after the recording.

三、听后填上韵母　Fill in the blanks with the finals you hear:

m ＿＿ f ＿＿　　x ＿＿ j ＿＿　　q ＿＿ zh ＿＿　　sh ＿＿ g ＿＿

h ＿＿ l ＿＿　　sh ＿＿ k ＿＿　　k ＿＿ d ＿＿　　r ＿＿ m ＿＿

k ＿＿ ch ＿＿　　j ＿＿ f ＿＿　　c ＿＿ q ＿＿　　＿＿ t ＿＿

四、听后填上声母　Fill in the blanks with the initials you hear:

＿＿ è ＿＿ ú　　　　　＿＿ ǎo ＿＿ āo　　　　　＿＿ iě ＿＿ ǎ

＿＿ uān ＿＿ uǎng　　＿＿ iě ＿＿ ì　　　　　＿＿ uē ＿＿ í

＿＿ uǒ ＿＿ ǐ　　　　＿＿ ǎo ＿＿ uì　　　　　＿＿ iǎo ＿＿ ū ＿＿ á

＿＿ ī ＿＿ ī ＿＿ ǐn　　＿＿ uě ＿＿ ōng ＿＿ òng ＿＿ àn

＿＿ uāng ＿＿ uǎn ＿＿ í ＿＿ ià

五、听后标出调号　Give the tone-marks:

huoche　　niunai　　youyi　　yiqian　　pingguo

gongchang　　huochai　　minzhu　　zhentou　　zhengfu

qianbiher　　feijichang

六、听后判断正误　Are the following statements true（√）or false（×）according to what you hear?

（1）他的西班牙语很好。　　（　　　）

（2）他会一点儿阿拉伯语。　　（　　　）

（3）他们不会汉语。　　　　　　　（　　）

（4）他会说日语。　　　　　　　　（　　）

七、听后选择正确答案：

Listen to the dialogues and circle the correct answcrs to the questions：

（1）情景：一个日本人和一个阿拉伯人谈话。

Situation：A Japanese and an Arabic are talking．

① a　　　b　　　c

② a　　　b　　　c

（2）情景：中国学生李大年和法国学生让谈话。

Situation：Li Danian，a Chinese student，and his French schoolmate Jean are talking．

生词：和　hé　and

① a　　　b

② a　　　b

③ a　　　b

八、听录音，口头回答问题　Answer the following questions.

第十三课　Lesson 13

一、听音节,边听边说(注意词重音)。
Listen the following syllables and read after the recording,paying attention to the word stress.

二、听声调,边听边说。
Listen to the tones of the following words and phrases and read after the recording.

三、画出你听到的音节　Underline one from each pair of syllables you hear:

jian	juan		juan	quan
qian	quan		zuan	juan
cuan	quan		guan	guang
shuan	xuan		kuan	kuang
xian	xuan		huan	huang

四、听后填上韵母　Fill in the blanks with the finals you hear:

j____ zh____　　z____ y____　　j____ k____　　q____ f____
c____ q____　　h____ j____　　x____ g____　　h____ s____
x____ ch____　　ch____ j____　　j____ k____　　g____ x____

五、听后把词语分成两组:
Divide the words into two groups and put them under the following tone sequences:

　　　　ˊ + ˋ　　　　　　　　　ˇ + ˋ

六、听后标出调号　Give the tone -marks:

jinlai　　　　meili　　　qiuchang　　zuanyan

qiangzhuang　　nü'er　　qingjia　　taijiquan

七、听后标图 **Mark out on the sketches what you hear in the recording：**

（1）

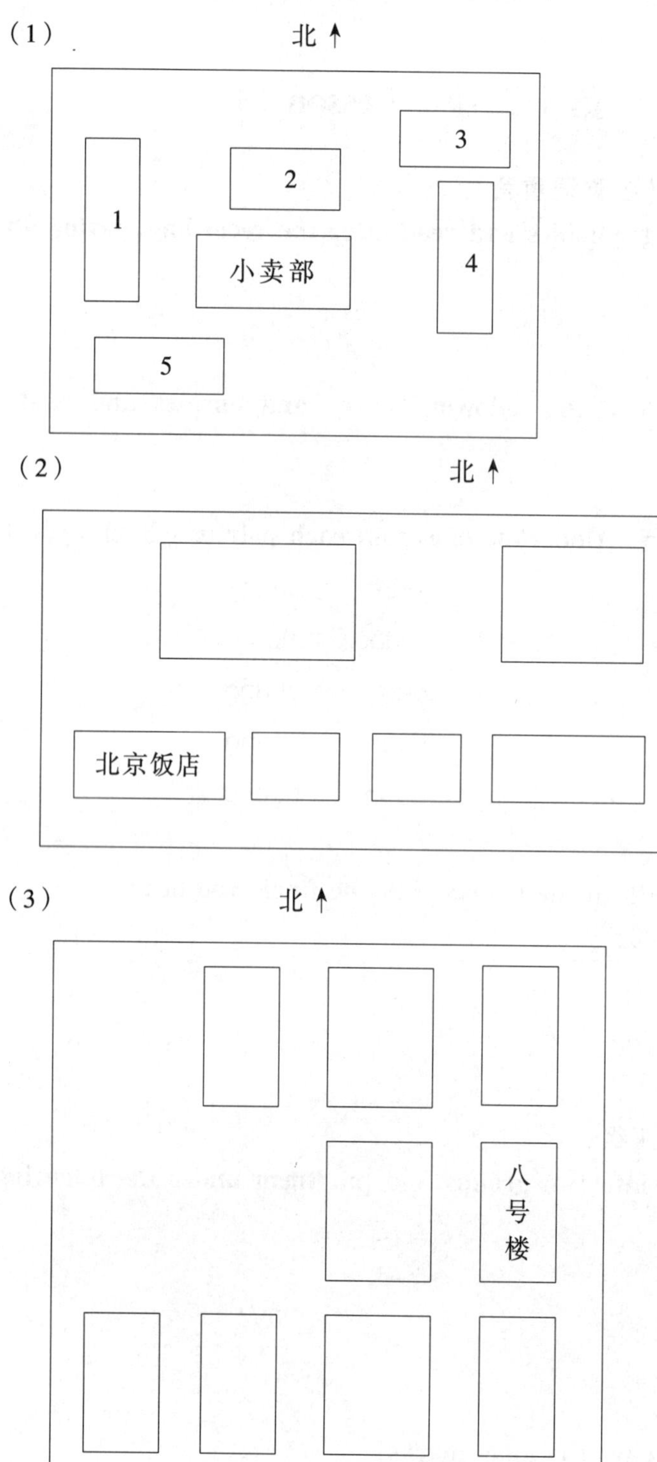

（2）

（3）

八、听录音，口头回答问题 **Answer the following questions.**

28

第十四课　Lesson 14

一、听音节,边听边说。

Listen the following words and read after the recording，paying attention to the stress of the second group of words.

二、听声调,边听边说。

Listen to the tones of the following words，phrases and the two proverbs in the third group and read after the recording.

三、画出你听到的音节　**Underline one from each pair of syllables you hear:**

（1） qi　　chi

qiao　chao

qiu　　chou

qin　　chen

qing　cheng

qian　chan

qiong　chong

（2） qi　　shi

qiao　shao

qiu　　shou

qing　sheng

qie　　shui

qian　shan

quan　shuan

四、听后填上声母　**Fill in the blanks with the initials you hear:**

____ǐ ____iú　　　____uí ____ù　　　____ēn ____iǎn

____óng ____ìng　　____iǎo ____ǒu　　____ěng ____éng

____èn ____ān　　　____ín ____áo　　　____ǒu ____ué

____uē ____ǎo　　　____ǎn ____ēng　　____òu ____uán

五、听后标出调号　**Give the tone-marks:**

（1） 汉语学院　　　中文系　　　哲学系

音乐学院　　　历史系　　　音乐系

体育学院　　　语言系　　　体育系

经济学院

（2）等什么　　　　　　等人
　　　等汽车　　　　　　去哪儿
　　　等谁　　　　　　　去友谊商店

（3）我学习中文。
　　　你学习英文。
　　　他可以说汉语。
　　　他会说西班牙语。
　　　我不会说德语，也不会说法语。

六、听后填空　**Listen to the passages and fill in the blanks**：
 （1）我弟弟和妹妹是＿＿＿＿＿＿＿＿＿＿＿＿的学生，我弟弟学习
  ＿＿＿＿＿＿，我妹妹学习＿＿＿＿＿＿。
 （2）阿里住＿＿＿＿＿＿号楼。
 （3）他们去＿＿＿＿＿＿＿＿＿＿。

七、听后选择正确答案：
Listen to the dialogues and circle the correct answers to the questions：
（1）情景：约翰在汽车站等一个朋友。他遇见一位等车的老教授，就随便谈了起来。

Situation: John is waiting for a friend at the bus stop, when he meets an old professor, who is also waiting there, and they started a small talk.

生词：和　hé　and

① a　　　b　　　c

② a　　　b

（2）情景：一个人询问郑教授的住址。

Situation: A man is asking where Professor Zheng lives.

① a　　　b　　　c

② a　　　b　　　c

八、听录音，口头回答问题　**Answer the following questions.**

第十五课　Lesson 15

一、听音节，边听边说。
Listen the following words and read after the recording，paying attention to the stresses of the second group of words.

二、听声调，边听边说。
Listen to the tones of the following words and phrases and the classical poem and read after the recording.

三、画出你听到的音节　**Underline one from each pair of syllables you hear：**

（1）	nián	niáng		（2）	chēn	zhēn
	liǎn	liǎng			chái	zhái
	jiān	jiāng			cǎi	zǎi
	qián	qiáng			shǎng	xiǎng
	xiàn	xiàng			róng	lóng
	yǎn	yǎng			qiǎo	jiǎo

四、听后填上韵母　**Fill in the blanks with the finals you hear：**

n ____ q ____　　n ____ z ____　　l ____ h ____

j ____ j ____　　d ____ l ____　　q ____ j ____

m ____ q ____　　h ____ x ____

五、听后标出调号　**Give the tone-marks：**

manyi　　qingsong　　huran　　san bu

shihou　　bi ye　　shang yue　　laoren

Mingnian wo qu Guangzhou xuexi yixue.

六、听后填空　**Listen to the dialogues and fill in the blanks：**

（1）情景：两个人谈论去看电影的事。

Situation: Two persons are talking about going to the movie.

填空:李大年这个星期日去________,下个星期日去________。

(2) 情景:两个人谈买词典的问题。

Situation: Two persons are talking about buying a dictionary.

填空:他们学校的书店在________号房间,那儿有________词典。

(3) 情景:明天是一个学生的生日,他想请同学们去宿舍玩。

Situation: Tomorrow is a student's birthday. He invites his classmates to his room.

生词:生日　shēngrì　birthday

　　　快乐　kuàilè　happy

填空:今天是________月________号。________号是一个学生的生日。

他请同学们________________。

七、听录音,口头回答问题　Answer the following questions.

第十六课　Lesson 16

一、语音练习　Pronunciation drills：

（1）边听边说　Repeat the following words.

（2）画出你听到的词语　Underline one from each pair of words you hear：

zhǐbāo	júzi	zūzi	wǔdǎo
jǐ bāo	jízi	zhūzi	fǔdǎo

liú xiě	chūnfēng	bàogào	jiǎndān
liú xué	chōngfēng	bāokuò	biǎndan

（3）听后给下面的谚语注音　Transcribe the proverb：

路遥知马力，日久见人心。

二、词重音练习　Word stress drill：

听后标出词重音　Underline the stress of each word：

上月　　　下月　　　去年　　　今年　　　昨天　　　明天　　　中学

大学　　　学院　　　外语　　　劳驾　　　邮局　　　旁边儿

工作　　　教授　　　汽车

三、听后选择正确答案：

Listen to the statements and the dialogue and circle the correct answers to the questions：

(1) a　　b

(2) a　　b

(3) a　　b

(4) a　　b

(5) a　　b　　c

(6) a　　b　　c

(7) a　　b

(8) a　　b　　c

(9) a b c

(10) 生词:和　hé　and

  答案:a b c

四、听录音,口头回答问题　Answer the following questions.

第十七课　Lesson 17

一、语音练习　Pronunciation drills：

（1）边听边说　Repeat the following words．

（2）画出你听到的词语　Underline one from each pair of words you hear：

$$\begin{cases} \text{yǔyán} \\ \text{yíyán} \end{cases} \quad \begin{cases} \text{liànxí} \\ \text{liángxí} \end{cases} \quad \begin{cases} \text{xīwàng} \\ \text{shīwàng} \end{cases} \quad \begin{cases} \text{xīfú} \\ \text{qūfú} \end{cases}$$

$$\begin{cases} \text{jícù} \\ \text{jìzhù} \end{cases} \quad \begin{cases} \text{cǎisè} \\ \text{cāicè} \end{cases} \quad \begin{cases} \text{érqiě} \\ \text{èrjiě} \end{cases} \quad \begin{cases} \text{gòngxiàn} \\ \text{kōngqián} \end{cases}$$

（3）听后给下面的谚语注音　Transcribe the following proverbs：

边学边问，才有学问。

不懂装懂，永是饭桶。

二、词重音练习　Word stress drills：

听后标出词重音　Underline the stress of each word：

现在　　起床　　早饭　　午饭　　晚饭　　上课

下课　　睡觉　　劳驾　　学院　　小学　　小卖部

三、句重音练习　Sentence stress drills：

（1）边听边说　Repeat the following sentences．

（2）听我问，你标出答句的重音：

Listen to the questions and underline the stress of each answer：

① 现在十点了。

② 现在九月了。

③ 今天二十八号。

④ 今天星期四。

⑤ 他明年去西班牙。

⑥ 我下星期日去长城。

⑦ 我一九七七年中学毕业。

四、听后选择正确答案：

Listen to the statements and the dialogues and circle the correct answers to the questions：

    （1）生词：时间　shíjiān　time

        答案：a　　b　　c

    （2）a　　b　　c

    （3）生词：开始　kāishǐ　to begin

        答案：a　　b　　c

    （4）a　　b　　c

    （5）a　　b　　c

    （6）a　　b　　c

    （7）a　　b　　c　　d

    （8）a　　b　　c

    （9）a　　b　　c

   （10）生词：只好　zhǐhǎo　to have to

        答案：a　　b

五、听录音，口头回答问题　**Answer the following questions.**

第十八课　Lesson 18

一、语音练习：Pronunciation drills：

（1）边听边说　Repeat the following words．

（2）画出你听到的词语　Underline one from each pair of words you hear：

chéngguǒ	tōngzhī	chuántǒng	chūfā
chéngguō	tóngzhì	chuàntōng	chǔfá
dàsǎo	gānjìng	dǎ jià	dàxuě
dǎsǎo	gǎnjǐn	dàjiā	dàxué
huǒchē	jíshǐ	hútòng	huānyíng
huòchē	jíshí	hùtōng	huànyǐng

（3）学说绕口令　Practice the tongue twister．

二、用阿拉伯数字写出你听到的钱数：

Write down the amounts of money you hear in Arabic numbers：

（1）　　　　（2）　　　　（3）　　　　（4）

（5）　　　　（6）　　　　（7）　　　　（8）

三、语调练习　Intonation practice．

边听边说（注意句末是升调还是降调）。

Listen and repeat，paying attention to the intonation of the sentences．

四、句重音练习　Sentence stress drills：

（1）边听边说　Repeat the following sentences．

（2）听我问，请你标出答句的重音：

Listen to the questions and underline the stress of each answer：

① 这枝铅笔四毛八。

② 这本杂志六块五。

③ 这张床八十九块五。

④ 这是阿里的本子。

⑤ 刘天华有汽车。

五、听后选择正确答案：

Listen to the dialogues and circle the correct answers to the questions:

（1）情景：约翰买圆珠笔。

Situation：John is buying a ball pen.

答案：a　　　b

（2）情景：阿里在商店买东西。

Situation：Ali is shopping in a shop.

答案：a　　　b

（3）情景：夏子在小卖部买东西。

Situation：Xiazi is shopping at a stall.

答案：a　　　b　　　c

六、听录音，口头回答问题　**Answer the following questions.**

第十九课　Lesson 19

一、语音练习　Pronunciation drills：

（1）边听边说　Repeat the following words．

（2）画出你听到的词语　Underline one from each pair of words you hear：

⎰ jìniàn ⎱ jǐ nián	⎰ huànxiǎng ⎱ huán xiāng	⎰ huà huār ⎱ huà huàr

⎰ jiàoshī ⎱ jiàoshì	⎰ jiěshì ⎱ jièshí	⎰ jīngjù ⎱ jǐngjù	⎰ kěqì ⎱ kèqi

⎰ lǐ fà ⎱ lì fǎ	⎰ lǎojiā ⎱ láo jià	⎰ xuéyuán ⎱ xuéyuàn	⎰ guìzi ⎱ guǐzi

二、语调练习　Intonation practice．

边听边说(注意句末是升调还是降调)。

Listen and repeat，paying attention to the intonation of the sentences．

三、句重音练习　Sentence stress drills：

（1）边听边说　Repeat the following sentences．

（2）听我问，请你标出答句的重音：

Listen to the questions and underline the stress of each answer：

① 我去琼楼饭店。

② 他看球赛。

③ 我学习哲学。

④ 我想借阿拉伯文杂志。

⑤ 我的词典五十三块六买的。

四、听后回答问题　Listen to the dialogues and answer the questions：

（1）情景：高开在邮局寄信。

Situation：Gao Kai is posting a letter in the post office．

（2）情景：刘天华在邮局。

Situation: Liu Tianhua is in the post office.

①

②

（3）情景：夏子在小卖部。

Situation: Xiazi is at the stall.

五、听录音，口头回答问题 Answer the following questions.

第二十课　Lesson 20

一、语音练习　Pronunciation drills：

（1）边听边说　Repeat the following words.

（2）画出你听到的词语　Underline one from each pair of words you hear：

jìnxíng	jièshào	lánqiú	kāishǐ
jìnqíng	yèxiào	liànqiú	kāishuǐ
báijiǔ	shūfu	kùzi	shuǐguǒ
páiqiú	shūhu	gǔzi	huí guó
sījī	dàidài	Qíncháo	wàijiāo
xíjī	tàitai	Qīngcháo	huáqiáo

（3）听后把词语分成两组：

Divide the words into two groups and put them under the following tone sequences：

$$´ + ´ \qquad\qquad ˇ + ´$$

（4）学说绕口令　Practice the tongue twister.

二、语调练习　Intonation practice.

边听边说（注意句末是升调还是降调）。

Listen and repeat，paying attention to the intonation of the sentences.

三、句重音练习　Sentence stress drills：

听我问，请你标出答句的重音：

Listen to the questions and underline the stress of each answer：

（1）他们有二百块人民币。

（2）他有十万美元。

（3）我换欧元。

（4）他有美元。

（5）在银行换外币。

四、数字练习　**Exercises on numberals:**

（1）用阿拉伯数字写出你听到的钱数：

Write down the amounts of money you hear in Arabic numbers：

①　　　②　　　③　　　④

⑤　　　⑥　　　⑦　　　⑧

⑨　　　⑩　　　⑪　　　⑫

（2）听后用汉字写出数字　Write the figures you hear in Chinese characters：

①　　　　　　　②

③　　　　　　　④

⑤　　　　　　　⑥

⑦　　　　　　　⑧

五、听后选择正确答案：

Lisen to the dialogues and circle the correct answers to the questions：

（1）情景：约翰在银行换外币。

Situation：John is changing money in the bank．

答案：a　　　b　　　c

（2）情景：一个日本学生想换外币。

Situation：A Japanese wants to change some money．

答案：a　　　b

六、听录音，口头回答问题　**Answer the following questions．**

第二十一课　Lesson 21

一、语音练习　Pronunciation drills:

（1）画出你听到的词语　Underline one from each pair of words you hear:

$\begin{cases}\text{bànlǐ}\\\text{bànlǔ}\end{cases}$　$\begin{cases}\text{róngyì}\\\text{róngyù}\end{cases}$　$\begin{cases}\text{bù mǎi}\\\text{bù měi}\end{cases}$　$\begin{cases}\text{fēnfāng}\\\text{fēngfān}\end{cases}$

$\begin{cases}\text{bǎibù}\\\text{běibù}\end{cases}$　$\begin{cases}\text{shānkǒu}\\\text{shāngkǒu}\end{cases}$　$\begin{cases}\text{kāifēng}\\\text{kāifàng}\end{cases}$　$\begin{cases}\text{rénchēng}\\\text{rénshēng}\end{cases}$

$\begin{cases}\text{shūhu}\\\text{shūfu}\end{cases}$　$\begin{cases}\text{dìdào}\\\text{dìdao}\end{cases}$　$\begin{cases}\text{shìfei}\\\text{shìfēi}\end{cases}$　$\begin{cases}\text{mǎimai}\\\text{mǎimài}\end{cases}$

（2）听后把词语分成四组：

Divide the words you hear into four groups and put them under the following tone sequences:

　´ ＋ －　　　　　´ ＋ ´　　　　　´ ＋ ˇ　　　　　´ ＋ `

（3）听写　Dictation（write in *pinyin*）:

① 　　　　② 　　　　③
④
⑤

二、语调练习　Intonation practice.

边听边说（注意句末是升调还是降调）。

Listen and repeat, paying attention to the intonation of the sentences.

三、句重音练习　Sentence stress drills.

四、听后回答问题　Listen to the dialogues and answer the questions:

（1）情景：阿里跟王老师和他儿子王小明谈话。

　　Situation：Ali is talking with Mr. Wang, his teacher, and Wang's son Wang

Xiaoming.

①

②

(2) 情景：夏子看贾红春家的照片。

Situation: Xiazi is looking at a picture of Jia Hongchun's family.

生词：照片　zhàopiàn　photograph

①

②

③

(3) 情景：约翰在故宫参观后找不到大门了，他问一个老人。

Situation: John could not find the way out after visiting the Palace Museum and ask an old man.

生词：大门　dàmén　gate

①

②

③

五、听录音，口头回答问题　Answer the following questions.

第二十二课　Lesson 22

一、语音练习　Pronunciation drills：

（1）画出你听到的词语　Underline one from each pair of words you hear：

{ jíbié { qūbié	{ zhù xiào { zhùjiào	{ qiǎohé { xiǎo hé	{ bùjiǔ { bùxiǔ
{ qiǎoshǒu { xiǎo shǒu	{ jiǎoqì { qiǎojì	{ qiūfēn { jiūfēn	{ jiā yóu { jiāo yóu
{ jùchǎng { jīchǎng	{ xiāoxi { xiūxi		

（2）听后给下面的古诗标出调号并朗读：

Listen to the poem，write down the tone-marks and then read aloud the poem：

Zao Fa Baidicheng

Zhao ci Baidi caiyun jian，Qian li Jiangling yi ri huan.

Liang an yuan sheng ti bu zhu，Qing zhou yi guo wan chong shan.

二、语调练习　Intonation practice.

边听边说（注意句末是升调还是降调）。

Listen and repeat，paying attention to the intonation of the sentences.

三、句重音练习　Sentence stress drills：

（1）听我问，请你标出答句的重音：

Listen to the questions and underline the stress of each answer：

① 这是床。

② 他是我朋友。

③ 这是音乐厅。

④ 他是我哥哥。

⑤ 这是我的钢笔。

⑥ 这是我的书。

⑦ 这是录音机。

⑧ 这是照相机。

(2) 听句子,说出每句的含义。

Listen to the sentences and tell what they imply.

四、听后回答问题:

Listen to the short passages and the dialogue and answer the questions:

(1) 生词:和　hé　and

　　①

　　②

(2) 生词:高兴　gāoxìng　happy

　　①

　　②

(3) 情景:一个外国人向三个小姐问路。

Situation：A foreigner is asking three girls the way.

生词:小姐　xiǎojie　　miss

　　　同志　tóngzhì　　comrade

　　①

　　②

五、听录音,口头回答问题　Answer the following questions.

第二十三课　Lesson 23

一、语音练习　Pronunciation drills：

（1）画出你听到的词语　Underline one from each pair of words you hear：

⌈qīngjìng ⌊qīnjìn	⌈xiànxiàng ⌊xiǎngxiàng	⌈shìjuàn ⌊shìjiàn	⌈jīnyú ⌊jīngyú
⌈xiānghuā ⌊xiānhuā	⌈míngyuè ⌊mínyuè	⌈qūxiàng ⌊qīxiàn	⌈juānqū ⌊jūnqū
⌈jīngxīn ⌊jīnxīng	⌈pínfán ⌊píngfán		

（2）听后给下面的绕口令注音并朗读：

Listen to，transcribe and read aloud the tongue twister：

小王和小黄，一块儿画凤凰。

小王画黄凤凰，小黄画红凤凰。

红凤凰、黄凤凰，画成活凤凰。

黄凤凰、红凤凰，望着小黄和小王。

二、语调练习　Intonation practice．

边听边说(注意句末是升调还是降调)。

Listen and repeat，paying attention to the intonation of the sentences．

三、句重音练习　Sentence stress drills：

（1）边听边画出有重读"几"的句子　Mark out the sentences with stressed 几：

① 你们房间有几张桌子？

② 宿舍里有几个人。

③ 书架上有几本杂志。

④ 桌子上有几本书？

⑤ 他念了几课课文？

⑥ 我要写几个汉字。

⑦ 我想去看几个同学。

⑧ 你买了几枝笔？

（2）听句子,说出每句的含义。

Listen to the sentences and tell what they imply.

四、听后选择正确答案:

Listen to the dialogues and circle the correct answers to the questions:

（1）情景:刘英给高明打电话。

Situation：Liu Ying is talking with Gao Ming on the phone.

① a b

② a b c

③ a b

（2）情景:阿里的同学和阿里谈话。

Situation：Ali's classmate is talking with Ali.

① a b

② a b

③ a b c

④ a b

五、听录音,口头回答问题 Answer the following questions.

第二十四课　Lesson 24

一、语音练习　Pronunciation drills：

（1）画出你听到的词语　Underline one from each pair of words you hear：

cāngcù	zībǔ	shànxīn	zhīzú
chángchù	zhībǔ	sànxīn	zìzhǔ
zōngzhǐ	zīshì	zhìzào	zòuyuè
zhōngzhǐ	zhīshi	zhízhào	zhòuyè
sīrén	sān céng		
shīrén	shānchéng		

（2）听后给下面的谚语注音并朗读：

Listen to, transcribe and read aloud the proverbs：

① 人往高处走，
　　水往低处流。

② 有志者自有千方百计，
　　无志者只感千难万难。

二、语调练习　Intonation practice.

边听边说（注意句末是升调还是降调）。

Listen and repeat, paying attention to the intonation of the sentences.

三、句重音练习　Sentence stress drills：

（1）听我问，请你标出答句的重音：

Listen to the questions and underline the stress of each answer：

① 看到第四课了。
② 应该看完第八页。
③ 你念第七个生词。
④ 我换完钱了。
⑤ 他写完这些汉字了。
⑥ 她没看完这本书。

(2) 听句子,说出每句的含义。

Listen to the sentences and tell what they imply.

四、听后选择正确答案:

Listen to the passage and the dialogue and circle the correct answers to the questions:

(1) 生词:和　hé and

　　① a　　　b　　　c

　　② a　　　b　　　c

　　③ a　　　b　　　c

(2) 情景:刘天华想借李大年的钢笔用用。

Situation: Liu Tianhua wants to borrow a pen from Li Danian.

　　① a　　　b

　　② a　　　b　　　c

　　③ a　　　b　　　c

五、听录音,口头回答问题　**Answer the following questions.**

第二十五课　Lesson 25

一、语音练习　Pronunciation drills：

（1）画出你听到的词语　Underline one from each pair of words you hear：

⌈qiézi	⌈qièshí	⌈chuántóur	⌈fāyán
⌊quézi	⌊quèshí	⌊chuángtóur	⌊fāyuán
⌈xiēzi	⌈huádòng	⌈xiǎomài	⌈zhuānchē
⌊xuēzi	⌊huódòng	⌊xiǎomèi	⌊zhuāng chē
⌈páiqiú	⌈yíxià		
⌊bái qiú	⌊yí jià		

（2）听写　Dictation（Write in *pinyin*）：

①

②

③

④

⑤

二、语调练习　Intonation practice．

边听边说（注意句末是升调还是降调）。

Listen and repeat，paying attention to the intonation of the sentences．

三、句重音练习　Sentence stress drills：

听我问，请你标出答句的重音：

Listen to the questions and underline the stress of each answer：

（1）我要纪念邮票。

（2）他买小孩儿衣服。

（3）他看三点半的电影。

（4）这是史密斯的床。

（5）他给哥哥写信。

（6）上午我们有四节课。

（7）我去换钱。

（8）阿里去打球。

四、听后选择正确答案：

Listen to the dialogue and the passage and circle the correct answers to the questions:

（1）情景:李双双和她的同屋打扫房间。

   Situation: Li Shuangshuang and her roommate are cleaning their room.

   生词:打扫　dǎsǎo　to clean（a room, etc.）

   　　　洗　　xǐ　　　to wash

   ① a　　b　　c

   ② a　　b

（2）生词:箱子　xiāngzi　suitcase

   ① a　　b

   ② a　　b

五、听录音,口头回答问题　Answer the following questions.

一、语音练习　**Pronunciation drills**：

（1）画出你听到的词语　Underline one from each pair of words you hear：

wàiyǔ	huánqiú	zhuāzhù	huáihèn
wèiyǔ	huáng qiú	zhuōzhù	huǐhèn
lúnzi	shàng chuán	huìyì	yí duàn
lóngzi	shàng chuáng	huáiyí	yí dùn
duìzi	shuǐlì		
dūnzi	shùnlì		

（2）听写　Dictation（Write in *pinyin*）：

①

②

③

④

⑤

（3）朗读你写的句子　Read aloud the sentences you have written.

（4）学说绕口令　Prctice the tongue twister.

二、句重音练习　**Sentence stress drills**：

（1）边听边说　Repeat the following sentences.

（2）边听边标出下面句子的重音：

Listen to the sentences and underline their stresses：

① 你上午去，还是下午去？

② 我喝牛奶，不喝咖啡。

③ 我们学习历史，他们学习哲学。

④ 那件脏衣服是史密斯的,不是我的。

三、听后选择正确答案:

Listen to the passage and the dialogues and circle the correct answers to the questions:

(1) ① a   b   c
   ② a   b   c
   ③ a   b   c

(2) 情景:安娜和刘天华从邮局出来,去冷饮店休息。

Situation: Coming out of the post office, Anna and Liu Tianhua are going to a coffee bar for a rest.

生词:汽水   qìshuǐ   aerated water

   ① a   b
   ② a   b

(3) 情景:今天是安娜的生日,很多人来她的房间向她表示祝贺。

Situation: Today is Anna's birthday. Many people come to her room to give their greetings.

生词:生日   shēngrì   birthday
      高兴   gāoxìng   glad, happy
      祝   zhù   to wish, to congratulate
      快乐   kuàilè   happy

   ① a   b
   ② a   b
   ③ a   b

四、听录音,口头回答问题   **Answer the following questions.**

第二十七课　Lesson 27

一、语音练习　Pronunciation drills：

（1）画出你听到的词语　Underline one from each pair of words you hear：

róngyi	xuéyuàn	Běijīng	liànxí
róngyī	xuéyuán	bèijǐng	liánxì
yǔyán	měitiān	Hànzì	rènshi
yùyán	méitián	hànzi	rénshì
jiàoshì	hēibǎn		
jiàoshī	hēibān		

（2）听后给下面的古诗注音并朗读：

Listen to, transcribe and read aloud the poem：

绝　句

两个黄鹂鸣翠柳，
一行白鹭上青天。
窗含西岭千秋雪，
门泊东吴万里船。

二、句重音练习　Sentence stress drills：

（1）边听边说　Repeat the following sentences.

（2）边听边回答，并标出答句的重音：

Answer the questions while you listen and underline the stress of each answer：

①

②

③

④

三、听后选择正确答案：

Listen to the passage and the dialogues and circle the correct answers to the questions：

（1）生词：但是　dànshì　but

  ① a b

  ② a b c

（2）情景：安娜在商店买衬衫。

  Situation：Anna is buying a blouse in a shop．

  ① a b

  ② a b

  ③ a b c

（3）情景：安娜在商店换衬衫。

  Situation：Anna is changing the blouse she bought in the shop．

  ① a b c

  ② a b

  ③ a b

四、听录音，口头回答问题　**Answer the following questions．**

第二十八课　Lesson 28

一、语音练习　Pronunciation drills:

（1）画出你听到的词语　Underline one from each pair of words you hear:

húzi	qīhēi	hànshān	chū hàn
fǔzi	qǐfēi	fān shān	chūfàn
yuánfèn	mùfāng	héngxíng	hōngdòng
yuànhèn	mùxiāng	fēngxíng	fēngdòng
gōngfèi	kāi huā		
gōnghuì	kāifā		

（2）听写　Dictation（Write in *pinyin*）：

①

②

③

④

⑤

（3）朗读你写的句子　Read aloud the sentences you have written.

二、句重音练习　Sentence stress drill.

（1）边听边说（注意"几"的重读和轻读）。

Listen and repeat the sentences, paying attention to the stressed and unstressed "几".

（2）听下面的句子，说出"两"在句子中的意思是"二"还是"几"。

Listen to the following sentences and tell whether the word "两" means "two" or "several".

三、听后选择正确答案:

Listen to the passage and the dialogues and circle the correct answers to the questions:

（1）① a　　　b

　　　② a　　　b

　　　③ a　　　b

（2）情景:阿里和安娜谈论琉璃厂。

　　　Situation：Ali and Anna are talking about Liulichang Street of Beijing.

　　　生词:工厂　　gōngchǎng　　factory

　　　① a　　　b

　　　② a　　　b

（3）情景:约翰问阿里去琉璃厂怎么坐车。

　　　Situation：John asks Ali which bus he should take to go to Liulichang Street.

　　　生词:动物园　　dòngwùyuán　　zoo

　　　　　 路　　　　lù　　　　　　　line（for bus number）

　　　① a　　　b

　　　② a　　　b

四、听录音,口头回答问题　**Answer the following questions.**

第二十九课　Lesson 29

一、语音练习　Pronunciation drills:

(1) 画出你听到的词语　Underline one from each pair of words you hear:

xiānhuā	shìyàn	jiǎnlì	qiānqiú
xiàn huā	shìyàng	jiǎnglì	qiǎngqiú
qiǎnxiǎn	liánxì	lǎonián	jiānchǎng
qiǎngxiǎn	liángxí	lǎoniáng	jiāngchǎng
jiānkè	jiānyìng		
jiǎng kè	jiāngyìng		

(2) 听写　Dictation (Write in *pinyin*):

①

②

③

④

⑤

(3) 朗读你写的句子　Read aloud the sentences you have written.

(4) 边听边说下面的谚语　Read aloud the proverbs you hear.

二、语调练习　Intonation practice.

听后回答(注意声调和降调)。

Listen and answer the questions, using correct intonation.

三、听后选择正确答案:

Listen to the dialogues and circle the correct answers to the questions:

(1) 情景:一个外国人问路。

Situation：A foreigner is asking the way.

生词：路　lù　line（for bus number）

① a　　b　　c

② a　　b

（2）情景：两个外国人谈论北京的公共汽车票价。

Situation：Two foreigners are talking about the bus fares in Beijing.

生词：空调　kōngtiáo　air-conditioning

① a　　b

② a　　b

四、听后画出去天坛公园的路线图：

Listen to the dialogue and draw a sketch showing the way to the Tiantan Park.

生词：天坛公园　Tiāntán Gōngyuán　Tiantan（The Temple of Heaven）Park

琼楼饭店

。

五、听录音，口头回答问题　Answer the following questions.

第三十课　**Lesson 30**

一、语音练习　**Pronunciation drills**：

（1）画出你听到的词语　Underline one from each pair of words you hear：

⌈ qìchē	⌈ láojià	⌈ huàn chē	⌈ yífu
⌊ qí chē	⌊ lǎojiā	⌊ huán chē	⌊ yīfu
⌈ huǒchē	⌈ dàxué	⌈ dànshì	⌈ yùxí
⌊ huòchē	⌊ dàxuě	⌊ dǎnshí	⌊ yùxǐ

（2）听写　Dictation（Write in *pinyin*）：

①

②

③

④

⑤

（3）朗读你写的句子　Read aloud the sentences you have written.

（4）学说绕口令　Prctice the tongue twister.

二、句重音练习：**Sentence stress drills**：

（1）听后根据句子的重音提问

Listen to the sentences then ask questions on the sentence stress.

（2）听我问，你标出答句的重音：

Listen to the questions and underline the stress of each answer：

① 不是第一个，是第六个。

② 不是第四张，是第五张。

③ 不是第二个，是第三个。

④ 不在二十七页，在二十九页。

三、听后回答问题。

Listen to the sentences and the dialogue and answer the questions.

四、听后选择正确答案：

Listen to the dialogues and circle the correct answers to the questions：

（1）情景：A 问 B 的座位。

　　Situation：A asks B whether he has a ticket for the play.

　　答案：a　　　b　　　c

（2）情景：A 问 B 谁来北京学习。

　　Situation：A asks B who is coming to study in Beijing.

　　① a　　　b

　　② a　　　b

（3）情景：B 在火车站送 A，跟 A 告别。

　　Situation：B sees A off at the station and says good-bye to A.

　　生词：同志　tóngzhì　comrade

　　答案：a　　　b　　　c

五、听录音，口头回答问题　**Answer the following questions.**

一、语音练习 Pronunciation exercises:

(1) 画出你听到的词语或短句:

Underline the wond/phrase/short sentence you hear from each pair:

⎧ shàng bān ⎩ xià bān	⎧ línjū ⎩ fēnjū
⎧ shàng jiē ⎩ shàngjí	⎧ júzi ⎩ jízi

⎧ Tā qù Shǒudū jīchǎng.
⎩ Tā qù Shǒudū jùchǎng.

⎧ Tā gāng xǐle zǎo.
⎩ Tā gāng xǐle jiǎo.

⎧ Tā xǐhuan nà tiáo hóng qúnzi.
⎩ Tā xǐhuan nà tiáo huáng qúnzi.

(2) 听写 Dictation:

①

②

③

④

⑤

(3) 读上面的句子 Read aloud the sentences in the Dictation.

(4) 学说绕口令 Practise the tongue twister.

二、句重音练习 Sentence stress practice:

听问题, 画出答句的重音

Listen to the following questions and mark out the sentence stresses of the answers:

（1）王师傅是我的邻居。

（2）我买了几斤葡萄。

（3）安娜买了四个苹果。

（4）约翰买的橘子不错。

（5）约翰买的橘子不错，苹果不好。

三、把下面的句子改成否定句　　**Turn the following negative**：

（1）

（2）

　（3）

（4）

（5）

四、听下面的句子，选择正确的解释：

Listen to the following sentences and circle a correct explanation to each one of them from the alternatives given：

（1）a　　　　b

（2）a　　　　b

（3）a　　　　b

（4）a　　　　b

（5）a　　　　b

五、听后回答问题：

Listen to the passage and the dialogues and answer the questions on them：

（1）

（2）情景：高开和王兰谈话。

Situation: Gao Kai and Wang Lan are talking.

①

②

（3）情景：张师傅在家门口遇见了王兰。

Situation: Master Zhang and Wang Lan meet at the doorway.

生词：菜　cài　vegetable

①

②

六、听录音，快速回答问题　Give prompt answers to the following questions.

第三十二课　Lesson 32

一、语音练习　Pronunciation exercises：

（1）画出你听到的词语或短句：

Underline the word/phrase/question you hear from each pair：

bóbo	dùzi	bízi	dú shū
pópo	tùzi	pízi	túshū

tāle yì jiān fáng
dāle yì jiān fáng

Nǐ de yīfu duō bu duō?
Nǐ de yīfu tuō bu tuō?

（2）边听边给下面的古诗注音　Transcribe the poem according to the recording：

登鹳鹊楼

白日依山尽，

黄河入海流。

欲穷千里目，

更上一层楼。

（3）朗读上面的诗　Read aloud the above poem.

二、句重音练习　Sentence stress practice：

（1）边听边说，注意句重音。

Repeat after the recording, paying attention to sentence stress.

（2）听我问，你选择答句，注意答句的重音：

Listen to the questions and circle the answer that gives the correct sentence stress from each three alternatives：

① a　　b　　c

② a　　b　　c

③ a　　b　　c

④ a　　b　　c

三、用"真"和"多么……啊"完成句子。

Complete the sentences using 真 and 多么 after the model.

（1）太阳　红

（2）颜色　好看

（3）东西　便宜

（4）这地方　有意思

（5）雨　大

（6）这件衣服　合适

（7）这个学校　大

四、听下面的句子,听后回答问题:

Listen to the following sentences and answer the questions on them:

（1）①

　　②

（2）

（3）

（4）

（5）

五、听后选择正确答案:

Listen to the dialogues and circle the correct answers to the questions from the alternatives given:

（1）情景:约翰请阿里去看话剧。

Situation：John invites Ali to a play.

答案:a　　b

（2）情景:早上安娜和史密斯讨论去哪儿玩。

Situation：Anna and Smith are discussing where to go in the morning.

生词:雨伞　yǔsǎn　umbrella

①a　　b

②a　　b

六、听录音,快速回答问题　**Give prompt answers to the following questions.**

第三十三课　Lesson 33

一、语音练习　Pronunciation exercises：

（1）画出你听到的词语或短句：

Underline the word/phrase/short sentence you hear from each pair：

$$\begin{cases} mùcái \\ mùchái \end{cases} \quad \begin{cases} cíxù \\ chíxù \end{cases} \quad \begin{cases} sìshí \\ shìshí \end{cases} \quad \begin{cases} sīrén \\ shīrén \end{cases}$$

$$\begin{cases} zāi\ huār \\ zhāi\ huār \end{cases} \qquad \begin{cases} Tāmen\ dōu\ suì\ le. \\ Tāmen\ dōu\ zuì\ le. \end{cases}$$

（2）听写　Dictation：

①

②

③

④

⑤

（3）读上面的句子　Read aloud the sentences in the Dictation．

二、句重音练习　Sentence stress practice：

（1）听后画出答句的重音：

Listen to the following questions and mark out the sentence stresses of the anwers：

① 我们上午学习四个小时。

② 要用三个多小时。

③ 小卖部九点半开门。

④ 我的表是十二点十三分。

⑤ 好吧,我又累又渴。

(2) 听后给下面的句子提出问题。

Listen to the sentences and ask questions on them.

三、听下面的句子,选择正确的解释:

Listen to the following sentences and circle a correct explanation to each one of them from the alternatives given:

(1) a b

(2) a b

(3) a b

(4) a b

(5) a b

四、听后选择正确答案:

Listen to the dialogues and circle the correct answers to the questions from the alternatives given:

(1) 情景:安娜和阿里在一起学习。

  Situation: Anna and Ali are doing their lessons together.

  答案:a b c

(2) 情景:约翰找钢笔。

  Situation: John is looking for his pen.

  答案:a b

(3) 情景:刘和李在书店门口儿。

  Situation: Liu and Li are in front of a bookshop.

  ① a b

  ② a b

五、听录音,快速回答问题 **Give prompt answers to the following questions.**

<h1 style="text-align:center">第三十四课　Lesson 34</h1>

一、语音练习　Pronunciation exercises：

（1）画出你听到的词语或短句：

Underline the word/phrase/short sentence you hear from each pair：

⎰ zīyuán	⎰ cūbù	⎰ zūzi
⎱ zhīyuán	⎱ chūbù	⎱ zhūzi
⎰ zēng bīng wǔshí wàn		⎰ Nǐ cāi ba.
⎱ zhēng bīng wǔshí wàn		⎱ Nǐ chāi ba.

（2）边听边给下面的古诗注音　Transcribe the poem according to the recording：

枫桥夜泊

月落乌啼霜满天，

江枫渔火对愁眠。

姑苏城外寒山寺，

夜半钟声到客船。

（3）朗读上面的诗　Read aloud the above poem.

二、句重音练习　Sentence stress practice：

（1）练习"都"的重读和轻读　Distinguish the stressed and unstressed 都．

听我问，你选择答句　Listen to the questions and circle the correct answers：

① a　　b

② a　　b

③ a　　b

④ a　　b

⑤ a　　b

⑥ a　　b

⑦ a　　b

⑧ a　　b

(2) 练习"才"的重读和轻读　Distinguish the stressed and unstressed 才.

听我问,你选择答句　Listen to the questions and circle the correct answers:

① a　　　b

② a　　　b

③ a　　　b

④ a　　　b

三、听下面的句子,选择正确答案:

Listen to the sentences and circle the correct answers to the questions from the alternatives given:

(1) a　　　b

(2) a　　　b

(3) a　　　b

(4) a　　　b

(5) a　　　b

四、听后回答问题:

Listen to the passage and the dialogues and then answer the questions on them:

(1) 生词:原谅　yuánliàng　to forgive

①

②

③

(2) 情景:约翰买完话剧票到了安娜的家。

Situation: John has got to Anna's home after buying the tickets for the play.

生词:骑　qí　to ride

①

②

(3) 情景:老王和小张谈爬山。

Situation: Lao Wang and Xiao Zhang are talking about mountaineering.

①

②

五、听录音,快速回答问题　Give prompt answers to the following questions.

二、句重音练习　**Sentence stress practice**：

第三十五课　Lesson 35

一、语音练习　**Pronunciation exercises**：

（1）画出你听到的词语或短句：

Underline the word/short sentence you hear from each pair:

| bàngōng | qiézi | shīfu | zhāoyáng |
| bānggōng | quézi | xīfú | qiáoliáng |

| Tā shì zhíxìngzi. | Tāmen zhèngzài zuò shìtí. |
| Tā shì jíxìngzi. | Tāmen zhèngzài zuò xítí. |

（2）边听边给下面的谚语注音：

Transcribe the proverbs according to the recording:

①　忠实的人,对人处处关心;

　　虚伪的人,对人当面奉承。

②　忠于诺言是君子,

　　不讲信用是小人。

③　种瓜得瓜,种豆得豆。

（3）朗读上面的谚语　Read aloud the above proverbs.

二、句重音练习　**Sentence stress practice**：

（1）听我问,你选择正确答案：

Listen to the questions and circle the correct answers to them from the alternatives given:

①　a　　　b　　　c

②　a　　　b　　　c

③　a　　　b　　　c

④　a　　　b　　　c

⑤　a　　　b　　　c

⑥　a　　　b　　　c

（2）听下面的句子,练习提问。

Listen to the sentences and ask questions on them.

三、听下面的句子,选择正确答案:

When you hear a sentence and the two alternative explanations, circle the one that is closer to the sentence in meaning:

(1) a   b

(2) a   b

(3) a   b

(4) a   b

(5) a   b

四、听后选择正确答案:

Listen to the passage and the dialogue and circle the correct answers to the questions from the alternatives given:

(1) 情景:安娜在公园遇见张正生。

Situation: Anna meets Zhang Zhengsheng in the park.

① a   b

② a   b   c

③ a   b   c

(2) 情景:史密斯在北海公园的一个冷饮店遇见了夏子和阿里。

Situation: Smith meets Xiazi and Ali in a coffee bar in Beihai Park.

① a   b

② a   b

③ a   b

④ a   b   c

五、听录音,快速回答问题   Give prompt answers to the following questions.

第三十六课　**Lesson 36**

一、语音练习　Pronunciation exercises：

（1）画出你听到的词语或短句：

Underline the word/phrase/short sentence you hear from each pair：

$\begin{cases}\text{zhīdào}\\\text{chídào}\end{cases}$　$\begin{cases}\text{zhīchí}\\\text{cí zhí}\end{cases}$　$\begin{cases}\text{chízi}\\\text{zhízi}\end{cases}$　$\begin{cases}\text{bú yào zhāi xialai}\\\text{bú yào chāi xialai}\end{cases}$

$\begin{cases}\text{yì zhāng zhīpiào}\\\text{yì zhāng jīpiào}\end{cases}$　$\begin{cases}\text{Nǐmen bié zhǎo le.}\\\text{Nǐmen bié chǎo le.}\end{cases}$

$\begin{cases}\text{Wǒmen qù fǎngwèn yí ge gōngzhǎng.}\\\text{Wǒmen qù fǎngwèn yí ge gōngchǎng.}\end{cases}$

（2）听写　Dictation：

①

②

③

④

⑤

（3）读上面的句子　Read aloud the sentences in the Dictation．

二、句重音练习　Sentence stress practice：

（1）听后说出句子的意思　Listen to the sentences and explain them．

（2）听后标出答句的重音：

Listen to the questions and mark the stresses of the answers：

① 我今天头疼。

② 不，我今天头疼。

③ 不,我今天才开始头疼。

④ 我今天头疼。

三、听下面的句子,听后填空　**Listen to the sentences and fill in the blanks:**

(1) 他应该挂______科。

(2) 她的病是______。

(3) 约翰试表以后知道______了。

(4) 大夫给了他______种药。大药片儿每天吃______片儿,小药
片儿每天吃______片儿。

(5) 他来______次中国了。

四、听后回答问题　**Listen to the dialogues and then answer the questions:**

(1) 情景:史密斯在医院看病。

Situation：Smith sees a doctor in the hospital．

①

②

(2) 情景:夏子在医院看病。

Situation：Xiazi sees a doctor in the hospital．

①

②

(3) 情景:张大夫给约翰看病。

Situation：Dr．Zhang is giving John a treatment．

①

②

五、听录音,快速回答问题　**Give prompt answers to the following questions．**

第三十七课　Lesson 37

一、语音练习　Pronunciation exercises：

(1) 画出你听到的词语或短句：

Underline the word/phrase/short-sentence you hear from each pair：

⌈ xīwàng	⌈ qījiān	⌈ shìshí	⌈ xūxīn
⌊ shīwàng	⌊ shíjiān	⌊ qíshí	⌊ shíxíng

⌈ guāfēn le	⌈ yí bàng miàobāo
⌊ guā fēng le	⌊ yíbànr miànbāo

⌈ liǎng tiáo jīnyú	⌈ Tā yǒu yì kē hóngxīng.
⌊ liǎng tóu jīngyú	⌊ Tā yǒu yì kē hóngxīn.

(2) 听后给下面的绕口令注音：

Transcribe the tongue twister according to the recording：

板凳宽，扁担长，

扁担要绑板凳上，

板凳不让扁担绑，

扁担非绑板凳上。

(3) 读上面的绕口令　Read aloud the above tongue twister.

二、听下面的句子，给"来"或"去"标上调号（注意它是读原调，还是读为轻声）：

Listen to the sentences and distinguish the stressed and unstressed 来/去. Give the tone marks wherever 来/去 is stressed：

(1) 阿里来中国半年了。

(2) 他拿来了一个录音机。

(3) 我们去长城照相。

(4) 我们带去两个篮球。

(5) 上星期我从张正生那儿借来一本词典。

(6) 我来借一本词典。

(7) 贾红春去美国两年了。

(8) 夏子的自行车我已经送去了。

三、听下面的句子,听后选择正确答案:

Listen to the sentences to the questions from the alternatives given:

(1) a   b

(2) a   b   c

(3) a   b

(4) a   b

(5) a   b

四、听后选择正确答案:

Listen to the passage and the dialogues and circle the correct answers:

(1) ① a   b   c

    ② a   b

    ③ a   b

    ④ a   b

(2) ① a   b   c

    ② a   b   c

(3) a   b

五、听录音,快速回答问题　**Give prompt answers to the following questions.**

第三十八课　Lesson 38

一、语音练习　Pronunciation exercises：

（1）画出你听到的词语或短句：

Underline the word/phrase/short sentence you hear from each pair：

| fānbù | ānjìng | běifāng | mùchuán |
| fēnbù | ēnqíng | běifēng | mùchuáng |

| bú xìn | fēngjǐng | jíjù |
| búxìng | fēngqíng | qíqū |

| xúnzhǎo chǎndì | Wǒ kànle qī yè. |
| xúnzhǎo chǎngdì | Wǒ kànle shí yè. |

（2）听写　Dictation：

①

②

③

④

（3）读上面的句子　Read aloud the sentences in the Dictation.

二、听下面的句子，给"来"或"去"标出实际的声调：

Listen to the sentences and mark the tone marks of 来/去 wherever they are stressed：

（1）你们上哪儿去？

（2）他们都去香山公园吗？

（3）我请了几位朋友来，你去做几个菜吧。

（4）客人们都来了，请您进屋去吧。

（5）妈妈刚才上街去了，她买了些牛肉来。

（6）糟糕！给妹妹的礼物我忘带来了。

三、听下面的句子,选择正确的解释:

Listen to the sentences and circle the correct explanations from the alternatives given:

(1) a   b

(2) a   b

(3) a   b

(4) a   b

(5) a   b

四、听后回答问题:

Listen to the dialogues and then answer the questions on them:

(1) 情景:晚上约翰回到宿舍看见了史密斯。

    Situation: John sees Smith when he is back to his room in the evening.

    ①

    ②

    ③

(2) 情景:星期日下午,安娜在院子里遇见了常大夫。

    Situation: It is Sunday afternoon now. Anna meets Dr. Chang in the courtyard.

    ①

    ②

五、听录音,快速回答问题　**Give prompt answers to the following questions.**

第三十九课　**Lesson 39**

一、语音练习　Pronunciation exercises：

（1）画出你听到的句子　Underline the sentence you hear from each pair：

Ānnà yǒu cáihuá.
Ānnà yǒu càihuār.

Zhāng Zǐqiáng mǎi yān.
Zhāng Zǐqiáng mǎi yán.

Nín yào táng ma?
Nín yào tāng ma?

Nà shì tā de qīzi bú shì?
Nà shì tā de qízi bú shì?

Língling ài chī xiányú.
Língling ài chī xiānyú.

（2）听后给下面的谚语注音　Transcribe the proverbs according to the recording：

① 生命在于运动。

② 饭后百步走，活到九十九。

③ 一懒生百病。

④ 一日三笑，不用吃药。

（3）朗读上面的谚语　Read aloud the above proverbs.

二、听后给下面的句子标出句重音：

Listen to the sentences and mark their stresses：

（1）五号跑得快。

（2）他骑得慢。

（3）这个队踢得不好。

（4）阿里汉语说得很好。

（5）他汉字写得怎么样？

（6）夏子乒乓球打得好，网球打得不好。

三、听下面的句子,并把它变成否定句:

Listen to the sentences and turn them negative:

(1)

(2)

(3)

(4)

(5)

(6)

四、听后回答问题　**Listen to the sentences and answer the questions on them:**

(1)

(2)

(3)

(4)

五、听后选择正确答案:

Listen to the dialogues and circle the correct answers to the questions from the alternatives given:

(1) 情景:同学们在教室商量星期日去哪儿玩儿,高老师进来了。

Situation: The students are discussing where to go on Sunday in the classroom when Mr. Gao comes in.

① a　　b

② a　　b

③ a　　b

(2) 听小相声《谈爱好》。

What's your hobby? (a cross talk).

① a　　b　　c

② a　　b

③ a　　b

六、听录音,快速回答问题　**Give prompt answers to the following questions.**

第四十课　Lesson 40

一、语音练习　**Pronunciation exercises:**

（1）画出你听到的短句　Underline the sentence you hear from each pair：

{ Tā hěn kèqi.
{ Tā hěn kěqì.

{ Wǒ zài kǎn shù.
{ Wǒ zài kàn shū.

{ Dōngdong cóng Shānxī lái.
{ Dōngdong cóng Shǎnxī lái.

{ Tā kāi yàofáng.
{ Tā kāi yàofāng.

{ Yí liè huǒchē kāilai le.
{ Yí liè huòchē kāilai le.

（2）听后给下面的古诗注音　Transcribe the poem according to the recording：

悯　农

锄禾日当午，

汗滴禾下土。

谁知盘中餐，

粒粒皆辛苦。

（3）朗读上面的诗　Read aloud the above poem.

二、听后用"一边…一边…"把两句话变为一句话：

Listen to the sentences and combine each pair into a sentence using 一边…一边… after the model:

例　Model：

他听音乐。他写汉字。——→他一边听音乐一边写汉字。

（1）

（2）

(3)

(4)

(5)

(6)

三、听下面的句子,判断句义的解释是否正确:

Listen to the sentences and tell whether the explanations are true（✓）or false（✗）:

(1)　　　(2)　　　(3)　　　(4)　　　(5)
(6)　　　(7)　　　(8)　　　(9)　　　(10)

四、听后选择正确答案:

Listen to the dialogues and circle the correct answers to the questions from the alternatives given:

(1) 情景:郑教授请约翰、汤姆、夏子在家里吃饭。

　　Situation: Prof. Zheng invites John, Tom and Xiazi to dinner at home.

　　生词:花篮儿　　huālánr　　　flower basket

　　　　　真正　　　zhēnzhèng　　true, real

　　① a　　b　　c

　　② a　　b　　c

　　③ a　　b　　c　　d

(2) 情景:安娜和夏子在宿舍谈话。

　　Situation: Anna and Xiazi are talking in their room.

　　生词:说明　　shuōmíng　　to show

　　① a　　b　　c

　　② a　　b　　c

　　③ a　　b

五、听录音,快速回答问题　**Give prompt answers to the following questions.**

第四十一课　Lesson 41

一、语音练习　Pronunciation exercises：

（1）边听边给下面的绕口令注音：

Transcribe the tongue twister according to the recording：

牛牛要吃河边柳，

妞妞赶牛牛不走，

妞妞护柳扭牛头，

牛牛扭头瞅妞妞，

妞妞扭牛牛更拗，

牛牛要顶小妞妞，

妞妞捡起小石头，

吓得牛牛扭头走。

（2）读上面的绕口令　Read aloud the above tongue twister．

（3）听写　Dictation：

①

②

③

④

⑤

二、用你听到的词语说一句话：

Make a sentence with each group of words you hear．

例　Model：

从，来——→他从日本来。

三、听下面的句子,听后选择正确答案:

Listen to the sentences and circle the correct answers to the questions from the alternatives given:

(1) a b c

(2) a b c

(3) a b c

(4) a b c

四、听后选择正确答案 **Listen to the dialogues and circle the correct answers:**

(1) 情景:史密斯吃完晚饭回到宿舍和阿里谈话。

Situation: Back to his room after supper, Smith talks with Ali.

答案:a b

(2) 情景:王老师带着儿子小华散步回来,在楼前遇见了刘师傅。

Situation: After a walk with his son Xiaohua, Mr. Wang meets Master Liu in front of his building.

① a b c

② a b

③ a b

④ a b

五、听录音,快速回答问题 **Give prompt answers to the following questions.**

第四十二课　**Lesson 42**

一、语音练习　Pronunciation exercises：

（1）听后给下面的谚语注音　Transcribe the proverbs according to the recording：

① 鱼好吃,腥难闻。

② 酒是冬天的火。

③ 酒吃头杯,茶喝二盏。

④ 先尝后买,才知好歹。

⑤ 一菜难合百人口味。

（2）听写　Dictation.

二、句重音练习　Sentence stress practice：

听下面的句子,标出"过"是轻读还是重读,并标出句重音:

Listen to the sentences and mark out the stressed 过 and the sentence stresses：

（1）他们过了马路,进了邮局。

（2）我去过那个小吃店。

（3）他还没有做完练习,过一会儿我们再去找他吧。

（4）约会的时间已经过了半个小时了,她还没到。

（5）你下车以后,往东走,过马路,就是首都剧场。

（6）那本书我看过三遍,过一会儿我洗完衣服给你讲讲。

三、听后用"次"或"遍"回答问题　Answer the questions using 次 or 遍：

（1）

（2）

（3）

（4）

（5）

（6）

四、听句子,听后回答问题:

Listen to the sentences and answer the questions on them：
（1）
（2）
（3）
（4）
（5）

五、听后选择正确答案　**Listen to the dialogues and circle the correct answers：**
（1）情景:汤姆跟李大年在小吃店吃饭。

Situation：Tom and Li Danian are eating in a snack bar．

生词:咸　　　xián　　　salty

豆腐　dòufu　　bean-curd（老豆腐　lǎodòufu　　rare bean-curd）

① a　　　b

② a　　　b　　　c

③ a　　　b　　　c

④ a　　　b

（2）情景:史密斯和约翰在宿舍谈话。

Situation：Smith and John are talking in their room．

① a　　　b

② a　　　b

③ a　　　b

④ a　　　b　　　c

六、听录音,快速回答问题　**Give prompt answers to the following questions．**

第四十三课　**Lesson 43**

一、语音练习　**Pronunciation exercises**：

（1）听后给下面的古诗注音　Transcribe the poem according to the recording：

秋　　思

洛阳城里见秋风，

欲作家书意万重。

复恐匆匆说不尽，

行人临发又开封。

（2）朗读上面的诗　Read aloud the above poem.

（3）听写　Dictation.

二、用你听到的词语说一句话，并将"着"放在句中：

Make a sentence in which 着 is used with each group of words：

例　Model：

　　拿，书——→他手里拿着两书本。

三、听下面的句子，听后回答问题：

Listen to the sentences and answer the questions on them：

（1）

（2）

（3）

（4）

（5）

四、听后选择正确答案:

Listen to the dialogue and the two passages and circle the correct answers to the questions:

(1) 情景:汤姆在路上遇见了约翰。

　　Situation: Tom meets John on the way.

　　生词:猴子　　hóuzi　　monkey

　　　　故事　　gùshi　　story

　　① a　　　b　　　c

　　② a　　　b

　　③ a　　　b

　　④ a　　　b

(2) a　　　b　　　c

(3) a　　　b　　　c

五、听录音,快速回答问题　Give prompt answers to the following questions.

第四十四课　**Lesson 44**

一、语音练习　Pronunciation exercises：

（1）边听边给下面的绕口令注音：

Transcribe the tongue twister according to the recording：

白石搭白塔，

白塔白石搭，

搭好白石塔，

石塔白又大。

（2）读上面的绕口令　Read aloud the above tongue twister.

（3）听写　Dictation.

二、用你听到的词语说一句话，并将"把"放在句中：

Make a 把 sentence with each group of words：

例　Model：

车票，交，列车员——→他把车票交给了列车员。

三、听下面的句子，选择与句子意思一致的解释：

Listen to the sentences and circle the explanations that are appropriate to them from the alternatives given：

（1）a　　b　　　　　　　　　（2）a　　b

（3）a　　b　　　　　　　　　（4）a　　b　　c

（5）a　　b　　c　　　　　　（6）a　　b

四、听后回答问题：

Listen to the dialogues and the story and answer the questions on them：

（1）情景：玲玲在北京火车站买票。

Situation：Lingling is buying tickets at the Beijing railway station．

①

②

③

(2) 情景:刘天华和玲玲刚上了火车,在放行李的时候,列车员来了。

Situation：Having got on their carriage，Liu Tianhua and Lingling are moving their luggage when the attendant comes．

①

②

③

④

(3) 生词:亲王　qīnwáng　prince

女王　nǚwáng　queen

亲爱　qīn'ài　dear

玩具　wánjù　toy

孙儿　sūn'ér　grandson（son's son）

价值　jiàzhí　value

①

②

③

五、听录音,快速回答问题　Give prompt answers to the following questions．

第四十五课　Lesson 45

一、语音练习　**Pronunciation exercises**：

（1）听后给下面的古诗注音　Transcribe the poem according to the recording：

还自广陵

天寒水鸟自相依，

十百为群戏落晖。

过尽行人都不起，

忽闻水响一齐飞。

（2）朗读上面的诗　Read aloud the above poem.

（3）听写　Dictation.

二、用你听到的词语说一句话，并将"着"放在句中：

Make a sentence in which 着 is used with each group of words：

例　Model：

躺，看——＞他躺着看书。

三、听下面的句子，听后选择正确答案：

Listen to the sentences and circle the correct answers to the questions from the alternatives given：

（1）a　　b

（2）a　　b　　c

（3）a　　b　　c

（4）a　　b

四、听后选择正确答案:

Listen to the passage and the dialogue and circle the correct answers to the questions from the alternatives given:

(1) 生词:招待　zhāodài　　　to treat

　　　　运往　yùnwǎng　　　to transport to

①　a　　　b　　　c

②　a　　　b　　　c

③　a　　　b

(2) 情景:安娜在路上遇见了汤姆。

　　Situation: Anna meets Tom on the way.

　　生词:故事　gùshì　　story

　　　　使　　shǐ　　　　to cause, to make

①　a　　　b

②　a　　　b

③　a　　　b

五、听录音,快速回答问题　**Give prompt answers to the following questions.**

第四十六课　**Lesson 46**

一、语音练习　**Pronunciation exercises：**

（1）边听边给下面的句子注音：

Transcribe the following signs according to the recording：

① 请勿吸烟

② 随手关门

③ 闲人免进

④ 小心火车

（2）读上面的句子　Read the above signs.

二、听写练习　**Dictation.**

（1）写句子　Write down the following sentences：

①

②

③

④

⑤

（2）听短文,请写下你听到的时间、地点和人名。

Listen to the following passage and take down the time, place and name.

三、听下面的句子,听后回答问题：

Listen to the sentences and answer the questions on them：

（1）

(2)

(3)

(4)

四、听后选择正确答案：

Listen to the dialogues and circle the correct answers to the questions from the alternatives given:

(1) 情景：一个老大爷在火车上，他快要下车了。

    Situation: An old man is about to get off the train.

    生词：收拾　shōushi　to pack up, to collect one's things

          趟　　tàng　　*a measure word*

    ① a　　b

    ② a　　b

    ③ a　　b

(2) 情景：早上，妈妈叫李大年起床。

    Situation: In the morning, mom calls Li Danian to get up.

    生词：约　yuē　to make an appointment

    ① a　　b

    ② a　　b　　c

    ③ a　　b

五、听录音，快速回答问题　Give prompt answers to the following questions.

第四十七课　**Lesson 47**

一、语音练习　**Pronunciation exercises**：

（1）边听边给下面的诗注音　Transcribe the poem according to the recording：

船

套在脚上的

是两只无名的小船

因为我们向往远方

就行走在生活的海洋上

也许我们到不了对岸

但永远朝着一个方向

（2）朗读上面的诗　Read aloud the above poem.

（3）听后把下面的句子变成正反疑问句，然后用否定句回答。

Turn the following into affirmo-negative questions and give the negative answers.

二、听写练习　**Dictation**：

（1）听写句子　Write down the following sentences：

①

②

③

④

⑤

（2）听下面的短文，边听边记下你听到的时间、地点、人名和数字。

Listen to the following passage and take down the time, place, name and figures.

96

三、听下面的句子,听后回答问题:

Listen to the sentences and answer the questions on them.

(1)

(2)

(3)

(4)

(5)

四、听后选择正确答案:

Listen to the dialogues and circle the correct answers to the questions from the alternatives given:

(1) 情景:阿里和汤姆在谈一条广告。

    Situation: Ali and Tom are talking about an advertisement.

    生词:健壮　jiànzhuàng　robust

        永远　yǒngyuǎn　forever, always

        像　　xiàng　　to be like

    ① a　　　b

    ② a　　　b

(2) 情景:阿里和汤姆谈晚上去看戏的事。

    Situation: Ali and Tom are planning to see a Beijing opera in the evening.

    生词:节目　jiémù　　recreational programme

        剧团　jùtuán　theatrical troupe

    ① a　　　b　　　c

    ② a　　　b　　　c

(3) 情景:约翰给东方旅馆九楼服务台打电话。(电话铃响)

    Situation: John is dialing the reception of Floor 9 of the Dongfang Hotel.

    答案:a　　　b　　　c

五、听录音,快速回答问题　**Give prompt answers to the following questions.**

第四十八课　**Lesson 48**

一、语音练习　Pronunciation exercises：

  （1）边听边给下面的句子注音：

    Transcribe the proverbs according to the recording：

    ① 三人同行，必有我师。

    ② 活到老，学到老。

    ③ 经一事，长一智。

    ④ 只要改，不怕晚。

  （2）读上面的句子　Read aloud the above proverbs．

二、听写练习　Dictations：

  （1）听写句子　Write down the folloving sentences：

    ①

    ②

    ③

    ④

    ⑤

  （2）听下面的短文，边听边记下你听到的时间、地点、人名和数字。

    Listen to the following passage and take down the time, place, name and figures．

三、听下面的句子,听后选择正确答案:

Listen to the sentences and circle the correct answers to the questions from the alternatives given:

(1) a   b

(2) a   b

(3) a   b

(4) a   b

(5) a   b

四、听后回答问题:

Listen to the dialogue and the passage and answer the questions on them:

(1) 情景:一个女青年在回家的路上看到一个小姑娘正在哭,就走过去。

    Situation: A girl is on her way home when she sees a little girl crying and goes up to her.

    生词:风   fēng   wind

          危险   wēixiǎn   dangerous

          技术员 jìshùyuán   technician

    ①

    ②

    ③

(2) 生词:小偷 xiǎotōu   pick-pocket

          打鼾 dǎ hān   to snore

          沙发 shāfā   sofa

    ①

    ②

    ③

五、听录音,快速回答问题 **Give prompt answers to the following questions.**

第四十九课　Lesson 49

（1）边听边给下面的绕口令注音：

Transcribe the tongue twister according to the recording：

大嫂子和大小子

一个大嫂子，一个大小子，

大嫂子跟大小子比包饺子；

不知是大嫂子包的饺子不如大小子，

还是大小子包的饺子不如大嫂子。

（2）读上面的绕口令　Read aloud the above tongue twister.

（3）听后把两句话合成比较句（一句用"比"，一句用"没有"）：

Combine each group of sentences into 1）a sentence using 比；and 2）a sentence using 没有：

例　Model：

上海饭馆儿多。北京饭馆儿不太多。

——→上海饭馆儿比北京多。

北京饭馆儿没有上海那么多。

①

②

③

④

⑤

二、听写练习　**Dictation**：

边听边记下数字和地点　Take down the places and figures.

"

三、听下面的句子,听后回答问题:

Listen to the sentences and answer the questions on them:

(1)

(2)

(3)

(4)

(5)

四、听后选择正确答案:

Listen to the dialogues and circle the correct answers to the questions from the alternatives given:

(1) 情景:甲从外地来北京住在旅馆,乙在一个学校工作,今天约好,来陪他游览。

Situation: A, who has just come to Beijing, is staying at a hotel and he has an appointment with B who works at a school and will take him go sightseeing in the city.

生词:游览　yóulǎn　to go sightseeing

　　　打算　dǎsuan　to plan

① a　　　b　　　c

② a　　　b　　　c

③ a　　　b　　　c

(2) 情景:约翰刚从中国南方参观回来,李大年去看他。

Situation: John has just come back from a visit to Southern China. Li Danian has come to see him.

生词:…极了　…jíle　　　extremely

　　　无锡　Wúxī　　　Wuxi, *a city in Jiangsu Province*

　　　风景　fēngjǐng　　　landscape

① a　　　b　　　c

② a　　　b　　　c

③ a　　　b　　　c　　　d

五、听录音,快速回答问题　**Give prompt answers to the following questions.**

第 五 十 课　Lesson 50

一、语音练习　**Pronunciation exercises**：

　　(1) 边听边给下面的谚语、格言注音：

　　Transcribe the proverbs and maxims according to the recording：

　　① 白日莫闲过，青春不再来。

　　② 书到用时方恨少。

　　③ 室雅何须大，花香不在多。

　　④ 穿衣戴帽，各人所好。

　　(2) 读上面的谚语、格言　Read aloud the above proverbs and maxims.

　　(3) 边听边记，然后说出主要意思。

　　Take notes while you listen and summarize orally what you hear.

二、把下面的句子改成比较句　**Turn the following into sentences of comparison**：

　　(1)

　　(2)

　　(3)

　　(4)

　　(5)

三、听下面的句子，边听边填表：

Listen to the following statements and fill in the forms while you listen：

(1)

汽水一瓶	啤酒一瓶	啤酒比汽水贵

(2)

上海人口	北京人口	北京人口比上海少

(3)

最高气温	最低气温	风力

(4)

最低气温	最高气温	风力

(5)

长江长	黄河长	长江比黄河长

四、听后回答问题 Listen to the dialogues and answer the questions on them:

（1）情景：甲请乙介绍北京的天气。

　　Situation: A asks B to tell him what the weather is like in Beijing.

　　①

　　②

　　③

（2）情景：天华的哥哥要去日本工作，走以前，天华和嫂子商量全家一起去逛公园。

　　Situation: Tianhua's brother is going to work in Japan. Before he leaves, Tianhua and his sister-in-law decide that the whole family go to a park.

　　生词：转　　zhuǎn　　　　　to turn

　　　　　风向　fēngxiàng　　　wind direction

　　①

　　②

　　③

　　④

　　⑤

五、听录音，快速回答问题 Give prompt answers to the following questions.

一、语音练习　Pronunciation exercises：

（1）边听边给下面的诗注音　Transcribe the poem according to the recording：

和童年留影对话

“你真是我吗？”

你用天真的笑回答了我。

“你真是我吗？”

回答不出。

因为我在寻找那颗失落的童心。

明天——相信我能回答：

“我就是你！”

（2）朗读上面的诗　Read aloud the above poem．

（3）听后把两个句子变成一个带"比"的句子：

Combine each group of sentences into one of comparison using 比：

①

②

③

④

⑤

二、边听边记下与下面问题有关的句子：

Listen to the story and take down the sentences that are relevent to the following questions：

生词：黑猫　　hēimāo　　　　black cat

　　　警长　　jǐngzhǎng　　　police officer

　　　只好　　zhǐhǎo　　　　could only but …

　　　坏蛋　　huàidàn　　　　bad egg

104

(1)

(2)

(3)

三、听下面的句子,听后回答问题:

Listen to the sentences and answer the questions on them:
(1)
(2)
(3)
(4)
(5)

四、听后选择正确答案:

Listen to the dialogues and circle the correct answers to the questions from the alternatives given:

(1) 情景:山田在公共汽车上碰见了安娜。

　　Situation：Shantian meets Anna on a bus．

　　① a　　　b

　　② a　　　b

(2) 情景:玲玲要去飞机场接人,可是下大雨了。

　　Situation：Lingling is going to meet someone at the airport，but it rains heavily．

　　生词：班　　　　bān　　　　flight

　　　　　雷阵雨　　léizhènyǔ　　thunder shower

　　① a　　　b

　　② a　　　b

五、听录音,快速回答问题　Give prompt answers to the following questions．

第五十二课　**Lesson 52**

一、语音练习　Pronunciation exercises:

(1) 边听边给下面的绕口令注音：

Transcribe the tongue twister according to the recording:

华华有两朵黄花儿，

红红有两朵红花儿。

华华要红花儿，

红红要黄花儿。

华华送给红红一朵黄花儿，

红红送给华华一朵红花儿。

华华有黄花儿和红花儿，

红红有红花儿和黄花儿。

两个笑得脸上像朵花儿。

(2) 读上面的绕口令　Read aloud the above tongue twister.

(3) 听后口头回答问题。

Listen to the sentences and answer the questions on them orally.

二、边听边记, 听后回答下面的问题:

Take notes while you listen and then answer the following questions:

(1)

(2)

三、听下面的句子, 听后回答问题:

Listen to the sentences and answer the questions on them:

(1)

(2)

(3)

(4)

(5)

四、听后选择正确答案:

Listen to the dialogues and circle the correct answers to the questions from the alternatives given:

(1) 情景:张正生老师和同学们讨论汉语节目表演的问题。

Situation: Mr. Zhang Zhengsheng is discussing with his students about what performance they should give on the Chinese evening party.

① a   b   c

② a   b   c

③ a   b   c

(2) 情景:夏子和安娜谈考试的成绩。

Situation: Xiazi and Anna are talking about how well they did in the recent examination.

生词:困难　kùnnan　difficult

① a   b   c

② a   b   c

五、听录音,快速回答问题　**Give prompt answers to the following questions.**

第五十三课　Lesson 53

（1）边听边给下面的古诗注音　Transcribe the poem according to the recording:

杂　诗

君自故乡来，

应知故乡事。

来日绮窗前，

寒梅着花未？

（2）朗读上面的诗　Read aloud the above poem.

（3）根据问题,标出答句的重音:

Mark the sentence stresses of the answers as suggested by the questions:

① 昨天的表演比上次强得多。

② 没有,他比平时早到了十分钟呢!

③ 不,比这儿暖和多了。

④ 不,除了约翰和安娜以外,我们都没去过。

⑤ 不,除了四川以外,我还想去乌鲁木齐看看。

二、听写练习　**Dictation**:

边听边记下每个节日的名称和时间:

Take down the names and dates of the holidays while you listen:

生词:政治性　　zhèngzhìxìng　political

元旦　　yuándàn　New Year's Day

正月　　zhēngyuè　the First month by the lunar calendar

初　　chū　*prefix used before numbers* 1 – 10 *to indicate the first ten days of a lunar month*

三、听下面的句子,听后回答问题:

Listen to the secntences and answer the questions on them:

(1)

(2)

(3)

(4)

(5)

四、听后填空　**Listen to the dialogues and then fill in the blanks:**

(1) 情景:中国学生贾红春和日本学生夏子谈节日。

Situation: Jia Hongchun, a Chinese student, and Xiazi, a Japanese student, are talking about festivals.

生词:除夕　chúxī　New Year's Eve

　　　亲戚　qīnqi　relative

① 中国的春节在农历______月______号。

② 初一早上人们吃过早饭就去亲戚朋友家______________。

③ 日本人现在不过________,只过________。

(2) 情景:大年在书店买书的时候遇见了约翰。

Situation: Danian meets John in the bookshop.

生词:画册　huàcè　picture album

　　　毛笔　máobǐ　Chinese brush for writing Chinese characters

① 约翰买了三本书,一本是________,一本是________,一本是________。另外,他还买了两种贺年片儿,一种是________,一种是________。

② 大年除了买书以外,还买了____________。

五、听录音,快速回答问题　**Give prompt answers to the following questions.**

第五十四课　Lesson 54

一、语音练习　**Pronunciation exercises**：

（1）边听边给下面的词语注音：

Transcribe the words and phrases according to the recording：

① 整整齐齐　　　　② 百花齐放

③ 艺术剧院　　　　④ 乘风破浪

⑤ 先进技术　　　　⑥ 为人民服务

⑦ 千奇百怪　　　　⑧ 九九八十一

（2）听写　Dictation：

①

②

③

④

二、听后把下面的"被"字句改成"把"字句：

Turn the 被-sentences into 把-sentences：

（1）

（2）

（3）

（4）

（5）

三、听下面的句子，听后选择正确答案：

Listen to the following sentences and circle the correct answers to the questions from the alternatives given：

（1）a　　b　　c

（2）a　　b　　c

（3）a　　b　　c　　d

（4）a　　b　　c

（5）a　　b　　c　　d

四、听后做练习　**Listen to the dialogue before you do the following exercises**:

情景:课间,安娜向高老师问一些关于中国人过春节的问题。

Situation: Anna asks Mr. Gao some questions about how Chinese celebrate the Spring Festival.

生词:除夕　　chúxī　　　New Year's Eve

　　　聊天　　liáo tiān　　to have a chat

　　　拜年　　bài nián　　to pay a New Year visit

　　　庆祝　　qìngzhù　　to celebrate

　　　活动　　huódòng　　activity

(1) 填空　Fill in the blanks:

①春节前一天叫________,也叫________。到了半夜十二点,人们互相
________________。这时候最________。

②北京的春天是从________月到________月。

(2) 选择正确答案:

Circle the correct answers to the questions from the alternatives given:

① a　　　b　　　c

② a　　　b　　　c　　　d

③ a　　　b

五、听故事,回答问题　**Listen to the story and then answer the questions**:

生词:斧子　fǔzi　axe

(1)

(2)

(3)

六、听录音,快速回答问题　**Give prompt answers to the following questions**.

第五十五课　Lesson 55

一、语音练习　Pronunciation exercises：

边听边给下面的词语注音：

Transcribe the words and phrases according to the recording：

(1) 玻璃制品

(2) 长途电话

(3) 蔬菜商店

(4) 长跑运动员

(5) 糊里糊涂

(6) 急急忙忙

(7) 精神焕发

(8) 八仙过海，各显其能。

二、听写　Dictation：

(1)

(2)

(3)

(4)

三、听下面的句子,听后选择正确解释：

Listen to the following sentences and circle the correct explanations from the alternatives given：

(1) a   b   c

(2) a   b   c

(3) a   b   c

(4) a   b   c

(5) a   b   c

四、听后做练习　Listen to the story before you do the following exercises：

生词：家长　　jiāzhǎng　　　parent or guardian of a child

　　　警察　　jǐngchá　　　 police（man）

藏　　cáng　　　hide
文章　wénzhāng　article

（1）选择正确答案　Circle the correct explanations from the alternatives given：
① a　　b　　c
② a　　b　　c
③ a　　b　　c
④ a　　b　　c

（2）回答下面的问题　Answer the following questions：
①
②
③
④
⑤

五、听录音,快速回答问题　Give prompt answers to the following questions.

录音文本　The Tapescript

第 一 课

一、听韵母。第一遍听,第二遍、第三遍跟读:

a o er ai ao an i iu ian iu u ua

二、听声母。第一遍听,第二遍、第三遍跟读:

b d t n l s g k h w y

三、听音节。第一遍听,第二遍、第三遍跟读:

ba bai ban bao bo bu bi bin

da dai dan dao du di diu dian

ta tai tan tao tu ti tian

na nai nan nao nu ni niu nin

la lai lan lao lu li liu lian lin

sa sai san sao su

ga gai gan gao gu gua

ka kai kan kao ku kua

ha hai han hao hu hua

ya yan yao yi yin

wa wai wan wo wu

四、听声调。第一遍听,第二遍、第三遍跟读:

(1) ā á ǎ à　　ū ú ǔ ù　　ī í ǐ ì

　　 āi ái ǎi ài　　ān án ǎn àn

(2) lā lá lǎ là　　bān bán bǎn bàn

　　 hū hú hǔ hù　　kāi kái kǎi kài

　　 niū niú niǔ niù　　lū lú lǔ lù

　　 gān gán gǎn gàn　　nū nú nǔ nù

　　 dāo dáo dǎo dào　　sū sú sǔ sù

　　 liān lián liǎn liàn　　tū tú tǔ tù

yīn yín yǐn yìn   wān wán wǎn wàn

yān yán yǎn yàn

五、听后画出声母：

（1）na   la   （2）san   lan

nao lao   sa   la

nu   lu   sai lai

（3）dan tan   （4）gao kao

dai tai   gu   ku

dian tian   gua kua

六、听后画出韵母：

（1） $b\begin{cases} a \\ ao \\ u \end{cases}$ （2） $t\begin{cases} ao \\ u \\ i \end{cases}$ （3） $h\begin{cases} a \\ an \\ ao \end{cases}$

（4） $i\begin{cases} iu \\ in \\ i \end{cases}$ （5） $y\begin{cases} a \\ ao \\ a \end{cases}$ （6） $w\begin{cases} a \\ u \\ o \end{cases}$

七、画出你听到的音节：

（1）tā   tǎ   （2）dá   dà

bái bǎi   bù   bú

hú   hǔ   huā huà

tāo táo   gǎo gào

liú liǔ   lù   lú

hǎi hái   wāi wài

sān sǎn   ér   èr

八、听后标出调号：

（1）lá   （2）nǔ   （3）dà   （4）sān

（5）yáo   （6）bài   （7）huá   （8）liǎn

（9）liú   （10）báo   （11）tǐ   （12）yí

九、练习对话：

(1) 情景：两个老朋友又见面了。

A：你好！

B：你好！

(2) 情景：在路上学生见到了老师。

A：您好！

B：你好！

(3) 情景：两个人第一次认识。

A：您好！

B：您好！

第 二 课

一、听韵母。第一遍听，第二遍、第三遍跟读：

（1）e ei en

（2）a o e er ai ei ao an en i iu ian in u ua

二、听声母。第一遍听，第二遍、第三遍跟读：

b m d t n l s g k h y w

三、听音节。第一遍听，第二遍、第三遍跟读：

da dai de dei den du dan diu

gai ge gei gen gao gan gu gua

mai me mei men mu man min mian

ka ke kai kei kao kan ken

ta tu ti tai tao tan tian te

nai nei nen nan nu niu nin nian

sai se sen sa san su

ya ye yao yan

wa wan wu wai wen

四、听声调。第一遍听，第二遍、第三遍跟读：

（1）ā á ǎ à   ē é ě è   ēi éi ěi èi

　　 ēn én ěn èn   āi ái ǎi ài

（2）māi mái mǎi mài   gēn gén gěn gèn

　　 tū tú tǔ tù   diān dián diǎn diàn

　　 hū hú hǔ hù   sēn sén sěn sèn

（3）lālā lālá lālǎ lālà lāla

　　 lálā lálá lálǎ lálà lála

　　 lǎlā lǎlá lǎlǎ lǎlà lǎla

　　 làlā làlá làlǎ làlà làla

(4) lāla   lála   lǎla   làla

     gūgu   lái ba   hǎode   kàn a

五、听后画出声母：

(1) da   ta   (2) gu   ku   hu

     dai   tai   gen   ken   hen

     di   ti   gao   kao   hao

     dao   tao   gua   kua   hua

     dan   tan   gan   kan   han

六、听后画出韵母：

(1) ben   ban   (2) lin   lian

     sen   san   diu   dian

     men   man   niu   nian

     nen   nan   miu   mian

     wen   wan

七、听后把每个音节的声韵母连在一起：

huā lín wǔ dào yě mèn tán gǎi

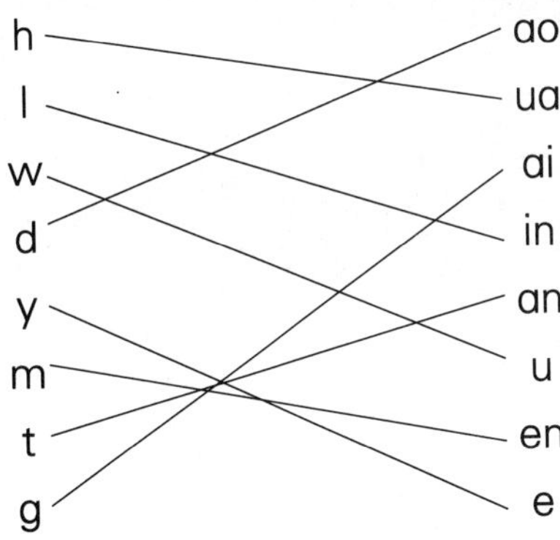

八、听后标出调号：

(1) mǔ mén gé bēi wǎn dāi tián kè

(2) bāyī máoyī gùkè yánsè dìtú

(3) mèimei bàba tāmen wǒde yéye

九、练习对话：

（1）情景：孩子给爸爸打电话。

　　A：您好，爸爸！

　　B：你好！

（2）情景：孩子给妈妈打电话。

　　A：您好，妈妈！

　　B：你好！

（3）情景：上课了，老师走进教室，师生互相问候。

　　A：你们好！

　　B：您好！

第 三 课

一、听韵母。第一遍听,第二遍、第三遍跟读:

    (1) ou   eng   ong   ui

    (2) a o e er ai ei ao ou an en eng ong i iu ian in

        u ua ui

二、听声母。第一遍听,第二遍、第三遍跟读:

    (1) p f sh r

    (2) b p m f d t n l s sh r g k h y w

三、听音节。第一遍听,第二遍、第三遍跟读:

    pa pan pen peng pou pu pian pin

    fa fan fen feng fei fu

    sha she shei shai shao shan shen sheng shou shu shua

    shui

    re rao rou ran ren reng rong ru rui

四、听声调。第一遍听,第二遍、第三遍跟读:

    (1) ōu   óu   ǒu   òu   ēng   éng   ěng   èng

         ōng   óng   ǒng   òng   uī   uí   uǐ   uì

    (2) pēng   péng   pěng   pèng

        ——   shuí   shuǐ   shuì

        fū   fú   fǔ   fù

    (3) lālā lālá lālǎ lālà lāla

        lálā lálá lálǎ lálà lála

        lǎlā lǎlá lǎlǎ lǎlà lǎla

        làlā làlá làlǎ làlà làla

    (4) pāndēng suīrán shēntǐ fūfù dōngbian

        línshī értóng niúnǎi róngyi shíhou

kǎoyā   běnlái   wǔdǎo   yǒuyì   lǎoshi

lùyīn   shìshí   lìshǐ   rèlèi   gùshi

（5）shǒudū   měitiān   kěnéng   rǎnhóng   fǔdǎo

yǒnggǎn   wǎnhuì   nǔlì   měige   wǎnle

五、辨韵母。画出你听到的音节：

（1）gai(✓)   gei   （2）ben(✓)   beng

shai   shei(✓)   pen   peng(✓)

pai   pei(✓)   fen   feng(✓)

mai(✓)   mei   shen(✓)   sheng

nai   nei(✓)   ren   reng(✓)

（3）man   men(✓)

nan   nen(✓)

shan(✓)   shen

ran(✓)   ren

han   hen(✓)

（4）gao   gou(✓)   gong

dao(✓)   dou   dong

rao   rou   rong(✓)

yao   you   yong(✓)

lao   lou(✓)   long

六、辨声母。画出你听到的音节：

beng(✓)   peng

tong(✓)   dong

gu   ku(✓)

shan   san(✓)

long   rong(✓)

fu(✓)   mu

七、听后标出调号：

（1）gòngtóng　　（2）gǎigé　　　（3）héshì　　　（4）bǎoguì

（5）dàhǎi　　　（6）měilì　　　（7）shídài　　　（8）pútao

（9）nèiróng　　（10）péngpài　　（11）shǒutào　　（12）gǔdài

八、听后填空：

（1）情景：A 向朋友介绍他的弟弟。

　　A：他是我弟弟，是大夫。她是我朋友。

　　B：你好！

　　C：你好！

　　B：你是老师吗？

　　C：是，我是老师。

　　他弟弟是　　大夫　　。

（2）情景：A 在 B 家看 B 的全家福照片。

　　A：你妹妹是大夫吗？

　　B：她是护士。我妈妈是大夫。

　　A：他是谁？

　　B：他是我哥哥，是工人。

　　他妈妈是　　大夫　　，妹妹是　　护士　　，哥哥是　　工人　　。

第 四 课

一、听韵母。第一遍听,第二遍、第三遍跟读:

（1）ang　uan　uo

（2）a　o　e　er　ai　ei　ao　ou　an　en　ang　eng　ong　i　iu　ian
in　u　ua　uo　ui　uan

二、听声母。第一遍听,第二遍、第三遍跟读:

（1）zh　ch

（2）b　p　m　f　d　t　n　l　s　zh　ch　sh　r　g　k　h　y　w

三、听音节。第一遍听,第二遍、第三遍跟读:

（1）
$\begin{cases} zha \\ cha \end{cases}$　$\begin{cases} zhai \\ chai \end{cases}$　$\begin{cases} zhao \\ chao \end{cases}$　$\begin{cases} zhou \\ chou \end{cases}$　$\begin{cases} zhan \\ chan \end{cases}$

$\begin{cases} zhen \\ chen \end{cases}$　$\begin{cases} zhang \\ chang \end{cases}$　$\begin{cases} zheng \\ cheng \end{cases}$　$\begin{cases} zhu \\ chu \end{cases}$　$\begin{cases} zhuo \\ chuo \end{cases}$

$\begin{cases} zhui \\ chui \end{cases}$　$\begin{cases} zhuan \\ chuan \end{cases}$

（2）
$\begin{cases} shan \\ ran \end{cases}$　$\begin{cases} shu \\ ru \end{cases}$　$\begin{cases} duan \\ tuan \end{cases}$　$\begin{cases} guo \\ kuo \end{cases}$　$\begin{cases} bang \\ pang \end{cases}$

$\begin{cases} bian \\ pian \end{cases}$　$\begin{cases} lin \\ nin \end{cases}$　$\begin{cases} shu \\ su \end{cases}$

（3）
$\begin{cases} nà \\ nàr \end{cases}$　$\begin{cases} zhā \\ zhār \end{cases}$　$\begin{cases} zhè \\ zhèr \end{cases}$　$\begin{cases} lán \\ lánr \end{cases}$　$\begin{cases} wán \\ wánr \end{cases}$

$\begin{cases} guǎn \\ guǎnr \end{cases}$　$\begin{cases} dèng \\ dèngr \end{cases}$　$\begin{cases} hái \\ háir \end{cases}$　$\begin{cases} zhū \\ zhūr \end{cases}$　$\begin{cases} mén \\ ménr \end{cases}$

四、听声调。第一遍听,第二遍、第三遍跟读:

（1）zhāng　　zháng　　zhǎng　　zhàng

chāng　　cháng　　chǎng　　chàng

zhuān　　zhuán　　zhuǎn　　zhuàn

chuān　　chuán　　chuǎn　　chuàn

piān　　pián　　piǎn　　piàn

tiān　　tián　　tiǎn　　tiàn

fū　　fú　　fǔ　　fù

hū　　hú　　hǔ　　hù

（2）lālā　lālá　lālǎ　lālà　lāla

　　　lálā　lálá　lálǎ　lálà　lála

　　　lǎlā　lǎlá　lǎlǎ　lǎlà　lǎla

　　　làlā　làlá　làlǎ　làlà　làla

（3）dōngfāng　　zhāopai　　chūbǎn　　chēzhàn　　zhāohu

　　　chénggōng　Chángchéng　chuántǒng　chéngshì　chúle

　　　zhuǎnbō　　chǎnchú　　chǎnpǐn　　chǎofàn　　wǎnshang

　　　chàng gē　　chuàn ménr　zhuànyǐ　　zhòngyào　　zhàngfu

（4）sān dár　　cháguǎnr　　zhàopiānr　　yìdiǎnr

　　　bǎobèir　　shǒutàor　　zài nǎr　　zhù zhèr

（5）Tiān'ānmén　　dàshǐguǎn　　bàngōngshì

　　　huǒchēzhàn　　shuǐguǒdiàn　　hèniánpiànr

五、辨声母。画出你听到的音节：

（1）zhi(✓)　　chi　　　　　zhen　　　chen(✓)

　　　zhu(✓)　　shu　　　　　shui　　　zhui(✓)

　　　zhai　　　chai(✓)　　　zhou(✓)　shou

　　　shang(✓)　chang　　　　shua(✓)　zhua

（2）gua(✓)　　kua　　　　　guan　　　kuan(✓)

　　　huo　　　guo(✓)　　　　huo　　　kuo(✓)

　　　gai　　　hai(✓)　　　　gong(✓)　kong

　　　kang(✓)　gang　　　　　gou　　　hou(✓)

六、辨韵母。画出你听到的音节：

  rou   ruo(✓)   rong

  zhao(✓)   zhuo   zhong

  shan(✓)   shang   sheng

  chou   chong(✓)   chao

七、听后标出调号：

（1）sēnlín   （2）zhēnlǐ   （3）shēnrù   （4）sōngshù

（5）huānténg   （6）shìchǎng   （7）fāngfǎ   （8）hóngsè

（9）yǎnchū   （10）běifēng   （11）duànliàn   （12）gōngchǎng

八、听后填"-r"：

（1）Yí dà dár.

（2）Zhēn méi fǎr.

（3）Tā shàng nǎr?

（4）Wǒ shàng nàr.

（5）Zhè ge wǎnr hěn hǎo.

九、听后选择正确答案：

（1）情景：学生们在楼前遇见了张老师。

  A、B、C：张老师好！

  D：你们好。你们上哪儿？

  A：李大年上食堂，刘天华上银行，我上商店。

  B：张老师，您上哪儿？

  D：我上医院。

问：谁上医院？

  a. 李大年   b. 刘天华   c. 张老师○

（2）情景：两个老人在路上相遇。

  A：您上哪儿？

  B：我上图书馆。

  A：上哪儿？上饭馆儿？

  B：图书馆！

问：他上哪儿？

    a．图书馆○   b．饭馆儿

十、听录音，口头回答问题：

（1）你上哪儿？

（2）张正生上哪儿？

（3）常志成上医院吗？

（4）谁上商店？

第 五 课

一、听韵母。第一遍听，第二遍、第三遍跟读：

a　o　e　er　ai　ei　ao　ou　an　en　ang　eng　ong　i　iu

ian　in　u　ua　uo　ui　uan

二、听声母。第一遍听，第二遍、第三遍跟读：

b	d	n	zh	sh	sh	g
p	t	l	ch	r	s	k

g	k	h
h	h	f

三、听音节。第一遍听，第二遍、第三遍跟读：

(1)

gua	zhuan	shua	guan	fu
hua	chuan	rua	huan	hu

bu	du
pu	tu

(2)

guo	huo	zhuo	zhan	chan
gua	hua	zhua	zhuan	chuan

gan	han
guan	huan

四、听声调。第一遍听，第二遍、第三遍跟读：

(1)　lālā　lālá　lālǎ　lālà　lāla

　　　lálā　lálá　lálǎ　lálà　lála

　　　lǎlā　lǎlá　lǎlǎ　lǎlà　lǎla

　　　làlā　làlá　làlǎ　làlà　làla

(2)　guā fēng　Zhōnghuá　shēntǐ　shāndòng　zhīshi

　　　dú shū　értóng　mínzhǔ　shídài　róngyi

shǒudū　　　lǐtáng　　　fǔdǎo　　　kǎo shì　　　ěrduo

diànchē　　　kèwén　　　dàshǐ　　　hùzhù　　　gàosu

（3）yīyuàn　　　rénmínbì　　　yóulǎntú　　　shìyīshì

bàogàohuì　　　Ālābówén

wúguǐ diànchē　diànshì zhuǎnbō

（4）bàba　　　zhàozhe　　　nuǎnhuo　　　wǎnshang　　　tàiyang

shuí de　　　guàntou　　　yílùshang　　　chàbuduō　　　shìyishì

（5）wàibianr　　　pángbiānr　　　niánhuàr　　　chàng gēr

dàshēngr　　　cháguǎnr　　　rèshuǐguǎnr

（6）bù　　　bù bān　　　bù zhuān　　　bù bái

bù lián　　　bù lěng　　　bù bǐ　　　bú shì

bú duì　　　bú rè　　　bú huì

五、听后把每个音节的声韵母连在一起：

zhao　chou　shai　sen　rong　huo　gan　fei

zh　　　　　　　　　ai
ch　　　　　　　　　an
sh　　　　　　　　　ao
s　　　　　　　　　en
r　　　　　　　　　ei
h　　　　　　　　　ong
g　　　　　　　　　uo
f　　　　　　　　　ou

六、听后填上声母：

zhāshi　　　zhīchí　　　zhēnshí　　　zhòngyào

chāisàn　　　chóngféng　　　zhēnchéng　　　péichèn

七、听后填上韵母：

zhànzhǎng　　　shénshèng　　　fǎngwèn　　　chángláng

chénggōng   wǎnshang   zhēnchéng   shānshang

八、听后标出调号：

tōngzhī   suíshí   diànshì   yóulǎn

zhuǎnwānr   huàbào   huǒchái   hǎoshì

九、听后选择正确答案：

(1) 情景：A 和 B 在食堂买饭。

  A：你吃什么？

  B：这是什么？

  A：这是馒头。那是包子。

  B：你吃馒头吗？

  A：不，我吃包子。

  B：我也吃包子。

问：他们吃什么？

  a. 馒头 b. 包子○

(2) 情景：李大年和刘天华在路上相遇。

  A：刘天华，你回宿舍吗？

  B：不，我上书店。你上哪儿？

  A：我上图书馆。你买书吗？

  B：对，我买书，也买画报。

问：刘天华上哪儿？

  a. 宿舍 b. 书店○ c. 图书馆

(3) 情景：A 向 B 询问银行在哪儿。

  A：那是银行吗？

  B：不，那是商店。你上银行吗？

  A：对，我上银行。你上哪儿？

  B：我也上银行。

问：他们上哪儿？

  a. 商店 b. 银行○

十、听录音，口头回答问题：

(1) 这是什么？

(2) 那是什么？

（3）你们上哪儿？

（4）他吃包子吗？

（5）你常常吃馒头吗？

（6）那是什么地方？

（7）你买什么？

第 六 课

一、听韵母。第一遍听,第二遍、第三遍跟读:

a o e er ai ei ao ou an en ang eng ong

i ie iu ian in ing u ua uo ui uan

二、听声母。第一遍听,第二遍、第三遍跟读:

(1) $\begin{cases} j \\ q \end{cases}$ $\begin{cases} j \\ zh \end{cases}$ $\begin{cases} q \\ ch \end{cases}$ $\begin{cases} x \\ sh \end{cases}$

(2) $\begin{cases} zh \\ ch \end{cases}$ $\begin{cases} sh \\ r \end{cases}$ $\begin{cases} b \\ p \end{cases}$ $\begin{cases} m \\ f \end{cases}$ $\begin{cases} d \\ t \end{cases}$

$\begin{cases} n \\ l \end{cases}$ $\begin{cases} g \\ k \end{cases}$

三、听音节。第一遍听,第二遍、第三遍跟读:

(1) $\begin{cases} ji \\ qi \\ xi \end{cases}$ $\begin{cases} jie \\ qie \\ xie \end{cases}$ $\begin{cases} jiu \\ qiu \\ xiu \end{cases}$ $\begin{cases} jian \\ qian \\ xian \end{cases}$ $\begin{cases} jin \\ qin \\ xin \end{cases}$ $\begin{cases} jing \\ qing \\ xing \end{cases}$

(2) $\begin{cases} bie \\ pie \end{cases}$ $\begin{cases} die \\ tie \end{cases}$ $\begin{cases} nie \\ lie \end{cases}$

(3) $\begin{cases} bin \\ bing \end{cases}$ $\begin{cases} pin \\ ping \end{cases}$ $\begin{cases} lin \\ ling \end{cases}$ $\begin{cases} min \\ ming \end{cases}$ $\begin{cases} nin \\ ning \end{cases}$

(4) $\left.\begin{matrix} g \\ k \\ h \end{matrix}\right\}an$ $\left.\begin{matrix} g \\ k \\ h \end{matrix}\right\}ang$ $\left.\begin{matrix} g \\ k \\ h \end{matrix}\right\}u$ $\left.\begin{matrix} g \\ k \\ h \end{matrix}\right\}ui$ $\left.\begin{matrix} g \\ k \\ h \end{matrix}\right\}uan$

四、听声调。第一遍听,第二遍、第三遍跟读:

(1) jiē jié jiě jiè │ qiū qiú qiǔ qiù

jiān　jián　jiǎn　jiàn　　qīn　qín　qǐn　qìn
jīng　jíng　jǐng　jìng　　xīng　xíng　xǐng　xìng

（2）qīngsōng　jíjí　　qīnyǒu　jīqì　　qīngchu

　　qiántiān　jiébái　　qiúchǎng　qiánjìn　jiéqi

　　jiěshuō　jǐnjí　　jiǎnshǎo　jiěshì　jiějie

　　jiànkāng　qìyóu　　jìnglǐ　　jiànzhù　xièxie

（3）qìchēzhàn　　lěngyǐndiàn　　jīqìrénr

（4）Qǐng nǐ gěi wǒ wǔ　běn Fǎwén shū.

（5）一、二、三、四、五、六、七、八、九、十

五、画出你听到的音节：

（1）ji　　　　qi(✓)　　　（2）bin (✓)　　bing

　　jie　　　qie(✓)　　　　pin　　　ping(✓)

　　jiu(✓)　qiu　　　　　　min(✓)　ming

　　jian　　qian(✓)　　　　nin　　　ning(✓)

　　jin　　 qin(✓)　　　　 lin　　　ling(✓)

　　jing(✓)　qing　　　　　xin(✓)　xing

六、听后填上声母：

jǐtǐ　　　　qìchē　　　qiūtiān　　　jiēshòu

qiántú　　jiànmiàn　　jǐnjí　　　　qínglǎng

七、听后填上韵母：

xīngqī　　jìnbù　　　pīngpāng　　yǐngshè

jīngshén　niánqīng　　rèliè　　　piēkāi

八、学说绕口令：

妈妈骑马，　　　　Māma qí mǎ,

马慢妈妈骂马；　　Mǎ màn māma mà mǎ;

妞妞轰牛，　　　　Niūniu hōng niú,

牛拗妞妞拧牛。　　Niú niù Niūniu níng niú.

九、听后选择正确答案：

（1）情景：A 在教室的窗台上看到一本画报，不知道是谁的。

    A：李大年，看，画报。

    B：这是谁的画报？你知道吗？

    A：我也不知道。

    B：是不是刘天华的画报？

    A：（喊）刘天华，这是你的画报吗？

    C：什么，我的画报？……啊，对，对，是我的画报。

    B：给你。

    C：谢谢。

    B：不谢。

问：那是谁的画报？

    a. 是李大年的画报　　　b. 是刘天华的画报○

（2）情景：阿里在路上遇见了李大年和他的姐姐。

    A：大年，你们上哪儿？

    B：阿里，你好。这是我姐姐。这是我朋友阿里。

    A：您好！

    C：您好！

    A：这是你的报，给你。

    B：谢谢。

    A：不谢。

问：那是谁的报？

    a. 是大年的报○　　　b. 是姐姐的报　　　c. 是阿里的报

十、听录音，口头回答问题：

    （1）这是谁的书？

    （2）那是谁的画儿？

    （3）这是你的纸吗？

    （4）你知道这是什么？

    （5）你知道那是谁的馒头？

    （6）那是姐姐的宿舍吗？

    （7）她是高老师的姐姐吗？

    （8）她是谁的姐姐？

    （9）那个青年是医生吗？

    （10）你给谁书？

第 七 课

一、听韵母。第一遍听,第二遍、第三遍跟读:

{a / e   {ao / ou   {an / ang   {ian / iang   {ang / iang   {en / eng

{in / ing

二、听声母。第一遍听,第二遍、第三遍跟读:

{b / p   {m / f   {d / t   {l / r   {j / q   {j / x   {q / x

{g / k / h   {zh / ch / sh / r

三、听音节。第一遍听,第二遍、第三遍跟读:

(1) {j / q / x}i   {j / q / x}ie   {j / q / x}iu   {j / q / x}ian   {j / q / x}iang

{n / l / q}iang   {g / k / h}u   {zh / ch / sh}u

(2) f{a / an / ang   p{ai / ei / ou   t{a / ao / an   ch{a / ou / ang

四、听声调。第一遍听,第二遍、第三遍跟读:

(1) niāng   niáng   niǎng   niàng

liāng   liáng   liǎng   liàng

jiāng   jiáng   jiǎng   jiàng

qiāng   qiáng   qiǎng   qiàng

xiāng   xiáng   xiǎng   xiàng

(2) fēijī   sēnlín   jīnshǔ   fāngxiàng

liánhuān   lánqiú   tíngzhǐ   nóngyè

Běijīng   yǒumíng   yǎnjiǎng   lǐngxiù

lùyīn   liànxí   mòxiě   duànliàn

(3) shǒudū   měitiān   mǎchē   jiǎndān

fǎguó   fǔzhú   qiǎngduó   wǔshí

yǒuyì   měilì   bǎohù   kěndìng

běnshi   nuǎnhuo   yǎnjing   wǎnshang

(4) huà huàr   xiāngshuǐr   xiàngpiānr

shuǐdiǎnr   huābiānr   mòshuǐr

(5) 一、   二、   三、   四、   五、   六、   七、   八、   九、   十

十、   九、   八、   七、   六、   五、   四、   三、   二、   一

五、听后填上声母：

s̲i   x̲ie   x̲iang   s̲ai   j̲iu   s̲ou   q̲ian   t̲u

六、画出你听到的音节：

(1) jiang(✓)   zhang   (2) jian(✓)   jiang

qian(✓)   jian   xian(✓)   xiang

xiu   jiu(✓)   zhan   zhang(✓)

jie   qie(✓)   chan(✓)   chang

gong   kong(✓)   xie   xiu(✓)

shan(✓)   xian   shan(✓)   shang

七、听后标出调号：

(1) jiǎndān   (2) wǔshí   (3) nǔlì   (4) nuǎnhuo

(5) ěrduo   (6) Fǎguó   (7) yìxiē   (8) kāishuǐ

138

八、听后选择正确答案：

(1) 情景：阿里想借摩托车用。

　　生词：用　yòng　　use

　　A：（敲门）你好，天华。

　　B：阿里，你好。

　　A：你有摩托车吗？

　　B：没有。你想用吗？

　　A：对，你知道谁有吗？

　　B：我同屋李大年有。

问：谁有摩托车？

　　a. 天华　　　b. 阿里　　　c. 李大年〇

(2) 情景：A 想借日文画报看。

　　A：高老师，您有日文画报吗？

　　B：没有，我有英文画报。你想看吗？

　　A：我不看英文画报。您知道哪儿借日文画报吗？

　　B：图书馆。图书馆有中文画报，也有日文画报、英文画报、法文画报、
　　　　西班牙文画报、德文画报、阿拉伯文画报。

　　A：太好了！谢谢您。

　　B：不谢。

问：高老师有什么画报？

　　a. 日文画报　　　b. 英文画报〇　　　c. 中文画报

九、听录音，口头回答问题：

　　(1) 你有照相机吗？

　　(2) 你有录音机吗？

　　(3) 你同屋有收音机吗？

　　(4) 你有姐姐吗？

　　(5) 你想借书吗？

　　(6) 谁有摩托车？

　　(7) 你想看电视吗？

　　(8) 你朋友想买什么书？

　　(9) 你有什么书？

　　(10) 那个青年是你同屋吗？

第 八 课

一、听韵母。第一遍听,第二遍、第三遍跟读:

$$\begin{Bmatrix} ian \\ iang \end{Bmatrix} \quad \begin{Bmatrix} in \\ ing \end{Bmatrix} \quad \begin{Bmatrix} u \\ uo \end{Bmatrix} \quad \begin{Bmatrix} ua \\ uo \end{Bmatrix} \quad \begin{Bmatrix} uan \\ uang \end{Bmatrix}$$

二、听声母。第一遍听,第二遍、第三遍跟读:

$$\begin{Bmatrix} z \\ c \end{Bmatrix} \quad \begin{Bmatrix} zh \\ ch \end{Bmatrix} \quad \begin{Bmatrix} s \\ sh \end{Bmatrix} \quad \begin{Bmatrix} sh \\ r \end{Bmatrix} \quad \begin{Bmatrix} b \\ p \end{Bmatrix} \quad \begin{Bmatrix} d \\ t \end{Bmatrix} \quad \begin{Bmatrix} g \\ k \end{Bmatrix}$$

$$\begin{Bmatrix} j \\ q \end{Bmatrix} \quad \begin{Bmatrix} x \\ sh \end{Bmatrix}$$

三、听音节。第一遍听,第二遍、第三遍跟读:

$$\begin{Bmatrix} z \\ c \\ s \end{Bmatrix}a \quad \begin{Bmatrix} z \\ c \\ s \end{Bmatrix}ai \quad \begin{Bmatrix} z \\ c \\ s \end{Bmatrix}ou \quad \begin{Bmatrix} z \\ c \\ s \end{Bmatrix}an \quad \begin{Bmatrix} z \\ c \\ s \end{Bmatrix}ang \quad \begin{Bmatrix} z \\ c \\ s \end{Bmatrix}ong$$

$$\begin{Bmatrix} z \\ c \\ s \end{Bmatrix}u \quad \begin{Bmatrix} z \\ c \\ s \end{Bmatrix}uan \quad \begin{Bmatrix} zh \\ ch \\ sh \end{Bmatrix}uang \quad \begin{Bmatrix} g \\ k \\ h \end{Bmatrix}uang$$

四、听声调。第一遍听,第二遍、第三遍跟读:

（1） zāogāo　　suīrán　　xiūlǐ　　yīguì　　cōngming

chuánshuō　cónglái　　yóu yǒng　zájì　　zánmen

zǎocāo　　bǐrú　　guǎngchǎng　cǎisè　　sǎngzi

zuòjiā　　qùnián　　Rìběn　　zàijiàn　　cuòwu

（2） xīngqīrì　　yóulǎntú　　xínglijià　　xiězìtái

zhíshēngfēijī　chūzū qìchē　chàbuduō　zhīshi fènzǐ

（3） yī　　　　yìbān　　　yìbiānr　　yìzhí　　　yìtóng

　　　 yìqǐ　　　 yìdiǎnr　　yídìng　　yíhuìr　　yílùshang

五、听后填上声母：

（1） zhìzào　　　（2） chēngzàn　　（3） chángchu　　（4） xīnzàng

（5） cāochǎng　　（6） cùshǐ　　　　（7） zǒngshì　　　（8） zǎocāo

六、画出你听到的音节：

（1） zhuan(√)　　　zhuang　　　　　zhong

　　　 chuan　　　　chuang　　　　　chong(√)

　　　 shuan　　　　shuang(√)

（2） guan　　　　　guang(√)　　　　gong

　　　 kuan(√)　　　kuang　　　　　kong

　　　 huan(√)　　　huang　　　　　hong

七、听后画出第四声和第二声连续的词语：

（1） yì zhāng　　　　　　（2） zhè chuáng

（3） nà bǎ　　　　　　　（4） xiàngpí

（5） cídài　　　　　　　（6） shì shéi

（7） zájì　　　　　　　　（8） liù mén

（9） shàng lóu　　　　　（10） bù gěi

八、听后回答问题：

（1）情景：一个学生和宿舍的管理人员谈话。

　　　 生词：明天　　míngtiān　　tomorrow

　　　 A：我的宿舍没有椅子。

　　　 B：是吗？有桌子没有？

　　　 A：有。

　　　 B：几张？

　　　 A：两张。也有两个柜子。

　　　 B：我上你宿舍看看。

　　　 A：好。

　　　　　（A 与 B 去 A 的宿舍，进屋看了家具）

　　B：你的宿舍有床、柜子、桌子，没有椅子。明天我给你两把。

　　A：谢谢你。

问：他的宿舍有什么？

(2) 情景：A 想借阿里的词典。

　　生词：在　zài　in, on, at

　　A：阿里，你有词典吗？

　　B：你要什么词典？

　　A：阿拉伯文的词典。

　　B：有。在宿舍。明天给你。

　　A：好，明天我看看。谢谢你。

　　B：不谢。

问：阿里有词典吗？

(3) 情景：阿里在商店买练习本。

　　A：小姐，我要买练习本。

　　B：您要哪种？

　　A：我要那种。

　　B：您买几本？

　　A：四本。

问：他买什么？

九、听录音，我说一个名词，请你在前边加上数词"一"和量词：

　　(1)床　　　　(2)桌子　　　　(3)纸　　　　(4)杂志

　　(5)画报　　　(6)书　　　　　(7)工人　　　(8)练习本

　　(9)柜子　　　(10)弟弟　　　(11)椅子　　　(12)馒头

　　(13)青年　　(14)大夫　　　(15)朋友　　　(16)词典

第 九 课

一、听韵母。第一遍听,第二遍、第三遍跟读:

(1) ü üe üan ün iao

(2) a o e i u ü

(3) $\begin{cases} i \\ u \\ ü \end{cases}$ $\begin{cases} ian \\ uan \\ üan \end{cases}$ $\begin{cases} üan \\ üe \end{cases}$ $\begin{cases} ian \\ iang \\ iao \end{cases}$

二、听声母。第一遍听,第二遍、第三遍跟读:

$\begin{cases} z \\ c \end{cases}$ $\begin{cases} zh \\ ch \end{cases}$ $\begin{cases} s \\ sh \end{cases}$ $\begin{cases} sh \\ r \end{cases}$ $\begin{cases} l \\ r \end{cases}$ $\begin{cases} n \\ r \end{cases}$ $\begin{cases} j \\ zh \end{cases}$

$\begin{cases} q \\ ch \end{cases}$ $\begin{cases} x \\ sh \end{cases}$ $\begin{cases} h \\ f \end{cases}$ $\begin{cases} f \\ w \end{cases}$

三、听音节。第一遍听,第二遍、第三遍跟读:

$\left.\begin{matrix} n \\ l \end{matrix}\right\}$ü $\left.\begin{matrix} n \\ l \end{matrix}\right\}$üe $\left.\begin{matrix} j \\ q \\ x \end{matrix}\right\}$u $\left.\begin{matrix} j \\ q \\ x \end{matrix}\right\}$ue $\left.\begin{matrix} j \\ q \\ x \end{matrix}\right\}$uan

$\left.\begin{matrix} j \\ q \\ x \end{matrix}\right\}$un $\left.\begin{matrix} j \\ q \\ x \end{matrix}\right\}$iao

四、听声调。第一遍听,第二遍、第三遍跟读:

(1)　qiānxū　　yuānbó　　yuēqǐng　　jūnduì　　yuānwang

　　　yuányīn　　xuéxí　　xúnzhǎo　　juésè　　qúnzi

　　　xǔduō　　lǚxíng　　liǎojiě　　qiǎnlǜ　　jiǎozi

　　　jùshuō　　rìyuán　　jùběn　　jiàoyù　　yuèbing

（2）quánlì yǐ fù　　　　liúxuéshēng　　yuánzhūbǐ

　　　yǔfǎshū　　　　　yuèlǎnshì　　　shòuhuòyuán

　　　yuè lái yuè chà　　yòu'éryuán　　yīnyuè xuéyuàn

　　　Běijīng Yǔyán Dàxué　　Guójì Jùlèbù

五、听后填上声母：

　　c̲hūf̲ā　　　z̲uòzhǔ　　　q̲uēxiàn　　　lǚyóu　　　zh̲īc̲hí

　　z̲uòy̲è　　　zh̲uóyuè　　c̲ùsh̲ǐ　　　c̲éngjīng　　juéx̲īn

六、听后填上韵母：

　　juéd̲ìng　　qūbié　　　xuǎnzé　　　　shàngxún

　　nǚ'ér　　　ji̲àoshì　　xu̲ānchuán　　miǎománg

七、画出你听到的词语：

$$\begin{cases} \text{qūtǐ} \\ \text{jùtǐ}(\checkmark) \end{cases} \quad \begin{cases} \text{xuéyuàn} \\ \text{juéyuán}(\checkmark) \end{cases} \quad \begin{cases} \text{lüèduó}(\checkmark) \\ \text{nüèdài} \end{cases}$$

$$\begin{cases} \text{liú xuè} \\ \text{liù juàn}(\checkmark) \end{cases} \quad \begin{cases} \text{xuǎnzé} \\ \text{juézé}(\checkmark) \end{cases} \quad \begin{cases} \text{yīyuàn}(\checkmark) \\ \text{yǔyán} \end{cases}$$

$$\begin{cases} \text{cǎisè} \\ \text{cāicè}(\checkmark) \end{cases} \quad \begin{cases} \text{xuānbù}(\checkmark) \\ \text{shuānzhù} \end{cases}$$

八、听后选择正确答案：

（1）情景：三个人在楼前相遇，谈去看什么。

　　　A：李大年、刘天华，你们去哪儿？

　　　B：我去首都剧场看京剧。

　　　C：我去首都电影院看电影。你呢？

　　　A：我不去看京剧，也不去看电影。我去看球赛。

　　　B：哪儿有球赛？

　　　A：首都体育馆。

　　　B：好，我也去看球赛。

　　　C：我也去。

　　问：他们去看什么？

a．电影　　　b．京剧　　　c．球赛〇

（2）情景：阿里和朋友谈看什么节目。

　　A：阿里，你知道吗？电影院有杂技。

　　B：哪儿有杂技？

　　A：电影院。

　　B：不对，不是电影院，是体育馆。

　　A：你去不去？

　　B：不去，我看电视，电视是京剧。

　　A：好，我也看京剧。

问：他们看什么？

　　a．电影　　　b．电视〇　　　c．杂技

（3）情景：一个人询问北京音乐厅在哪儿。

　　A：小姐，请问这儿是不是音乐厅？

　　B：不，这儿不是音乐厅，是电影院。

　　A：我去北京音乐厅听音乐。你知道北京音乐厅吗？

　　B：知道，在那儿。

　　A：谢谢你。

　　B：不谢。

问：他去哪儿？

　　a．电影院　　　b．音乐厅〇

九、听录音，口头回答问题：

（1）你去哪儿？

（2）他去哪儿？

（3）你去不去北京饭店？

（4）他回不回学校？

（5）你看不看杂技？

（6）李大年去不去体育场？

（7）阿里看不看京剧？

（8）你想不想看电影？

（9）刘天华去不去听音乐会？

（10）这儿是不是首都体育馆？

一、听韵母。第一遍听,第二遍、第三遍跟读:

   (1) a　ai　ao　an　ang

   (2) e　er　ei　en　eng

   (3) i　ia　iao　ie　iu　ian　in　iang　ing　iong

   (4) u　ua　uo　ui　uan　un　uang

   (5) ü　üe　üan　ün

二、听音节。第一遍听,第二遍、第三遍跟读:

dun	zun	zhun	sun	run	gun
tun	cun	chun	shun	lun	kun

jun	jiong
qun	qiong
xun	xiong

三、听声调。第一遍听,第二遍、第三遍跟读:

   (1) yī　　yígòng　yípiàn　yìbān　yìbiān　yìtóng
      yì huí　yìqǐ　　yì liǎng

   (2) bù　　bù'ān　　bù chī　bùrú　　bù yíyàng
      bùguǎn　　bù lěng　　bù zěnmeyàng　　búcuò
      búdàn　　chàbuduō

   (3) sǔnshī　zǎocāo　zǔguó　lǚxíng　shǒubiǎo
      fǔdǎo　jiǒngkùn　zhǔnbèi　jiějie　zǎoshang

   (4) gāngbǐ　hēibǎn　niúnǎi　píjiǔ　　yǔfǎ
      shuǐguǒ　kùnjiǒng　wò shǒu

   (5) Zhǎnlǎnguǎn li yǒu hǎojǐ bǎi zhǒng zhǎnlǎnpǐn.

四、学说绕口令：

一个小孩子，	Yí ge xiǎo háizi,
拿双新鞋子，	Ná shuāng xīn xiézi,
看见大茄子，	Kànjiàn dà qiézi,
放下新鞋子，	Fàngxia xīn xiézi,
去拾大茄子，	Qù shí dà qiézi,
忘了新鞋子。	Wàngle xīn xiézi.

五、画出你听到的词语：

jīchǎng jùchǎng(✓)	jūnqū(✓) juānqū	jūnrén qióngrén(✓)
jīnyú jīngyú(✓)	qūxiàn qīxiàn(✓)	chūnfēng(✓) chōngfēng
chéngqīng céngjīng(✓)	píqiú píjiǔ(✓)	shìjuàn(✓) shìjiàn
yīngxióng(✓) yīngyǒng		

六、画出你听到的词语：

十一 十七	七号楼 一号楼	十号楼 四号楼	311 331	5030 5300	6060 6006

七、听后选择正确答案：

（1）情景：学生和老师互问住址。

生词：晚上　wǎnshang　evening

A：张老师，您住几号楼？

B：十七号。

A：十一号？

B：不是十一号，是十七号。你住哪儿？

A：我住六号楼三〇九房间。

B：好，晚上我去看你。再见。

A：再见。

问：张老师住几号楼？

　　a．十一　　　b．十七〇　　　c．六

（2）情景：贾红春接到了李大年的电话。

生词：很　hěn　evry

A：喂，我是贾红春。你是谁？

B：我是李大年。我在琼楼饭店。

A：啊，你好，大年。晚上我想去看你。你住多少号房间？

B：我住 1204。

A：电话号码是多少？

B：也是 1204。你住九号楼吗？

A：不，我还住六号楼。刘天华住九号楼。

B：刘天华？他好吗？

A：他很好。晚上我们去饭店看你。

B：好，晚上再见。

A：再见。

问：谁住九号楼？
　　a．贾红春　　　b．李大年　　　c．刘天华〇

八、听录音，口头回答问题：

（1）你住几号楼？多少号房间？

（2）阿里住几号楼？

（3）九号楼的电话号码是多少？

（4）你们学校的电话号码是多少？

（5）你还住八号楼吗？

（6）晚上你还去食堂吗？

（7）晚上你还看电视吗？

（8）你的房间是多少号？

（9）你常常在哪儿听音乐？

（10）你们在哪儿买东西？

第 十 一 课

一、听音节。第一遍听，第二遍跟读：

(1)

$\left.\begin{array}{l}zh\\ch\\sh\end{array}\right\}uai$ $\left.\begin{array}{l}g\\k\\h\end{array}\right\}uai$ $\left.\begin{array}{l}zh\\ch\\sh\end{array}\right\}un$ $\left.\begin{array}{l}g\\k\\h\end{array}\right\}un$

$\left.\begin{array}{l}j\\q\\x\end{array}\right\}un$ $\left.\begin{array}{l}j\\q\\x\end{array}\right\}iong$

(2)

$g\left\{\begin{array}{l}ua\\uai\end{array}\right.$ $zh\left\{\begin{array}{l}ua\\uai\end{array}\right.$ $t\left\{\begin{array}{l}ao\\ou\end{array}\right.$ $n\left\{\begin{array}{l}iao\\uo\end{array}\right.$

$ch\left\{\begin{array}{l}uan\\uang\end{array}\right.$ $g\left\{\begin{array}{l}e\\uo\end{array}\right.$

二、听声调。第一遍听，第二遍跟读：

(1)

yīfu	xiāoxi	pútao	mántou	dǒngle
yǐzi	mùtou	bànfǎ	chàbuduō	bú kèqi
guàibude				

(2)

zhuānxīn	jiāotōng	guójiā	lóutī	zǎocān
hǎijūn	kuàichē	chènyī		

(3)

yāoqiú	guānhuái	tóngxué	lánqiú	zǒuláng
chuǎimó	rèqíng	nèiróng		

(4)

pīngpāngqiú	shōuyīnjī	kēxuéyuàn
túshūguǎn	Yíhé Yuán	yóuyǒngchí
yǔmáoqiú	zhǎnlǎnguǎn	bàngōnglóu
dàshǐguǎn	yuèlǎnshì	zìxíngchē
yǒuhǎo fǎngwèn	rèliè huānyíng	
tǐyù bǐsài	cānjiā yànhuì	

三、画出你听到的音节：

(1) zhuai(√)　zhuan　　　　(2) mao　　　miao(√)

　　chuai　　chuan(√)　　　　dao(√)　　diao

　　shuai　　shuan(√)　　　　nao　　　niao(√)

　　guai(√)　guan　　　　　　lao(√)　　liao

　　kuai(√)　kuan　　　　　　tao(√)　　tiao

　　huai　　 huan(√)　　　　　pao　　　piao(√)

四、听后填上声母：

(1) kuàizi　　(2) qíguài　　(3) huīsè　　(4) guìzi

(5) tòngkuai　(6) shuāidǎ　 (7) huáiniàn　(8) suīrán

(9) shuàilǐng　(10) chuǎicè　(11) guā fēng　(12) kuǎtái

五、听后标出调号：

(1) Chī xīcān zuò zuǒcè.

　　Chī zhōngcān zuò yòucè.

　　Tā zuò zuǒcè chī xīcān.

　　Wǒ chī zhōngcan zuò yòucè.

(2) Tā yǒu shí zhāng chuáng.

　　Nǐ yǒu shí zhāng chuáng.

　　Wǒmen dàjiā quán yǒu shí zhāng chuáng.

六、听后填空：

(1) 这是美国电影,不是英国电影。

　　这是美国电影。

(2) 他听德国音乐,不听日本音乐。

　　他听德国音乐。

(3) 这不是美国银行,也不是西班牙银行,是法国银行。

　　这是法国银行。

(4) A:你看什么画报？

　　B:有法文画报吗？

　　A:有,给你。

他看<u>法文</u>画报。

七、听后选择正确答案：

（1）情景：三个人在路上相遇。

生词：和　　hé　　and

A：你们好！

B：你好，贾红春。这是我的朋友——夏子。

A：你好！我姓贾，叫贾红春。

C：你好！我是日本学生，叫夏子。

A：你们去哪儿？

B：我和夏子去看电影。

A：什么电影？

B：中国电影，电影的名字是《我的朋友们》。你去不去看？

A：不去。我和刘天华去看杂技。再见！

B：再见！

C：再见！

问：①电影的名字是什么？

　　a.《我们的朋友》　　　b.《我的朋友们》○　　　c.《我的朋友》

②贾红春去看什么？

　　a.电影　　　b.杂技○

（2）情景：A在路上问书店在哪儿。

A：小姐，请问这个学校有书店吗？

B：什么？商店？有，在十一号楼。

A：不是商店，是书店，我想买书。

B：书店也有。

A：在哪儿？

B：在一号楼。

A：谢谢您。

B：不客气。

问：①A想上哪儿？

　　a.商店　　　b.书店○

②书店在几号楼？

　　a.十一号楼　　b.一号楼○

八、听后回答问题：

情景：一个学生去张老师家。

A：(敲门)张老师住这儿吗？

B：(开门)住这儿，我爸爸不在。

A：我叫阿里，是美国学生。

B：您请进，请坐。

A：你叫什么名字？

B：我叫张华。您请喝茶。

A：谢谢。

　　(张老师回来了)

A：张老师，您好！

C：啊，是阿里，你好！请坐，请坐，不要客气。

问：(1) 阿里是哪国人？

　　(2) 张华是谁？

九、听录音，口头回答问题：

(1) 你是学生吗？

(2) 你是英国学生吗？

(3) 你的朋友是不是学生？

(4) 您贵姓？

(5) 你同屋叫什么名字？你们住几号楼？

(6) 你的同屋是不是德国学生？

(7) 你喝不喝茶？

(8) 夏子是哪国学生？她住几号房间？

(9) 你们学校有多少学生？

第 十 二 课

一、听音节，边听边说：

（1）

```
b⎫        d⎫        z⎫        d⎫        d⎫
 ⎬a        ⎬a       c⎬a        ⎬e        ⎬ie
p⎭        t⎭        s⎭        t⎭        t⎭

j⎫        g⎫        j⎫        j⎫
q⎬ie      k⎬u       q⎬un      q⎬iong
x⎭        h⎭        x⎭        x⎭
```

（2）

```
 ⎧an        ⎧ian        ⎧uan        ⎧u         ⎧iu
p⎨          q⎨        sh⎨          f⎨         d⎨
 ⎩ang       ⎩iang       ⎩uang       ⎩ou        ⎩iao

 ⎧en        ⎧in         ⎧ou         ⎧ie        ⎧ie
r⎨          l⎨          r⎨          j⎨         x⎨
 ⎩eng       ⎩ing        ⎩ong        ⎩ue        ⎩ue
```

二、听声调，边听边说：

（1）értóng　　érzi　　nǚ'ér　　ěrduo　　ěrjī　　èr bǎi

（2）quānr　　wánr　　yǎnr　　huàr　　yìdiǎnr

yíxiàr　　yíhuìr　　xiǎoháir　　shǒujuànr　　míngxìnpiànr

（3）guǎngbō　　yǎnchū　　kǎchē　　yǔyī　　Běijīng

yǎnyuán　　yǒumíng　　lǚxíng　　zǒngjié　　lǐtáng

zǒnglǐ　　liǎojiě　　yǔfǎ　　yǒuhǎo　　guǎngchǎng

bǐsài　　gǎnxiè　　fǎngwèn　　kǎoshì　　fǒudìng

xǐhuan　　nuǎnhuo　　sǎngzi　　yǎnjing　　zěnme

（4）jì shēngcí　　xiě Hànzì　　tīng lùyīn　　zuò liànxí

dǎ diànhuà　　　kàn diànshì　　　chuān yīfu

xūxīn xuéxí　　　zhuān xīn zhì zhì　　　zhùyì fāyīn

guāngmíng zhèngdà　　jiāqiáng yǒuyì　　　shí shì qiú shì

máf<u>an</u>　　　　xièj<u>ué</u>　　　　qúnzh<u>òng</u>　　　　sh<u>ā</u>ng<u>ā</u>ng

hu<u>ā</u>lánr　　　shu<u>ǎ</u>ngkuài　　　k<u>ě</u>ndìng　　　　rénm<u>ín</u>

k<u>ā</u>ichu<u>àng</u>　　　j<u>ū</u>nfú　　　　còuqi<u>ǎo</u>　　　　értóng

四、听后填上声母：

<u>k</u>èfú　　　<u>z</u>ǎo<u>c</u>āo　　tiě<u>t</u>ǎ　　<u>k</u>uāng<u>u</u>ǎng　　<u>j</u>iě<u>sh</u>ì

<u>q</u>uē<u>x</u>í　　<u>s</u>uǒyǐ　　<u>b</u>ǎoguì　　<u>x</u>iǎo<u>s</u>ū<u>d</u>á

<u>s</u>ī<u>zh</u>ī<u>p</u>ǐn　<u>x</u>uě <u>zh</u>ōng <u>s</u>òng <u>t</u>àn　　<u>sh</u>uāng <u>g</u>uǎn <u>q</u>í <u>x</u>ià

五、听后标出调号：

huǒchē　　　niúnǎi　　　yǒuyì　　　yǐqián　　　píngguǒ

gōngchǎng　　huǒchái　　　mínzhǔ　　　zhěntou　　　zhèngfǔ

qiānbǐhér　　fēijīchǎng

六、听后判别正误：

（1）他会英语、法语。他不会汉语，会一点儿西班牙语。
　　　他的西班牙语很好。（╳）

（2）他不会英语，会说一点儿阿拉伯语。他学习法语。
　　　他会一点儿阿拉伯语。（✓）

（3）他们会一点儿德语、汉语。他们不会法语、西班牙语。他们学习西班牙
　　　语。
　　　他们不会汉语。（╳）

（4）我可以说日语，我不会阿拉伯语。
　　　他会说日语。（✓）

七、听后选择正确答案：

（1）情景：一个日本人和一个阿拉伯人谈话。
　　　A：你是哪国人？
　　　B：我是阿拉伯人，叫阿里。你是中国人吗？
　　　A：不是，我是日本人，叫夏子。你会说日语吗？
　　　B：不会。你会说阿拉伯语？

A：也不会。太好了,我们可以常常说汉语。

问：①夏子是哪国人?

　　　a．中国人　　b．日本人○　　　c．阿拉伯人

　　②他们可以常常说什么语?

　　　a．日语　　b．阿拉伯语　　c．汉语○

(2) 情景:中国学生李大年和法国学生让谈话。

　　生词:和　　hé　and

　　A：你是新同学吗?

　　B：是,我叫让,是法国留学生。你也是北京大学的学生吗?

　　A：是,我叫李大年,在北大学习中文。你学习什么?

　　B：我也学习中文。你会说法语不会?

　　A：不会。我会说英语,还会说一点儿西班牙语。

　　B：我可以去你的房间看你吗?

　　A：可以。我住十七号楼,去我房间喝茶好吗?

　　B：太好了。

问：① 让和李大年都是北京大学的学生吗?

　　　a．是○　　b．不是

　　② 李大年会说什么语?

　　　a．法语　　b．英语○

　　③ 他们去谁的房间喝茶?

　　　a.让　b.李大年○

八、听录音,口头回答问题:

　　(1) 你会英语吗?

　　(2) 约翰会说阿拉伯语吗?

　　(3) 你同屋会说西班牙语吗?

　　(4) 你会说什么语?

　　(5) 你是哪国人?

　　(6) 你朋友可以说法语吗?

　　(7) 你是北京大学的学生吗?

　　(8) 你的同学是日本人吗?

　　(9) 你在哪个大学学习?

　　(10) 你学习什么?

　　(11) 在中国你有新朋友吗?

第 十 三 课

一、听音节,边听边说(注意词重音):

    yīshēng   lǎoshī   gōngrén   sùshè   shāngdiàn

    yínháng   huàbào   zhīdào   kěyǐ   liànxí

    liànxí

    dōngbianr   xībianr   nánbianr   běibianr

    jīntiān   míngtiān   zuótiān

二、听声调,边听边说:

(1) gānjing   xiānsheng   yìsi   dōngxi   shūshu

        tóufa   bízi   késou   shuí de   guàntou

        wǎnshang fùqin   sǎngzi   tàiyang   yuèliang

(2) gāngbǐ   xiūlǐ   shēntǐ   hēibǎn

        píjiǔ   quántǐ   yóulǎn   niúnǎi

        shuǐguǒ   xǐ zǎo   shǒubiǎo fǔdǎo

        dàshǐ   wò shǒu   shàngwǔ xiàwǔ

(3) kōngqì   jīdàn   shēngdiào xūyào

        pínglùn   xuélì   hánjià   yúkuài

        yǒuyì   jiǎngzuò   cǎisè   zǎofàn

        zàijiàn   Hànzì   shìyàn   zhèngzài

(4)学说绕口令:

    十是十,四是四。十四是十四,四十是四十。

    十四不是四十,四十也不是十四。

三、画出你听到的音节:

    jian   juan(✓) | cuan(✓)   quan

    qian(✓)   quan | shuan   xuan(✓)

xian xuan(✓)   guan guang(✓)

juan quan(✓)   kuan(✓) kuang

zuan(✓) juan   huan huang(✓)

四、听后填上韵母：

jiǎnzhuāng zuānyán   juān kuǎn qiánfāng

cuànquán huángjiàng   xiànguān huànsuàn

xuānchuán chuàngjiàn   jìnkuàng guāngxiàn

五、听后把词语分成两组：

      ´ + `        ˇ + `

（2）yángròu   （1）yǐhòu

（3）yánsè   （4）bǐsài

（6）nénggòu   （5）lǐngxiù

（9）táishàn   （7）hǎoshì

（10）shíyàn   （8）jǔbàn

六、听后标出调号：

jìnlái   měilì   qiúchǎng   zuānyán

qiángzhuàng   nǚ'ér   qǐng jià   tàijíquán

七、听后标图：

（1）A：劳驾，邮局在哪儿？

  B：在小卖部旁边儿。

  A：小卖部旁边儿有邮局吗？

  B：有，我知道，在小卖部东边儿。

  A：谢谢你。

  B：没什么。

问：邮局在几号楼？

（2）A：劳驾，请问国际俱乐部在哪儿？

  B：在友谊商店北边儿。

  A：我也不知道友谊商店在哪儿。

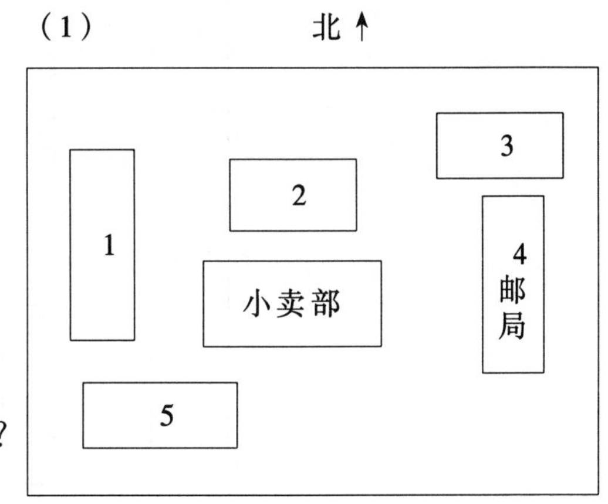

B：北京饭店呢？

A：北京饭店我知道。

B：友谊商店在北京饭店的东边儿。国际俱乐部在友谊商店的北边儿。

A：我知道了，谢谢。

B：没什么。

问：国际俱乐部在哪儿？

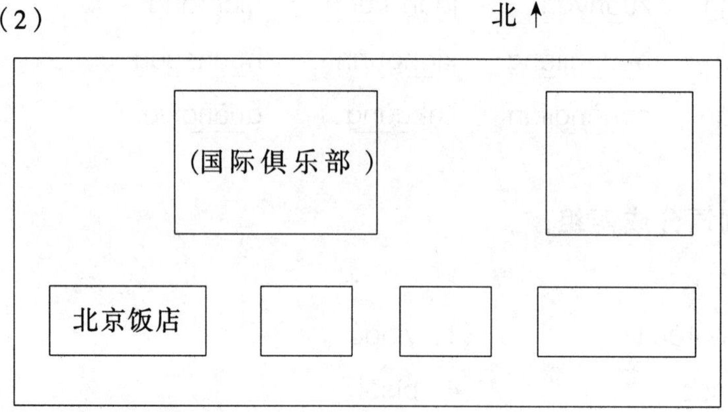

（3）A：小姐，请问四号楼在哪儿？

B：你知道八号楼吗？

A：知道。

B：八号楼西边是五号楼，四楼在五号楼的北边儿。

A：谢谢。

B：不客气。

问：四号楼在哪儿？

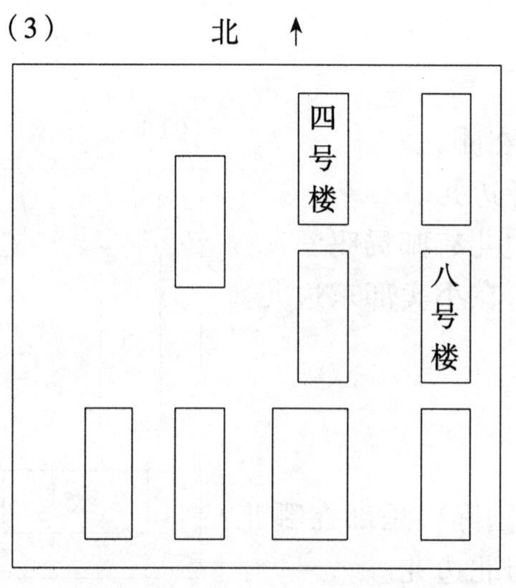

八、听录音,口头回答问题：

    （1）你前边儿是谁？

    （2）你旁边儿是谁？

    （3）你后边儿是谁？

    （4）你左边儿是谁？

    （5）你右边儿是谁？

    （6）谁在你东边儿？

    （7）谁在你西边儿？

    （8）谁在你北边儿？

    （9）谁坐你南边儿？

  （10）请问,外交公寓在哪儿？

第 十 四 课

一、听音节,边听边说：

(1)

zhīdào / chídào	chūxí / zhǔxí	shēnzhǎn / shēngchǎn	Zhōngwén / chōngfèn
zhīshi / jīqì	zhìdù / jìshù	shēngzhǎng / tīngjiǎng	zhèngquè / jīngquè
chī fàn / qīxiàn	chuān yī / quántǐ	chōu yān / qiūtiān	chūntiān / qúnzhòng

(2)（注意下面词的重音）

dǎrǎo　　piányi　　háishi　　jìniàn

wàibianr　　yánsè　　yǐjing　　gōngzuò

gōngzuò　　jiàoshòu　　qìchē　　qǐchuáng

二、听声调,边听边说：

(1)

lánqiú / lǎnchóng	értóng / ěrchuí	yóuyú / yǒumíng	liánhé / liǎnpén
jīchē / jízhōng	qīngchūn / qíngtiān	Fēizhōu / féiròu	huāngzhāng / huángjīn

(2) quántǐ cānjiā　　　　rèqíng fúwù

rì xīn yuè yì　　　　fúzhuāng zhǎnlǎn

sècǎi xuànlì　　　　chī xīn wàng xiǎng

(3) 听教师读下面的谚语,然后边听边说：

① 至亲不如好友。　　　Zhìqīn bùrú hǎo yǒu.

②在你遇到困难的时候,帮助　　Zài nǐ yùdào kùnnan de
　你的人才是真正的朋友。　　shíhou, bāngzhù nǐ de rén cái
　　　　　　　　　　　　　　shì zhēnzhèng de péngyou.

三、画出你听到的音节：

（1）qi(√)　　　chi　　　　　　（2）qi　　　　　　shi(√)

　　qiao　　　chao(√)　　　　　　qiao(√)　　　shao

　　qiu(√)　　chou　　　　　　　　qiu　　　　　shou(√)

　　qin　　　 chen(√)　　　　　　 qing　　　　 sheng(√)

　　qing(√)　cheng　　　　　　　 qie(√)　　　shui

　　qian　　　chan(√)　　　　　　 qian(√)　　shan

　　qiong(√)　chong　　　　　　　 quan　　　 shuan(√)

四、听后填上声母：

qǐqiú　　　　 shuí qù　　　　shēngiǎn　　　 chóngjìng

qiǎoshǒu　　 shěngchéng　　chènshān　　　Qíncháo

chǒujué　　　 quēshǎo　　　 chǎnshēng　　 shòu quán

五、听后标出调号：

（1）汉语学院　　　　中文系　　　　哲学系
　　 音乐学院　　　　历史系　　　　音乐系
　　 体育学院　　　　语言系　　　　体育系
　　 经济学院

（2）等什么　　　　　等人
　　 等汽车　　　　　去哪儿
　　 等谁　　　　　　去友谊商店

（3）我学习中文。
　　 你学习英文。
　　 他可以说汉语。
　　 他会说西班牙语。
　　 我不会说德语，也不会说法语。

六、听后填空：

（1）我在语言大学学习英语。我妹妹在北京大学学习哲学。我弟弟也在北
　　 京大学学习，他学习经济。他们不在一个系。

　　 我弟弟和妹妹是北京大学的学生，我弟弟学习经济，我妹妹学习哲学。

（2）我住四号楼,<u>阿里和约翰</u>也住那儿。

　　阿里住__四__号楼。

（3）A：您等车？

　　B：等车。

　　A：您上哪儿？

　　B：上国际俱乐部,我在那儿工作。

　　A：我也去那儿。车来了,咱们上车吧。

　　他们去<u>国际俱乐部</u>。

七、听后选择正确答案：

（1）情景：约翰在汽车站等一个朋友。他遇见一位等车的老教授,就随便谈
　　　了起来。

　　生词：和　　hé　　and

　　约　翰：您等汽车？

　　老教授：是啊,您也等车？

　　约　翰：不,我等一个朋友。您在哪儿工作？

　　老教授：我在中国音乐学院工作。我来语言大学看一个朋友。您在语
　　　　　　言大学工作吗？

　　约　翰：不,我在这里学习。……您看,汽车来了,您上车吧。再见。

　　老教授：再见。

　　问：① 谁等汽车？

　　　　　a．约翰　　b．老教授○　　　c．约翰和老教授

　　　　② 老教授在哪儿工作？

　　　　　a．语言大学　b．中国音乐学院○

（2）情景：一个人询问郑教授的住址。

　　A：小姐,请问郑教授住几号楼？

　　B：郑教授？ 是外语系的郑教授吗？

　　A：对,对,您认识他？

　　B：认识,我也在外语系工作。他住十号楼。这是十四号楼,十四号楼
　　　　的西边是四号楼,四号楼的北边是十号楼。

　　A：谢谢。

　　问：① B和郑教授是哪个系的老师？

　　　　　a．外语系○　　b．汉语系　　　c．体育系

　　　　② 郑教授住几号楼？

162

　　a．十四号楼　　b．十号楼〇　　c．四号楼

八、听录音,口头回答问题：

(1) 你等汽车吗？

(2) 你等谁？

(3) 你在哪儿工作？

(4) 你在哪儿学习？

(5) 你在哪个系学习？

(6) 你学习什么？

(7) 你认识贾红春吗？

(8) 你认识郑教授吗？

(9) 明天谁来看你？

第 十 五 课

一、听音节，边听边说：

(1)
| rónɡyi | ɡuānɡrónɡ | rèqínɡ | fùráo |
| lónɡzhònɡ | hǎilónɡ | lètǔ | fùlǎo |

| chābié | cháshuǐ | hùxiānɡ | kǒnɡpà |
| chēlún | chěsuì | ɡùxiānɡ | ɡǒnɡɡù |

(2)（注意下面词的重音）

jīntiān　　　zuótiān　　　mínɡtiān　　　shànɡwǔ

xiàwǔ　　　biāozhǔn　　　zuòwèi　　　wàiɡuó

xiūlǐ　　　niánjì　　　lǎorén　　　wèi shénme

二、听声调，边听边说：

(1)
| miànbāo | chènyī | qìchē |
| měi tiān | chěnɡ xiōnɡ | qǐfā |

| wèntí | lǜchá | yùyán |
| wěnhé | lǚxínɡ | yǔyán |

| yòuyì | càidiàn | qìnɡzhù |
| yǒuyì | cǎidiàn | qǐnɡ zuò |

| mèimei | dìdi | ɡuìzi |
| mǔqin | jiějie | ɡuǐzi |

(2)　niánqīnɡrén　　　　níhónɡdēnɡ　　hánɡkōnɡxìn

　　　pīnɡpānɡqiú　　　quán lì yǐ fù　yīxuéyuàn

　　　lěnɡyǐndiàn　　　fúwùyuán　　　mǎmahūhū

　　　hùxiānɡ fǎnɡwèn　　　　　　yǒuhǎo wǎnɡlái

　　　zhùyì fāyīn　　　　　　　　duōduō ɡuānzhào

(3)听教师读下面的古诗，然后边听边说：

静夜思　　　　　　　　Jìnɡ Yè Sī

床前明月光，　　　　　　Chuánɡ qián mínɡ yuèɡuānɡ,

疑是地上霜。   Yí shì dì shàng shuāng.
举头望明月，   Jǔ tóu wàng míngyuè,
低头思故乡。   Dī tóu sī gùxiāng.

三、画出你听到的音节：

（1）nián　　　niáng(✓)　　（2）chēn(✓)　　zhēn

liǎn(✓)　　liǎng　　　　　chái　　　zhái(✓)

jiān　　　jiāng(✓)　　　　cǎi(✓)　　zǎi

qián　　　qiáng(✓)　　　　shǎng(✓)　　xiǎng

xiàn(✓)　　xiàng　　　　　róng(✓)　　lóng

yǎn　　　yǎng(✓)　　　　qiǎo(✓)　　jiǎo

四、听后填上韵母：

niánqīng　　niàngzào　　liánhuān　　jiǎngjīn

dòngliáng　　qínjiǎn　　miǎnqiǎng　　huànxiǎng

五、听后标出调号：

mǎnyì　　　qīngsōng　　hūrán　　　sàn bù

shíhou　　　bì yè　　　shàng yuè　　lǎorén

Míngnián wǒ qù Guǎngzhōu xuéxí yīxué.

六、听后填空：

（1）情景：两个人谈论去看电影的事。

A：李大年，明天是星期日，我们去看电影。你去不去？

B：我的一个朋友昨天来北京了。她住在北京饭店。明天我去看她。

咱们下星期日去，可以吗？

A：也可以。

B：谢谢你们。

李大年这个星期日去看一个朋友，下个星期日去看电影。

（2）情景：两个人谈买词典的问题。

A：贾红春，你桌子上的新书我可以看看吗？

B：可以，那是一本新词典，汉语词典。

Ａ：哪个书店有？

Ｂ：我们学校的书店有。

Ａ：是吗？我不知道，在哪儿？那儿有英语词典吗？

Ｂ：在这个楼 127 号房间。你可以去那儿看看。

他们学校的书店在<u>127</u>号房间，那儿有<u>汉语</u>词典。

（3）情景：明天是一个学生的生日，他想请同学们去宿舍玩。

　　　生词：生日　shēngrì　birthday

　　　　　　快乐　kuàilè　happy

Ａ：同学们，明天是我的生日，……

Ｂ：你的生日？

Ａ：9 月 28 号是我的生日。我想请你们去我的房间喝茶。

（众）：好！（大家鼓掌，以示祝贺）生日快乐！

Ａ：谢谢，谢谢！

今天是<u>9</u>月27号。<u>28</u>号是一个学生的生日。他请同学们<u>去他的房间喝茶</u>。

七、**听录音，口头回答问题：**

（1）今天几号了？

（2）今天几月几号了？

（3）今天星期几？

（4）明天几号？

（5）昨天几号？

（6）昨天星期几？

（7）一个星期有几天？

（8）星期日你去看球赛吗？

（9）星期日他去看球赛吗？你呢？

（10）星期日你学习吗？

（11）星期六你们工作吗？

第 十 六 课

一、语音练习：

（1）边听边说：

{zhūzi / zūzi	{jízi / júzi	{zhǐbāo / jǐ bāo	{wǔdǎo / fǔdǎo
{jiǎndān / biǎndan	{bàogào / bāokuò	{liú xué / liú xiě	{chūnfēng / chōngfēng

（2）画出你听到的词语：

{zhǐbāo / jǐ bāo(✓)	{júzi(✓) / jízi	{zūzi / zhūzi(✓)
{wǔdǎo / fǔdǎo(✓)	{liú xiě(✓) / liú xué	{chūnfēng(✓) / chōngfēng
{bàogào(✓) / bāokuò	{jiǎndān(✓) / biǎndān	

（3）听后给下面的谚语注音：

路遥知马力，　　Lù yáo zhī mǎ lì,
日久见人心。　　Rì jiǔ jiàn rénxīn.

二、词重音练习：

听后标出词重音：

上月	下月	去年	今年	昨天	明天	中学	大学
学院	外语	劳驾	邮局	旁边儿	工作	教授	汽车

三、听后选择正确答案：

（1）今天四月五号。我们下月去长城。

　　问：他们几月去长城？

　　　　a. 四月　　b. 五月○

（2）他们今年去英国，明年去法国。

　　问：他们什么时候去法国？

　　　　a. 今年　　b. 明年○

（3）今天九月十一号，我们去故宫，明天去颐和园。

    问：他们什么时候去颐和园？

        a．九月十一号　　b．九月十二号○

（4）我 1998 年上大学，在大学学习五年。

    问：他什么时候大学毕业？

        a．1998 年　　b．2003 年○

（5）我在 1991 年小学毕业，1997 年中学毕业，2001 年大学毕业。

    问：他在中学学习几年？

        a．五年　　b．六年○　　c．七年

（6）高开是中国学生，他 1994 年去德国一个大学学习。他在那儿学习四年。

    问：高开哪年毕业？

        a．1994 年　　b．1996 年　　c．1998 年○

（7）今年夏子在北京语言大学学习汉语，明年九月去北京大学。她要学习
经济。

    问：夏子要在北京大学哪个系学习？

        a．中文系　　b．经济系○

（8）A：咱们四月去长城，五月去故宫，下月呢？

    B：六月咱们去颐和园，好吗？

    A：可以。

    问：现在是几月？

        a．四月　　b．五月○　　c．六月

（9）A：阿里，你在中国学习几年？

    B：在语言大学学习一年汉语，明年去北京大学学习哲学。我在北京大
学要学习四年。

    问：他在中国学习几年？

        a．一年　　b．四年　　c．五年○

（10）生词：和　hé　and

    A：我们明天去香山，你去不去？

    B：我这个星期日不去。下星期我妈妈来北京，我和她一块儿去。

    问：她和妈妈什么时候去香山？

        a．明天　　b．这个星期日　　c．下星期○

四、听录音,口头回答问题:

(1) 今天几号了?

(2) 今天星期几了?

(3) 昨天你上哪儿了?

(4) 明天你去故宫吗?

(5) 昨天你去香山了吗?

(6) 今天你去颐和园不去?

(7) 你明年去哪儿学习?

(8) 你哪年中学毕业?

(9) 你哪年大学毕业?

(10) 你什么时候回国?

第 十 七 课

一、语音练习：

（1）边听边说：

xīfú	yǔyán	liànxí	érqiě
qūfú	yíyán	liángxí	èrjiě
xīwàng	gòngxiàn	jícù	cǎisè
shīwàng	kōngqián	jìzhù	cāicè

（2）画出你听到的词语：

yǔyán(✓)	liànxí(✓)	xīwàng
yíyán	liángxí	shīwàng(✓)
xīfú(✓)	jícù	cǎisè
qūfú	jìzhù(✓)	cāicè(✓)
érqiě	gòngxiàn(✓)	
èrjiě(✓)	kōngqián	

（3）听后给下面的谚语注音：

边学边问，才有学问。Biān xué biān wèn, cái yǒu xuéwen.

不懂装懂，永是饭桶。Bù dǒng zhuāng dǒng, yǒng shì fàntǒng.

二、词重音练习：

听后标出词重音：

现<u>在</u>　　起<u>床</u>　　早<u>饭</u>　　午<u>饭</u>　　晚<u>饭</u>　　上<u>课</u>

下<u>课</u>　　睡<u>觉</u>　　劳<u>驾</u>　　学<u>院</u>　　小<u>学</u>　　小卖<u>部</u>

三、句重音练习：

（1）边听边说：

① 现在四月。

② 现在十一月。

170

③ 今天十月十号。

④ 今天十一月十五号。

⑤ 现在八点半。

⑥ 现在十二点一刻了。

⑦ 现在差一刻七点。

(2) 听我问，你标出答句的重音：

①	现在几点了？	现在十点了。

②	现在几月了？	现在九月了。

③	今天几号？	今天二十八号。

④	今天星期几？	今天星期四。

⑤	他什么时候去西班牙？	他明年去西班牙。

⑥	你什么时候去长城？	我下星期日去长城。

⑦	你什么时候中学毕业？	我一九七七年中学毕业。

四、听后选择正确答案：

(1) 生词：时间　shíjiān　time

(听收音机)"嘟、嘟、嘟、嘟、嘟、嘀——，北京时间十二点整。"

问：现在几点？

　　a. 2:00　　b. 10:00　　c. 12:00○

(2) (听收音机)"嘟、嘟、嘟、嘟、嘟、嘀——，北京时间七点整。"

问：现在几点？

　　a. 7:00○　　b. 1:00　　c. 4:00

(3) 生词：开始　kāishǐ　to begin

A：球赛几点开始？

B：七点半。

问：球赛几点开始？

　　a. 7:00　　b. 7:30○　　c. 1:30

（4）A：晚上电视几点开始？

　　B：六点五十五。

　　问：电视几点开始？

　　　　a. 6:55○　　　b. 5:50　　　c. 6:05

（5）A：你们下午几点上课？

　　B：两点半。

　　问：他们下午几点开始上课？

　　　　a. 12:00　　　b. 14:30○　　　c. 2:00

（6）A：你早上几点起床？

　　B：差一刻七点。

　　问：他早上几点起床？

　　　　a. 6:45○　　　b. 7:00　　　c. 7:15

（7）A：你早上几点钟吃早饭？

　　B：我不吃早饭。我七点半起床，八点上课，没有时间吃早饭。

　　问：他早上几点吃早饭？

　　　　a. 7:30　　　b. 8:00　　　c. 7:00　　d. a、b、c 都不对○

（8）夏子在中文系学习汉语。她上午八点上课，十二点下课。她下午不上
　　课，在宿舍学习。

　　问：夏子几点下课？

　　　　a. 12:00○　　　b. 2:00　　　c. 8:00

（9）今天是星期日。张正生七点三刻起床。吃了早饭他去香山了。在香山
　　饭店他吃了午饭，就去颐和园了。下午五点半他回学校，六点去食堂。

　　问：张正生在哪儿吃晚饭？

　　　　a. 香山　　　b. 学校○　　　c. 颐和园

（10）生词：只好　zhǐhǎo　to have to

　　A：你吃饭了吗？

　　B：吃了。你上哪儿，小李？

　　A：现在食堂有饭没有了？

　　B：没有了。你去饭馆儿吧。

　　A：我只好去饭馆儿了。

　　问：小李吃饭了没有？

　　　　a. 吃了　　　b. 没吃○

172

五、听录音, 口头回答问题：

  （1）现在几点？

  （2）你们几点下课？

  （3）你们几点吃午饭？

  （4）早上你几点起床？

  （5）晚上你学习吗？

  （6）晚上你几点睡觉？

  （7）你早上吃早饭不吃？

  （8）今天下午你去图书馆吗？

  （9）现在几月了？

  （10）星期六晚上你看电影吗？

第 十 八 课

一、语音练习：

（1）边听边说：

⌈ chūfā	⌈ tōngzhī	⌈ chéngguǒ	⌈ chuántǒng
⌊ chǔfá	⌊ tóngzhì	⌊ chéngguō	⌊ chuàntōng
⌈ dǎ jià	⌈ dǎsǎo	⌈ dàxué	⌈ gānjìng
⌊ dàjiā	⌊ dàsǎo	⌊ dàxuě	⌊ gǎnjǐn
⌈ hútòng	⌈ huānyíng	⌈ huǒchē	⌈ jíshǐ
⌊ hùtōng	⌊ huànyǐng	⌊ huòchē	⌊ jíshí

（2）画出你听到的词语：

⌈ chéngguǒ(✓)	⌈ tōngzhī	⌈ chuántǒng(✓)
⌊ chéngguō	⌊ tóngzhì(✓)	⌊ chuàntōng
⌈ chūfā(✓)	⌈ dàsǎo	⌈ gānjìng(✓)
⌊ chǔfá	⌊ dǎsǎo(✓)	⌊ gǎnjǐn
⌈ dǎ jià	⌈ dàxuě	⌈ huǒchē
⌊ dàjiā(✓)	⌊ dàxué(✓)	⌊ huòchē(✓)
⌈ jíshǐ	⌈ hútòng(✓)	⌈ huānyíng(✓)
⌊ jíshí(✓)	⌊ hùtōng	⌊ huànyǐng

（3）学说绕口令：

吃葡萄,不吐葡萄皮儿;Chī pútao,bù tǔ pútaopír;

不吃葡萄,倒吐葡萄皮儿。Bù chī pútao,dào tǔ pútaopír.

二、用阿拉伯数字写出你听到的钱数：

（1）八毛四　　　　　（2）九毛三　　（3）二块七毛一

（4）五块零六　　　　（5）三块七　　（6）二十四块三毛九

（7）二十九块零七分　（8）九十七块七毛一

三、语调练习：

边听边说(注意句末是升调还是降调)：

（1）Nǐ děng chē↗?　　　　　　　　Wǒ děng chē↘.

174

（2）Nǐ mǎi shū ↑?　　　　　Wǒ mǎi shū ↓.

（3）Tā qù Běijīng ↑?　　　　Tā qù Běijīng ↓.

（4）Tā shì nǐ tóngwū ↑?　　　Duì, tā shì wǒ tóngwū ↓.

（5）Nǐ yě qù kàn Jiǎ Hóngchūn ↑?　　Wǒ yě qù kàn Jiǎ Hóngchūn ↓.

（6）Zhè shì nǐ de shōuyīnjī ↑?　　Bù, bú shì wǒ de shōuyīnjī ↓.

（7）Xiàzǐ yǒu mótuōchē ↑?　　　Tā yǒu mótuōchē ↓.

（8）Nà shì Yuēhàn de fángjiān ↑?　　Duì, nà shì Yuēhàn de fángjiān ↓.

（9）Tā xiǎng jiè zhàoxiàngjī ↑?　　Shì, tā xiǎng jiè zhàoxiàngjī ↓.

（10）Yì zhī qiānbǐ yì máo ↑?　　　Bù, yì zhī qiānbǐ sì máo bā ↓.

四、句重音练习：
（1）边听边说：
　　① 这枝笔<u>四毛八</u>。

　　② 那枝圆珠笔<u>一块二</u>。

　　③ 这种练习本<u>八毛八</u>。

　　④ 那本书<u>九块三毛五</u>。

　　⑤ 我的词典<u>三十五块四</u>。

（2）听我问，请你标出答句的重音：
　　① 这枝铅笔<u>多少</u>钱?　　　这枝铅笔<u>四毛八</u>。

　　② 这本杂志<u>多少</u>钱?　　　这本杂志<u>六块五</u>。

　　③ 这张床<u>多少</u>钱?　　　这张床<u>八十九块五</u>。

　　④ 这是<u>谁</u>的本子?　　　这是<u>阿里</u>的本子。

　　⑤ <u>谁</u>有汽车?　　　<u>刘天华</u>有汽车。

五、听后选择正确答案：
（1）情景：约翰买圆珠笔。
　　A：您买什么?
　　B：我想买圆珠笔, 有吗?
　　A：有, 您看, 您要哪种?

B：多少钱一枝？

A：这种一块五，那种一块二。

B：我要一块二的。

A：您还要别的吗？

B：不要了。

问：约翰的圆珠笔多少钱？

    a．一块五   b．一块二〇

（2）情景：阿里在商店买东西。

A：您买什么？

B：有钢笔吗？

A：有，您要哪种？有三块六的，五块八的，十一块九的，二十三块七的。

B：要五块八的

问：阿里的钢笔多少钱？

    a．五块八〇   b．六块八

（3）情景：夏子在小卖部买东西。

A：我买铅笔。

B：您要哪种？有八毛一的，四毛八的，还有八毛五的。

A：我要四毛八的。请问，里边有多少枝？

B：有十枝。您还要别的吗？

A：我还想买练习本。

B：练习本在那边儿买。

A：谢谢。

问：她买什么了？

    a．铅笔   b．练习本   c．铅笔、练习本〇

六、听录音，口头回答问题：

（1）你有几枝笔？

（2）你有什么笔？

（3）你的圆珠笔多少钱？

（4）你的练习本多少钱一个？

（5）小卖部的铅笔多少钱一枝？

（6）昨天你买东西了吗？

（7）你的书多少钱一本？

（8）你的词典多少钱？

（9）食堂的包子多少钱一个？馒头呢？

（10）请问，学校宿舍一个月多少钱？

（11）小卖部卖什么？

第 十 九 课

一、语音练习：

（1）边听边说：

| huà huār | huànxiǎng | jìniàn | jiàoshī |
| huà huàr | huán xiāng | jǐ nián | jiàoshì |

| jiěshì | jīngjù | kěqì | lǎojiā |
| jièshí | jǐngjù | kèqi | láo jià |

| lǐ fà | guìzi | xuéyuán |
| lì fǎ | guǐzi | xuéyuàn |

（2）画出你听到的词语：

| jìniàn | huànxiǎng | huà huār |
| jǐ nián(✓) | huán xiāng(✓) | huà huàr(✓) |

| jiàoshī(✓) | jiěshì(✓) | jīngjù(✓) |
| jiàoshì | jièshí | jǐngjù |

| kěqì | lǐ fà(✓) | lǎojiā |
| kèqi(✓) | lì fǎ | láo jià(✓) |

| xuéyuán(✓) | guìzi(✓) |
| xuéyuàn | guǐzi |

二、语调练习：

边听边说(注意句末是升调还是降调)：

(1) Zhè shì shū ma ↑?

(2) Wǒ qù, tā ne ↑?

(3) Nín děng chē ma ↑?

(4) Tā shì nǐ gēge ma ↑?

(5) Nǐ qù kàn māma ma ↑?

(6) Zhè shì tā de ↓.

(7) Wǒ qù Xiāng Shān le ↓.

(8) Wǒ chī miànbāo le ↓.

（9）Zhè shì wǒ gēge ↓ .

（10）Nà zhāng huàr shì gēge de ↓ .

三、句重音练习：

（1）边听边说：

 ① 我要寄两封<u>信</u>。

 ② 这是<u>书</u>。

 ③ 信箱在<u>里边儿</u>。

 ④ 我买<u>信封</u>。

 ⑤ 我看<u>电影</u>。

 ⑥ 我<u>看</u>。

 ⑦ 我去<u>音乐厅</u>。

 ⑧ 我<u>去</u>。

 ⑨ 你看<u>电影</u>吗？——我看<u>电影</u>。

 ⑩ 你看<u>电影</u>不看？——我<u>看</u>电影。

 ⑪ 你看<u>电影</u>还是看电视？——我看<u>电视</u>。

 ⑫ 你看<u>什么</u>电影？——我看<u>中文</u>电影。

 ⑬ 谁看杂技？——<u>阿里</u>看杂技。

 ⑭ 约翰去哪儿了？——他去<u>邮局</u>了。

（2）听我问，请你标出答句的重音：

 ① 你<u>去</u>不去琼楼饭店？ 我<u>去</u>琼楼饭店。

 ② 他看<u>什么</u>？ 他看<u>球赛</u>。

 ③ 您在北京大学学习<u>什么</u>？ 我学习<u>哲学</u>。

 ④ 你借<u>什么</u>杂志？ 我想借<u>阿拉伯文</u>杂志。

 ⑤ 你的词典<u>多少钱</u>买的？ 我的词典<u>五十三块六</u>买的。

四、听后回答问题：

（1）情景：高开在邮局寄信。

 A：先生，寄封信。

 B：寄平信，还是航空信？

 A：平信。

 B：邮票六毛。你还要别的吗？

 A：不要了。

问：他寄什么信？

（2）情景：刘天华在邮局。

179

A：先生，寄两封航空信。

B：两封十二块八。您还要别的吗？

A：有纪念邮票吗？

B：有，您要哪种？

A：我看看。一共有多少种？

B：七种。

A：一种买一套。

问：① 寄一封航空信多少钱？

②他买了多少套纪念邮票？

(3) 情景：夏子在小卖部。

A：小姐，我买信封。

B：一块二一沓儿，您要几沓儿？

A：一沓儿几个？

B：一沓儿十个。

A：要三沓儿。

问：她买了多少个信封？

五、听录音，口头回答问题：

(1) 你们学校有邮局吗？

(2) 在中国寄平信多少钱？

(3) 寄到北京饭店的信多少钱？

(4) 寄到日本的航空信多少钱？

(5) 寄到法国的航空信多少钱？

(6) 寄到你们国家的航空信多少钱？

(7) 你有纪念邮票吗？

(8) 昨天你寄信了吗？

(9) 我可以看看你的纪念邮票吗？

(10) 你是日本人还是中国人？

(11) 你是英国人还是德国人？

(12) 明天你去故宫还是去看杂技？

第二十课

一、语音练习：

（1）边听边说：

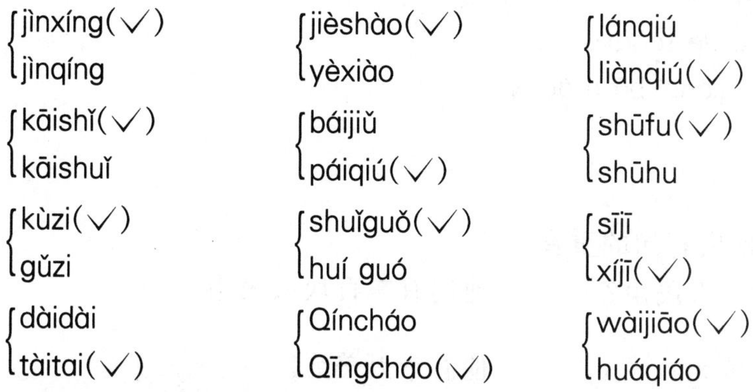

- jìnxíng（✓）／ jìnqíng
- jièshào（✓）／ yèxiào
- lánqiú ／ liànqiú（✓）
- kāishǐ（✓）／ kāishuǐ
- báijiǔ ／ páiqiú（✓）
- shūfu（✓）／ shūhu
- kùzi（✓）／ gǔzi
- shuǐguǒ（✓）／ huí guó
- sījī ／ xíjī（✓）
- dàidài ／ tàitai（✓）
- Qíncháo ／ Qīngcháo（✓）
- wàijiāo（✓）／ huáqiáo

（2）画出你听到的词语：

（内容同上）

（3）听后把词语分成两组：

′ + ′	ˇ + ′
① tóngxué	③ tǒngchóu
② xuéxí	⑤ biǎoyáng
④ shíyán	⑥ zhǔrén
⑦ chángcháng	⑨ lǎonián
⑧ yóujú	⑩ shěnchá
⑪ shénqí	⑫ měixué

（4）学说绕口令：

大哥有大锅，	Dàgē yǒu dà guō,
二哥有小锅。	Èrgē yǒu xiǎo guō.
大哥要换二哥的小锅，	Dàgē yào huàn èrgē de xiǎo guō,
二哥不换大哥的大锅。	Èrgē bú huàn dàgē de dà guō.

二、语调练习：

边听边说（注意句末是升调还是降调）：

（1）Zhè shì shuí ↑?

（2）Duōshǎo qián ↑ ?

（3）Nǐ shénme shíhou qǐ chuáng ↑ ?

（4）Nǐ xiǎng qù yóujú ↑ ?

（5）Tā huì shuō Fǎyǔ ↑ ?

（6）Zhè shì Lǐ Dànián ↓ .

（7）Xiàzǐ qù yínháng ↓ .

（8）Gěi nǐ qián ↓ .

（9）Tā shì wǒ de tóngxué ↓ .

（10）Liǎng zhī qiānbǐ bā máo ↓ .

三、句重音练习：

听我问，请你标出答句的重音：

（1）他们有<u>多少</u>人民币？　　　　他们有<u>二百</u>块人民币。

（2）他有<u>多少</u>美元？　　　　　　他有<u>十万</u>美元。

（3）您换<u>什么</u>外币？　　　　　　我换<u>欧元</u>。

（4）阿里有美元还是<u>日元</u>？　　　他有<u>美元</u>。

（5）在<u>哪儿</u>换外币？　　　　　　在<u>银行</u>换外币。

四、数字练习：

（1）用阿拉伯数字写出你听到的钱数：

① 100 块　　② 1,000 块　　③ 10,000 块　　④ 150 块

⑤ 1,500 块　　⑥ 15,550 块　　⑦ 2,070 块　　⑧ 2,007 块

⑨ 46,751 块　　⑩ 101 块　　⑪ 1,001 块　　⑫ 100,003 块

（2）听后用汉字写出数字：

① 176　　② 5,003　　③ 20,601　　④ 20,020

⑤ 20,200　　⑥ 22,000　　⑦ 20,002　　⑧ 496,717

五、听后选择正确答案：

（1）情景：约翰在银行换外币。

A：先生，我换钱。我有美元，换人民币。

B：今天牌价是一百美元换八百六十三块六毛四人民币。您换多少？

A：我换三百五十美元。

B：请您填这张表。

A：您看，可以吗？

B：可以。

A：对了，我想问问，这儿能换欧元吗？

B：能换。您的人民币是三千零二十二块七毛四，请数数。

A：对了。谢谢。

问：他换什么钱了？

  a．美元　　b．人民币○　　c．欧元

(2) 情景：一个日本学生想换外币。

A：夏子，银行可以换外币吗？

B：可以。

A：哪儿有银行？

B：我们学校有。

问：在哪儿可以换外币？

  a．学校　　b．银行○

六、听录音，口头回答问题：

(1) 你知道银行在哪儿吗？

(2) 你知道在哪儿换外币吗？

(3) 你们国家的钱叫什么名字？

(4) 昨天你去银行了吗？上月呢？

(5) 你们国家有多少人？

(6) 请你数数你们班有多少人？

(7) 上星期你填表了吗？

第二十一课

一、语音练习：

（1）画出你听到的词语

{ bànlǐ
{ bànlǚ(✓)

{ róngyì
{ róngyù(✓)

{ bù mǎi
{ bù měi(✓)

{ fēnfāng(✓)
{ fēngfān

{ bǎibù(✓)
{ běibù

{ shānkǒu(✓)
{ shāngkǒu

{ kāifēng
{ kāifàng(✓)

{ rénchēng
{ rénshēng(✓)

{ shūhu
{ shūfu(✓)

{ dìdào
{ dìdao(✓)

{ shìfei
{ shìfēi(✓)

{ mǎimai(✓)
{ mǎimài

（2）听后把词语分成四组：

´ + —　　　　　´ + ´　　　　　´ + ˇ　　　　　´ + ˋ

① guójiā　③ tuánjié　② píngguǒ　④ xuéxiào

⑧ juéxīn　⑦ wénxué　⑥ qíngjǐng　⑤ hánjià

⑨ Fángshān　⑩ yóujú　⑪ qínggǎn　⑫ yídìng

⑬ chuángdān　⑯ cóngqián　⑭ língsǎn　⑮ mínyòng

（3）听写（用汉语拼音写）：

① xiǎo péngyou　　② lǎo xiānsheng

③ sìshí jǐ gōngjīn　　④ Lǎo xiānsheng qīshíjiǔ suì le.

⑤ Tā qù yínháng huàn rénmínbì.

二、语调练习：

边听边说（注意句末是升调还是降调）

（1）Nà shì shénme ↑?

（2）Nín duō dà niánji le ↑?

（3）Hái yào biéde ma ↑?

（4）Nǐmen chī mántou ↑?

(5) Tā shì wǒ péngyou ↓ .

(6) Yì dár xìnfēng shì shí ge ↓ .

(7) Bú yào biéde le ↓ .

(8) Zhè shì zánmen de ↓ .

三、句重音练习：

（1）边听边说：

    ① 这个小孩儿多大了？   他七岁了。

    ② 你二十几了？   我二十三了。

    ③ 你弟弟几岁了？   五岁多了。

    ④ 她哥哥真胖,有多重？   七十几公斤。

    ⑤ 您多大年纪了？   我六十多了。

    ⑥ 他八十多了吧？   他八十四了。

（2）听下面的句子,说出每句的含义是什么：

    ① 今天他不去医院。

    ② 今天他不去医院。

    ③ 今天他不去医院。

    ④ 今天他不去医院。

四、听后回答问题：

（1）情景：阿里跟王老师和他儿子王小明谈话。

    A：王老师,你们好！

    B：你好！小明,这是阿里叔叔,叫叔叔。

    C：叔叔好！

    A：你好,小明。你几岁了？

    C：三岁多了。

    A：三岁？你个子真高啊！有一米吧？

    C：差一点儿。

    问：① 小明多大了？

        ② 小明有一米高吗？

（2）情景：夏子看贾红春家的照片。

    生词：照片　　zhàopiàn　　photograph

    A：我可以看看照片吗？

    B：可以,你看吧。

    A：这是你弟弟吧？他多大了？

B：你猜猜。

A：十二三了吧？

B：今年十一岁。

A：十一？他有多重？

B：四十多公斤。

A：是吗？真胖啊！那是你爸爸吧？他个子真高，有两米吧？

B：一米九五，他在北京体育大学工作，是老师。现在年纪大了，不工
　　作了。

A：他是谁？

B：我叔叔，爸爸的弟弟。他个子不高，是音乐学院的老师。

问：① 她弟弟多大了？

　　② 她的爸爸在哪儿工作？有多高？

　　③ 她的叔叔高不高？在哪儿工作？

(3) 情景：约翰在故宫参观后找不到大门了，他问一个老人。

　　生词：大门　　dàmén　　gate

　　A：老先生，请问故宫的大门在哪儿？

　　B：别客气，我还不老呢。

　　A：啊，那，那您多大年纪了？

　　B：不大，今年差半岁八十。

　　A：八十还不老吗？

　　B：不老，我还工作呢！（笑）你找大门，是吧？大门在右边儿。

　　A：谢谢您了。

　　B：不客气。

　　问：① 老人今年多大年纪了？

　　　　② 约翰找什么？

　　　　③ 大门在哪边儿？

五、听录音，口头回答问题：

　　(1) 那个小朋友几岁了？

　　(2) 你猜那个老先生多大年纪了？

　　(3) 你的朋友个子有多高？

　　(4) 上星期你寄了几封信？

　　(5) 王兰的弟弟胖不胖？有多重？

（6）你有几枝铅笔？我借一枝可以吗？

（7）郑教授在哪儿工作？他工作多少年了？

（8）我有几本新画报，你想看吗？

（9）你什么时候毕业？

（10）你去邮局了吗？买纪念邮票了吗？

第二十二课

一、语音练习：

（1）画出你听到的词语：

{ jíbié / qūbié(✓) }　　{ zhù xiào / zhùjiào(✓) }　　{ qiǎohé(✓) / xiǎo hé }

{ bùjiǔ / bùxiǔ(✓) }　　{ qiǎoshǒu / xiǎo shǒu(✓) }　　{ jiǎoqì(✓) / qiǎojì }

{ qiūfēn(✓) / jiūfēn }　　{ jiā yóu / jiāoyóu(✓) }　　{ jùchǎng(✓) / jīchǎng }

{ xiāoxi / xiūxi(✓) }

（2）听后给下面的古诗标出调号并朗读：

早发白帝城　　　　　Zǎo Fā Báidìchéng

朝辞白帝彩云间，　　　Zhāo cí Báidì cǎiyún jiān,

千里江陵一日还。　　　Qiān lǐ Jiānglíng yí rì huán.

两岸猿声啼不住，　　　Liǎng àn yuán shēng tí bú zhù,

轻舟已过万重山。　　　Qīng zhōu yǐ guò wàn chóng shān.

二、语调练习：

边听边说（注意句末是升调还是降调）：

（1）Xìnxiāng zài nǎr↑?

（2）Nǐ èrshi jǐ↑?

（3）Tā mǎile jǐ zhī bǐ↑?

（4）Jīntiān xīngqī jǐ↑?

（5）Xiànzài chà shí fēn liù diǎn↓.

（6）Wǒmen bù mǎi xìnzhǐ↓.

（7）Tā mǎile jǐ zhī bǐ↓.

（8）Tāmen bú qù Shǒudū Jùchǎng↓, qù Shǒudū Tǐyùguǎn↓.

三、句重音练习：

    (1) 听我问,请你标出答句的重音：

        ① 这是<u>什么</u>?　　　　　这是<u>床</u>。
        ② 他是<u>谁</u>?　　　　　　他是我<u>朋友</u>。
        ③ 这是<u>音乐厅</u>吗?　　　这是音乐厅。
        ④ 他是<u>你哥哥</u>不是?　　他是<u>我</u>哥哥。
        ⑤ 这是<u>谁</u>的钢笔?　　　这是<u>我</u>的钢笔。
        ⑥ 这是<u>谁</u>的书?　　　　这是<u>我</u>的书。
        ⑦ 这是<u>录音机</u>吗?　　　这是<u>录音机</u>。
        ⑧ 这是<u>照相机</u>吗?　　　这是<u>照相机</u>。

    (2) 听句子,说出每句的含义：

        ① 这是<u>我</u>的钢笔。
        ② <u>这</u>是我的钢笔。
        ③ 这是我的<u>钢笔</u>。
        ④ 他多<u>大</u>?
        ⑤ 他多<u>高</u>?
        ⑥ 他多<u>重</u>?
        ⑦ 我认识那个<u>年轻人</u>。
        ⑧ <u>我</u>认识那个年轻人。

四、听后回答问题：

    (1) 生词：和　hé　and

        在中国,我们一般都不问年轻女人的年龄。你可以问小孩儿和老人的年龄。问小孩儿年龄,可以说"几岁"或者"多大"。问年龄大的人,可以说"多大年纪"或者"多大岁数"。问年龄大的人千万别说"几岁",问年龄小的人也不应该说"多大岁数"。

    问：① 在中国,可以问年龄大的人"几岁"吗?

        ② 在中国,问年龄小的人"多大岁数",可以吗?

    (2) 生词：高兴　gāoxìng　happy

        日本学生夏子在电影院问一个老人几岁了。老人不太高兴,旁边儿的一个年轻人说："中国人问老人年龄,不说'几岁了',要说'多大年纪了'或者'多大岁数了'。"夏子知道自己不对,说："对不起,我是日本人,我不知道怎么问,您千万别生气。"老人笑了。夏子和旁边儿的年轻人也笑了。

    问：① 老人为什么生气?

189

　　　　② 夏子为什么笑了？

　（3）情景：一个外国人向三个小姐问路。
　　　　　生词：小姐　　xiǎojie　　miss
　　　　　　　　　同志　　tóngzhì　comrade
　　　　A：同志，请问去首都剧场怎么坐车？
　　　　ＢＣＤ(三位小姐)：(笑)
　　　　A：你们笑什么？
　　　　B：我们现在一般不叫年轻女人"同志"，叫"小姐"。
　　　　A：对不起，我不知道。
　　　　C：没关系。
　　　　D：您去首都剧场，是吧？ 在北京饭店旁边坐汽车，首都剧场在北京饭
　　　　　　店北边儿。
　　　　B：听懂了吗？
　　　　A：懂了，懂了。谢谢你们。
　　问：① 三个小姐为什么笑？
　　　　② 首都剧场在哪儿？

五、听录音，口头回答问题：
　（1）中国人怎样问小孩儿的年龄？
　（2）中国人怎样问年轻人的年龄？
　（3）中国人怎样问老人的年龄？
　（4）你们一般问年轻女人的年龄吗？
　（5）应该怎么问别人的年龄？
　（6）你来中国学习历史，还是哲学？
　（7）你说得不对，别人生气了，可以怎么说？
　（8）别人说"对不起"，你可以怎么说？
　（9）你毕业的时候多大？
　（10）下午不上课的时候，你一般做什么？

第二十三课

一、语音练习：

（1）画出你听到的词语：

$\begin{cases} \text{qīngjìng}(\checkmark) \\ \text{qīnjìn} \end{cases}$ $\begin{cases} \text{xiànxiàng}(\checkmark) \\ \text{xiǎngxiàng} \end{cases}$ $\begin{cases} \text{shìjuàn}(\checkmark) \\ \text{shìjiàn} \end{cases}$

$\begin{cases} \text{jīnyú}(\checkmark) \\ \text{jīngyú} \end{cases}$ $\begin{cases} \text{xiānghuā}(\checkmark) \\ \text{xiānhuā} \end{cases}$ $\begin{cases} \text{míngyuè} \\ \text{mínyuè}(\checkmark) \end{cases}$

$\begin{cases} \text{qūxiàng}(\checkmark) \\ \text{qīxiàn} \end{cases}$ $\begin{cases} \text{juānqū}(\checkmark) \\ \text{jūnqū} \end{cases}$ $\begin{cases} \text{jīngxīn} \\ \text{jīnxīng}(\checkmark) \end{cases}$

$\begin{cases} \text{pínfán} \\ \text{píngfán}(\checkmark) \end{cases}$

（2）听后给下面的绕口令注音并朗读：

小王和小黄，	Xiǎo Wáng hé Xiǎo Huáng,
一块儿画凤凰。	yíkuàir huà fènghuáng.
小王画黄凤凰，	Xiǎo Wáng huà huáng fènghuáng,
小黄画红凤凰。	Xiǎo Huáng huà hóng fènghuáng.
红凤凰、黄凤凰，	Hóng fènghuáng、huáng fènghuáng,
画成活凤凰。	huàchéng huó fènghuáng.
黄凤凰、红凤凰，	Huáng fènghuáng, hóng fènghuáng,
望着小黄和小王。	wàngzhe Xiǎo Huáng hé Xiǎo Wáng.

二、语调练习：

边听边说（注意句末是升调还是降调）：

（1）Yǒu xìnzhǐ ma ↑?

（2）Zuótiān nǐ shàng nǎr le ↑?

（3）Xiànzài jǐ diǎn le ↑?

（4）Zhè shì tā jiějie ba ↑?

（5）Xìnxiāng zài lǐbianr ↓.

（6）Zhè shì tā jiějie ↓.

（7）Wǒ jīnnián sìshíjiǔ le ↓.

（8）Tā mǎi liànxíběn ne ↓.

三、句重音练习：

  （1）边听边画出有重读"几"的句子：

    ① 你们房间有几张桌子？

    ② 宿舍里有几个人。

    ③ 书架上有几本杂志。

    ④ 桌子上有几本书？

    ⑤ 他念了几课课文？

    ⑥ 我要写几个汉字。

    ⑦ 我想去看几个同学。

    ⑧ 你买了几枝笔？

  （2）听句子，说出每句的含义：

    ① 他在休息。

    ② 他在念课文。

    ③ 他现在写汉字呢。

    ④ 我们明天考试。

    ⑤ 你刚才做什么呢？

    ⑥ 他们听录音呢。

四、听后选择正确答案：

  （1）情景：刘英给高明打电话。

    A：喂，我是北京语言大学。你是哪儿？

    B：我是北京大学。你是高明吗？

    A：我是高明。你是……

    B：我是刘英。

    A：刘英？你好！你什么时候来北京了？

    B：昨天。你现在做什么呢？

    A：我在复习。

    B：什么？休息？

    A：复习！我在念课文，写汉字，做练习，准备明天的考试。

    B：是吗？我想去看你，可以吗？

    A：今天晚上不行，明天吧。明天我们一块儿吃晚饭好吗？

    B：好，明天见。

  问：① 高明是哪个学校的学生？

    a. 北京大学　　b. 北京语言大学〇

    ② 刘英打电话的时候，高明在做什么？

　　　　a．复习○　　b．休息　　c．考试
　　③ 明天他们一块儿做什么？
　　　　a．考试　　b．吃晚饭○

（2）情景：阿里的同学和阿里谈话。
　　A：阿里，昨天晚上我去宿舍看你，你同屋说你去打球了。
　　B：是啊，晚上我一般不学习，去国际俱乐部打球，或者看电影。
　　A：你有这本书的录音吗？
　　B：有，你要听吗？
　　A：我没有这本书的课文录音，我想借你的录音听听。
　　B：可以，下午你去我宿舍吧。
问：① 阿里晚上一般做什么？
　　　　a．学习　　b．打球或者看电影○
　　② 他什么时候去阿里宿舍了？
　　　　a．昨天晚上○　　b．今天下午
　　③ 阿里和同学说话的时候是上午、下午，还是晚上？
　　　　a．上午○　　b．下午　　c．晚上
　　④ 他要借什么？
　　　　a．一本书　　b．课文的录音○

五、听录音，口头回答问题：
　　（1）你们在做什么呢？
　　（2）他们在复习语法吗？
　　（3）你旁边儿的同学写汉字呢吗？
　　（4）谁念课文呢？
　　（5）你刚才听广播了吗？
　　（6）下午我们一块儿打球吧。
　　（7）星期六你们休息吗？
　　（8）你们什么时候考试？
　　（9）你们听录音的时候，老师在做什么？
　　（10）你一般什么时候复习？

第二十四课

一、语音练习：

（1）画出你听到的词语：

{ cāngcù
{ chángchù（✓）

{ zībǔ
{ zhībǔ（✓）

{ shànxīn（✓）
{ sànxīn

{ zhīzú（✓）
{ zìzhǔ

{ zōngzhǐ（✓）
{ zhōngzhǐ

{ zīshì（✓）
{ zhīshi

{ zhìzào
{ zhízhào（✓）

{ zòu yuè（✓）
{ zhòuyè

{ sīrén（✓）
{ shīrén

{ sān céng（✓）
{ shānchéng

（2）听后给下面的谚语注音并朗读：

① 人往高处走，　　　Rén wǎng gāochù zǒu,
　 水往低处流。　　　Shuǐ wǎng dīchù liú.

② 有志者自有千方百计，　Yǒuzhìzhě zì yǒu qiān fāng bǎi jì,
　 无志者只感千难万难。　Wúzhìzhě zhǐ gǎn qiān nán wàn nán.

二、语调练习：

边听边说（注意句末是升调还是降调）：

（1）Nǐmen xuédào dì jǐ kè ↑？

（2）Zhè ge xiǎoháir jīnnián jǐ suì ↑？

（3）Shuí qù Yīnyuè Xuéyuàn ↑？

（4）Tā shénme shíhou bìyè ↑？

（5）jì liǎng fēng xìn ↓.

（6）Wǒ bú huì yòng ↓.

（7）Wǒmen zài shítáng chī fàn ↓.

（8）Yígòng wǔshí měiyuán ↓.

三、句重音练习：

 （1）听我问，请你标出答句的重音：

  ① 你看到第几课了？   看到第四课了。

  ② 应该看完第几页？   应该看完第八页。

  ③ 我念第几个生词？   你念第七个生词。

  ④ 你换完钱了吗？   我换完钱了。

  ⑤ 他没写完这些汉字吧？ 他写完这些汉字了。

  ⑥ 她看完这本书没有？ 她没看完这本书。

 （2）听句子，说出每句的含义：

  ① 我复习完第二十课了。

  ② 我复习完第二十课了。

  ③ 我复习完第二十课了。

四、听后选择正确答案：

 （1）生词：和 hé and

   约翰和阿里是同学。他们明天第三节和第四节考试。约翰已经复习完了。阿里还没有复习完，他复习到第十五课了。他在准备明天的考试。阿里有一个问题，他不懂"还"的意思。约翰告诉了他"还"的意思，也告诉了他怎么用这个词。

   阿里说："谢谢你，约翰。"约翰说："咱们是同学，应该互相学习，互相帮助。"

 问：① 他们什么时候考试？

   a. 明天 b. 第三节和第四节 c. 明天第三节和第四节○

  ② 谁复习完了？

   a. 阿里 b. 约翰○ c. 阿里和约翰

  ③ 谁不懂"还"的意思？

   a. 阿里○ b. 约翰 c. 阿里和约翰

 （2）情景：刘天华想借李大年的钢笔用用。

  A：大年，你现在做什么呢？

  B：听广播呢。

  A：我想用一下儿你的钢笔。

  B：你用吧，我做完练习了。你做完没有？

  A：还没有呢，我做到第六页了，还有三页。

  B：晚上咱们一块儿练习汉字怎么样？

A：那太好了。晚上我来你宿舍。几点？

B：七点半吧。

问：① 谁用谁的钢笔？

　　　　a. 刘天华用李大年的〇　　　b. 李大年用刘天华的

② 他们的练习一共多少页？

　　　　a. 六页　　　b. 三页　　　c. 九页〇

③ 晚上他们做什么？

　　　　a. 做练习　　　b. 听广播　　　c. 写汉字〇

五、听录音,口头回答问题：

（1）你们学到第几课了？

（2）你们学完第几课了？

（3）你们学完第二十四课没有？

（4）这课的生词你都懂了吗？

（5）"准备"这个词的意思你懂不懂？ 你能告诉我这个词的意思吗？

（6）第二十五课在第几页？

（7）今天下午你帮助安娜写汉字吗？

（8）我想用用你的照相机可以吗？

（9）我们应该互相学习,互相帮助,对不对？

（10）你昨天第四节上课了没有？

（11）明天的课你准备没准备？

<h1 align="center">第二十五课</h1>

一、语音练习：

（1）画出你听到的词语：

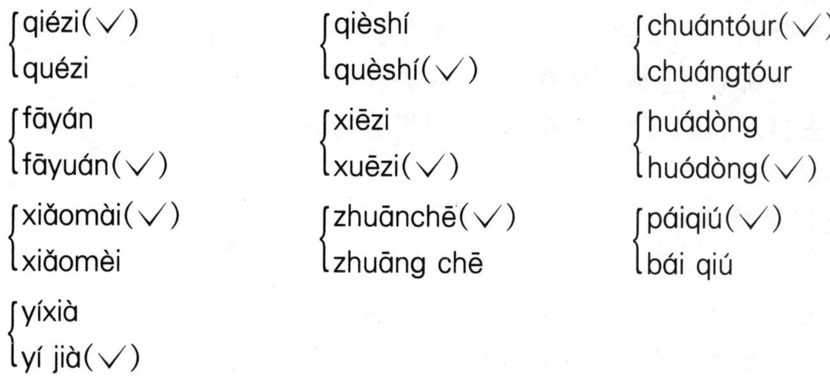

（2）听写（用汉语拼音写）：

① Tā de fángjiān hěn gānjing.

② Yuēhàn hé Shǐmìsī zhù yí ge sùshè, tāmen de dōngxi dōu hěn zhěngjié.

③ Zuótiān Xiàzǐ mǎile liǎng jiàn xīn yīfu hé yì shuāng bùxié.

④ Tā zài fùxí yǔfǎ ne, bú qù dǎ qiú.

⑤ Wǒmen dì yī jié xuéxí kèwén, dì sì jié xiě Hànzì.

（3）朗读你写的句子。

二、语调练习：

边听边说（注意句末是升调还是降调）：

（1）Nín yě qù ma ↑?

（2）Tā shì nín de mèimei ma ↑?

（3）Shuí zài wàibianr ↑?

（4）Nǎ ge shì nǐ dìdi ne ↑?

（5）Tā de shū zài zhuōzi shang、dì shang ↓.

（6）Xiànzài qī diǎn èrshíliù le ↓.

（7）Xuésheng de fángjiān lǐ dōu yǒu guìzi ↓.

（8）Nà běn zázhì tā gěi bàba le ↓.

三、句重音练习：

听我问，请你标出答句的重音：

(1) 你要<u>什么</u>邮票？　　　　　　　我要<u>纪念</u>邮票。

(2) 他买<u>什么</u>衣服？　　　　　　　他买<u>小孩儿</u>衣服。

(3) 他看<u>几点</u>的电影？　　　　　　他看<u>三点半</u>的电影。

(4) 这是<u>谁</u>的床？　　　　　　　　这是<u>史密斯</u>的床。

(5) 他给<u>谁</u>写信？　　　　　　　　他给<u>哥哥</u>写信。

(6) 上午你们有<u>几节</u>课？　　　　　上午我们有<u>四节</u>课。

(7) 你去<u>买邮票</u>，还是去<u>换钱</u>？　　我去<u>换钱</u>。

(8) <u>你</u>去打球，还是<u>阿里</u>去打球？　<u>阿里</u>去打球。

四、听后选择正确答案：

(1) 情景：李双双和她的同屋打扫房间。

　　生词：打扫　　dǎsǎo　　to clean（a room，etc.）

　　　　　洗　　　xǐ　　　　to wash

A：双双，咱们的房间应该打扫了。

B：是啊。

A：你看，桌子上、柜子上、书架上、床下都是土，咱们先打扫一下儿。

B：好。

　　（二人打扫屋子）

A：现在干净了吧。

B：我的枕头和被子都脏了，应该洗了。

A：我的衣服也脏了。明天是星期日，咱们一块儿洗吧。

问：① 她们刚才做什么了？

　　　a. 洗衣服了　　　b. 房间脏了　　　c. 打扫房间了○

　　② 星期日他们做什么？

　　　a. 打扫房间　　　b. 洗被子、枕头和衣服○

(2) 生词：箱子　　xiāngzi　　suitcase

　　　　昨天我去夏子的房间了。她的房间很整洁。桌子上、书架上、柜子上都没有土。被子、枕头和别的东西也都很干净。在她的房间里，我没有看到鞋。她告诉我，不用的鞋都在床下的箱子里。夏子真是一个爱干净的人。

问：①夏子的房间怎么样？

　　　a. 很整洁○　　　b. 没有土

　　② 夏子的房间里有没有鞋？

198

　　　　a．有○　　　b．没有

五、听录音，口头回答问题：

（1）你和谁住一个房间？

（2）你们的宿舍楼干净不干净？

（3）你同屋书架上的书多不多？

（4）你房间里的东西都很整洁，是不是？

（5）谁的衣服脏了？

（6）你的桌子下有土没有？

（7）你看，地上有什么？

（8）晚上睡觉，你用不用被子和枕头？

（9）你看，老师那双鞋怎么样？

（10）一双鞋有几只？

（11）你爱看电影，还是爱看球赛？

第二十六课

一、语音练习：

（1）画出你听到的词语：

⎧ wàiyǔ(✓)	⎧ huánqiú(✓)	⎧ zhuāzhù(✓)
⎩ wèiyǔ	⎩ huáng qiú	⎩ zhuōzhù
⎧ huáihèn(✓)	⎧ lúnzi	⎧ shàng chuán(✓)
⎩ huǐhèn	⎩ lóngzi(✓)	⎩ shàng chuáng
⎧ huìyì	⎧ yí duàn(✓)	⎧ duìzi
⎩ huáiyí(✓)	⎩ yí dùn	⎩ dūnzi(✓)
⎧ shuǐlì(✓)		
⎩ shùnlì		

（2）听写（用汉语拼音写）：

① Ānnà jièshàole Měiguó de yí ge xuéxiào.

② Zhè jiàn yīfu shì nǐ de ba, zhēn hǎokàn.

③ Zhèxiē shì shuí de? Zěnme fàngzài wǒ de yǐzi shang le?

④ Guìzi li yǒu qìshuǐr hé píjiǔ, nǐ xiǎng hē shénme?

⑤ Lǐ lǎoshī huídále xuéshengmen de wèntí.

（3）朗读你写的句子。

（4）学说绕口令：

长虫绕着砖堆转，　Chángchong ràozhe zhuānduī zhuàn,
转完砖堆钻砖堆。　Zhuànwán zhuānduī zuān zhuānduī.

二、句重音练习：

（1）边听边说：

① 你去，还是他去？

② 那只鞋不是他的，是我的。

③ 你学习英文，还是学习法文？

④ 你用钢笔，还是铅笔？

⑤ 你喝茶，还是喝咖啡？

⑥ 我喝牛奶,不喝啤酒。

⑦ 你会英文吗? 会。

⑧ 你会英文,还是会法文? 我会英文。

⑨ 先生,我买钢笔。

⑩ 我买钢笔,不买铅笔。

（2）边听边标出下面句子的重音:

① 你上午去,还是下午去?

② 我喝牛奶,不喝咖啡。

③ 我们学习历史,他们学习哲学。

④ 那件脏衣服是史密斯的,不是我的。

三、听后选择正确答案:

（1）约翰和安娜是同学,他们在一个班学习。一天下午,安娜去约翰的宿舍看他。

约翰的床不整洁,椅子也很脏,上边儿有很多土,还放了一只鞋。安娜问他脏椅子是谁的。他说是同屋史密斯的。

史密斯回来了。安娜认识史密斯,他知道史密斯很爱整洁。她问史密斯:"这把脏椅子是你的?"史密斯笑了,安娜和约翰也笑了。

问: ① 约翰和谁是同学?

    a. 史密斯　　b. 安娜○　　c. 约翰

② 谁的椅子很脏?

    a. 史密斯　　b. 安娜　　c. 约翰○

③ 谁爱整洁?

    a. 史密斯○　　b. 安娜　　c. 约翰

（2）情景:安娜和刘天华从邮局出来,去冷饮店休息。

生词:汽水　 qìshuǐ　 aerated water

A:刘天华,我的纪念邮票怎么样?

B:很好,你的信封也很好,上边儿的画儿很好看。

A:我想休息休息,喝点什么。

B:你看,那边儿有个冷饮店。我们去喝汽水儿吧。

A:什么叫"冷饮店"?

B:冷饮店是卖啤酒、汽水儿、牛奶和咖啡的地方。

A:卖饭吗?

B：不卖,卖饭的地方叫饭馆儿。

问：① 安娜在邮局买什么了?

    a. 纪念邮票和信纸　　b. 纪念邮票和信封○

② 冷饮店卖饭不卖?

    a. 卖　　b. 不卖○

(3) 情景：今天是安娜的生日,很多人来她的房间向她表示祝贺。

生词：生日　　shēngrì　　birthday

　　　高兴　　gāoxìng　　glad, happy

　　　祝　　　zhù　　　　to wish, to congratulate

　　　快乐　　kuàilè　　　happy

(在音乐声和谈笑声中)

A：今天是我的生日。同学们和朋友们来我的宿舍,我很高兴,谢谢你们。

B：祝你生日快乐!

C：祝你生日快乐!

A：谢谢,谢谢你们。这里有汽水儿和啤酒,请你们自己喝吧,都别客气。

　(敲门声)

A：请进! 啊,张老师,您也来了,您请坐。

D：今天是你的生日,祝你生日快乐!

A：谢谢您,您来了,我真高兴。张老师,您喝啤酒还是喝汽水儿?

D：我喝汽水儿吧。

A：张老师,我给您介绍一下儿,他是我哥哥,……

D：他叫安东,在北京大学学习。

　(张老师和安东笑)

E：张老师是我去年的老师。

A：哦,对不起,我怎么一点儿也不知道呢?

D：没关系,我也不知道你是安东的妹妹啊! (对众人)同学们,今天是安娜的生日。我们都很高兴。来,我们一块儿祝安娜生日快乐。

众人：(对安娜)祝你生日快乐!

　(碰杯声)

问：① 今天是谁的生日?

    a. 安娜○　　b. 安东

② 张老师喝什么了?

    a. 啤酒　　b. 汽水儿○

③ 张老师认识安东吗?
　　a. 认识○　　b. 不认识

四、听录音, 口头回答问题:

(1) 老师的桌子上有什么?

(2) 你们班谁的房间不太整洁?

(3) 上课的时候, 你常常回答老师的问题吗?

(4) 对不起, 我不应该问这个问题。(用"没关系"或"没什么"回答)

(5) 你朋友的衣服好看, 还是你姐姐的衣服好看?

(6) 你看, 他找什么呢?

(7) 请帮助我一下儿, 行不行?

(8) 他去银行换外币, 什么时候回来?

(9) 安娜怎么不爱吃糖呢?

(10) 你爱喝什么?

(11) 请你给我介绍一下儿你们班。

第二十七课

一、语音练习：

（1）画出你听到的词语：

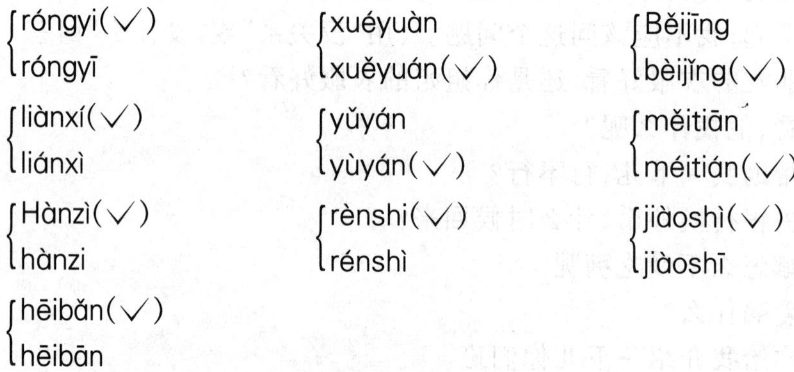

（2）听后给下面的古诗注音并朗读：

绝　句　　　　　　　　　　　　　　Juéjù

两个黄鹂鸣翠柳，　　　　　　Liǎng ge huánglí míng cuìliǔ,

一行白鹭上青天。　　　　　　Yì háng báilù shàng qīngtiān.

窗含西岭千秋雪，　　　　　　Chuāng hán xī lǐng qiānqiū xuě,

门泊东吴万里船。　　　　　　Mén bó Dōngwú wàn lǐ chuán.

二、句重音练习：

（1）边听边说：

① 这双鞋样子好看。

② 这件衬衫颜色好。

③ 他们的房间地很干净。

④ 那件衣服颜色太深。

⑤ 她的汽车样子很好看。

（2）边听边回答，并标出答句的重音：

① 你的皮鞋样子怎么样？

② 他的衣服颜色好不好？

③ 她的鞋样子好看不好看？

④ 安娜的衬衫样子好不好？

三、听后选择正确答案：

（1）生词：但是　　dànshì　but

　　　　　　星期日史密斯去商店买皮鞋。有一双皮鞋，颜色是黄的，样子很好看。史密斯试了试，小了一点儿。有一双黑颜色的皮鞋不大不小，不肥不瘦，很合适，但是样子不好看。商店的小姐告诉他，友谊商店的皮鞋样子好。他想下星期日去友谊商店看看。

　　问：① 什么颜色的皮鞋样子好看？

　　　　　　a．黄色的○　　　　b．黑色的

　　　　② 他买皮鞋了没有？什么颜色的？

　　　　　　a．买了，黄色的　　　b．买了，黑色的　　　c．没买○

（2）情景：安娜在商店买衬衫。

　　　　A：您买什么？

　　　　B：我想买件衬衫。

　　　　A：您要什么颜色的？

　　　　B：蓝颜色的，浅蓝的。

　　　　A：您看这件合适不合适？

　　　　B：可以试试吗？

　　　　A：可以，您可以回去试一下儿，不合适可以来换。

　　　　B：好，多少钱？

　　　　A：八十七块。在那边儿交钱。

　　问：① 她买了什么颜色的衬衫？

　　　　　　a．蓝的　　　b．浅蓝的○

　　　　② 她在商店试衬衫没有？

　　　　　　a．试了　　　b．没试○

　　　　③ 这种衬衫多少钱一件？

　　　　　　a．八十七块○　　　b．七十八块　　　c．八十一块

（3）情景：安娜在商店换衬衫。

　　　　A：小姐，我想换换这件衬衫。

　　　　B：您什么时候买的？

　　　　A：昨天，今天星期一，不，是上星期六。我回去试了一下儿，瘦了点儿，想换一件肥一点儿、长一点儿的。

　　　　B：好。您看这件怎么样？

A：长短、肥瘦合适，但是颜色深了一点儿。有浅点儿的吗？

B：您看这件呢？

A：这件很好。谢谢您。

B：没什么。

问：① 她什么时候买的衬衫？

　　a．昨天　　　b．星期一　　　c．上星期六○

② 她的衬衫怎么不合适？

　　a．肥了一点儿　　　b．瘦了一点儿○

③ 她换没换衬衫？

　　a．换了○　　　b．没换

四、听录音，口头回答问题：

（1）你的皮鞋样子怎么样？

（2）谁的皮鞋样子好看？

（3）你的衬衫是什么颜色的？

（4）阿里有红颜色的衬衫吗？

（5）北京商店的录音机贵不贵？

（6）什么东西是白色的？

（7）什么东西是黑色的？

（8）什么东西是黄色的？

（9）什么东西是蓝色的？

（10）日本的汽车便宜，还是德国的汽车便宜？

第二十八课

一、语音练习：

（1）画出你听到的词语：

{ húzi(✓)　　{ qīhēi　　　{ hànshān(✓)
{ fǔzi　　　　{ qǐfēi(✓)　 { fān shān

{ chū hàn(✓)　{ yuánfèn(✓) { mùfāng(✓)
{ chūfàn　　　 { yuànhèn　　 { mùxiāng

{ héngxíng　　 { hōngdòng(✓) { gōngfèi(✓)
{ fēngxíng(✓) { fēngdòng　　 { gōnghuì

{ kāi huā
{ kāifā(✓)

（2）听写（用汉语拼音写）：

① Zuótian wǒ zài Qiónglóu Fàndiàn yùjiànle Ālǐ.

② Chángchéng lí zhèr hěn yuǎn.

③ Nǐ cóng fúzhuāngdiàn chūlai shàng nǎr le?

④ Xiàwǔ wǒmen gēn lǎoshī yìqǐ qù Liúlichǎng.

⑤ Běijīng gōnggòng qìchē de shòupiàoyuán dàbùfen shì nǚde.

（3）朗读你写的句子。

二、句重音练习：

（1）边听边说（注意"几"的重读和轻读）：

① 他二十几了？

② 他二十几岁了吧？

③ 这些东西有三十几公斤。

④ 这些东西有三十几公斤？

⑤ 这座楼有十几米高。

⑥ 这座楼有十几米高？

⑦ 他买了几张画儿。

⑧ 他买了<u>几</u>张画儿?

(2) 听下面的句子,说出"两"在句子中的意思是"二"还是"几":
① 昨天我去琉璃厂买了<u>两</u>张<u>画儿</u>,没买别的。(几)
② 他买了<u>两</u>张画儿,一张很<u>贵</u>,一张很<u>便宜</u>。(二)
③ 小姐,我买<u>两</u>张票。(二)
④ 晚上我们班去看<u>电影</u>,我去买两张票。(几)
⑤ 我买了<u>两</u>本书,给<u>姐姐</u>一本,给<u>弟弟</u>一本。(二)
⑥ 他买了两本书,还买了几个<u>练习本</u>。(几)
⑦ 她有<u>两</u>双皮鞋和<u>三</u>件衬衫。(二)
⑧ 星期日我洗了两件衣服,还看了一个<u>电影</u>。(几)

三、听后选择正确答案:

(1) 高开和王兰从服装店出来,遇见了张正生。张正生想去琉璃厂买几张画儿,但是不知道怎么坐车。高开也想去琉璃厂买两枝笔。他对王兰说:"咱们跟他一起去看看吧?"

　　公共汽车站离服装店很近。他们三个人上了车,一人买了一张一块钱的票,没用十分钟就到了琉璃厂。

问:① 高开和王兰在哪儿遇见了张正生?
　　　a. 服装店<u>里</u>　　b. 服装店外边儿○
② 高开去琉璃厂做什么?
　　　a. 买几张画儿○　　b. 买两枝笔
③ 从服装店到琉璃厂,汽车票多少钱?
　　　a. 一块○　　b. 五毛

(2) 情景:阿里和安娜谈论琉璃厂。
　　生词:工厂　　gōngchǎng　　factory
　　A:昨天我去看你,你不在。
　　B:是吗? 对不起,我去琉璃厂了。
　　A:琉璃厂? 那是什么工厂?
　　B:不是工厂。琉璃厂是一个地方的名字,那儿有很多商店卖书、卖笔、卖画儿。你看这些中国画儿和笔,是从那儿买的。
　　A:这些画儿真好。琉璃厂离这儿远不远?
　　B:不太远。下星期我和我哥哥一起去,你跟我们一块儿去吧。
　　A:那太好了。
　　问:① 琉璃厂离这儿远不远?

a．不远　　b．不太远○
② 他们什么时候还去琉璃厂？
　　a．星期日　　b．下星期○

(3) 情景：约翰问阿里去琉璃厂怎么坐车。
　　生词：动物园　　dòngwùyuán　　zoo
　　　　　路　　　　lù　　　　　　　line (for bus number)

A：阿里，你知道去琉璃厂怎么坐车吗？

B：知道，你想去买中国画儿，是吗？

A：是啊，我想买两张画儿，还想买点儿别的东西。

B：你知道动物园吗？

A：知道。

B：你坐公共汽车到动物园，从动物园换 15 路汽车到琉璃厂站下。

A：可以坐电车吗？动物园前边儿有很多电车。

B：不行，电车不去琉璃厂。

问：① 去琉璃厂在哪儿换车？
　　　a．动物园○　　b．琉璃厂站
　　② 去琉璃厂可以坐电车吗？
　　　a．可以，电车很多　　b．不行，电车不到琉璃厂○

四、听录音，口头回答问题：
　(1) 你从哪儿来？
　(2) 你们上午从几点到几点上课？
　(3) 刚才休息的时候你遇见老高了吗？
　(4) 你们学校离哪个商店近？
　(5) 坐汽车便宜，还是坐电车便宜？
　(6) 你们学校旁边儿有公共汽车站吗？
　(7) 北京的汽车票贵不贵？
　(8) 北京的汽车售票员怎么样？
　(9) 你跟谁住一个房间？
　(10) 请你给我介绍一下琉璃厂，好吗？

第二十九课

一、语音练习：

（1）画出你听到的词语：

$\begin{cases} \text{xiānhuā}(\checkmark) \\ \text{xiàn huā} \end{cases}$ $\begin{cases} \text{shìyàn} \\ \text{shìyàng}(\checkmark) \end{cases}$ $\begin{cases} \text{jiǎnlì} \\ \text{jiǎnglì}(\checkmark) \end{cases}$

$\begin{cases} \text{qiānqiú} \\ \text{qiǎngqiú}(\checkmark) \end{cases}$ $\begin{cases} \text{qiǎnxiǎn}(\checkmark) \\ \text{qiǎngxiǎn} \end{cases}$ $\begin{cases} \text{liánxì}(\checkmark) \\ \text{liángxí} \end{cases}$

$\begin{cases} \text{lǎonián}(\checkmark) \\ \text{lǎoniáng} \end{cases}$ $\begin{cases} \text{jiānchǎng} \\ \text{jiāngchǎng}(\checkmark) \end{cases}$ $\begin{cases} \text{jiānkè} \\ \text{jiǎng kè}(\checkmark) \end{cases}$

$\begin{cases} \text{jiānyìng}(\checkmark) \\ \text{jiāngyìng} \end{cases}$

（2）听写（用汉语拼音写）：

① Zhèng Jiàoshòu hé shòupiàoyuán zài tán huà.

② Zǎoshang hé wǎnshang zuò chē de rén hěn duō, chē shang hěn jǐ.

③ Wǒmen xuéxiào yǒu sì ge shāngdiàn, sān ge shítáng, chī fàn hé mǎi
dōngxi dōu hěn fāngbiàn.

④ Zài Běijīng zuò shí duō zhàn cái yí kuài qián, zhēn piányi.

⑤ Xià chē yǐhòu yìzhí wǎng dōng zǒu jiù dàole Yǔyán Dàxué.

（3）朗读你写的句子。

（4）边听边说下面的谚语：

① 真金不怕火炼，   Zhēn jīn bú pà huǒ liàn,
脚正不怕鞋歪。   Jiǎo zhèng bú pà xié wāi.

② 世上无难事，   Shìshang wú nán shì,
只怕有心人。   Zhǐ pà yǒuxīn rén.

二、语调练习：

听后回答（注意升调和降调）：

（1）汽车票很便宜↓，是不是↑？

（2）汽车比较挤↓，是不是↑？

（3）在北京坐汽车比较方便↓，是不是↑？

（4）我们是不是在这一站下车↑？

（5）他是不是下车了↑？

（6）是不是往南走↑？

（7）是不是坐出租汽车方便↑？

三、听后选择正确答案：

（1）情景：一个外国人问路。

　　生词：路　lù　line（for bus number）

　　A：劳驾,去北京饭店怎么坐车？

　　B：你在这儿坐 1 路或 4 路,到王府井下车,过马路就到了。

　　A：到什么地方下车？

　　B：王府井,王—府—井。

　　A：王府井,远不远？

　　B：不远,坐四站就到了。

　　A：这两路车是一直往东开吗？

　　B：是,一直往东。

问：① 去北京饭店可以坐几路汽车？

　　　a. 11 路　　　b. 46 路　　　c. 1 路或 4 路○

　　② 从那儿坐汽车去北京饭店,要坐几站？

　　　a. 十站　　　b. 四站○

（2）情景：两个外国人谈论北京的公共汽车票价。

　　生词：空调　kōngtiáo　air-conditioning

　　A：北京的汽车票真贵,是不是？

　　B：我想不贵。

　　A：坐一站两块钱,还不贵吗？

　　B：坐一站两块？ 不对吧。

　　A：真的,我昨天坐了。

　　B：你坐的几路车？

　　A：826 路公共汽车。

　　B：826 路车是空调车,比别的车贵。826 路公共汽车坐几站都是两块。
　　　别的车不是。别的车坐一站到十站是一块,坐十站到二十站是一块
　　　五或者两块。

　　A：坐小公共汽车贵不贵？

　　B：不太贵,从动物园到颐和园才两块钱。

问：① 826 路公共汽车坐四站多少钱？

　　　　　a．一块〇　　　b．两块
　　　② 331 路公共汽车坐四站多少钱？
　　　　　a．五毛　　　b．一块〇

四、听后画出去天坛公园的路线图：

生词：天坛公园　　Tiāntán Gōngyuán　　Tiantan（The Temple of Heaven）Park

A：高开，从琼楼饭店去天坛公园怎么坐车？

B：从琼楼饭店去天坛公园很方便。你坐地铁到前门，从前门再换 20 路公
　　共汽车到天坛站下，下车以后过马路，一直往东走，就是天坛公园。

A：坐地铁的人多吗？

B：有时候比较挤，星期六和星期日坐车的人很多。

　　　琼楼饭店　　　　　前门　　　　　　　　　　　天坛
　　　　〇　　　　　　　　〇　　　　　　　　　　　　〇

　　地铁　　20 路公共汽车

五、听录音，口头回答问题：

（1）昨天上午你和王老师谈话了没有？

（2）在北京，坐出租汽车方便不方便？

（3）坐地铁的人多不多？

（4）邮局离这儿远不远？往哪边儿走？

（5）你毕业以后做什么工作？

（6）用"比较"回答下面的问题：

　　　① 小卖部的啤酒贵不贵？

　　　② 学校食堂的饭怎么样？

　　　③ 他的摩托车样子怎么样？

（7）用"才"回答下面的问题：

　　　① 你们班有多少学生？

　　　② 高老师的孩子多大了？

　　　③ 你的词典多少钱？

　　　④ 现在几点了？

212

第 三 十 课

一、语音练习：

（1）画出你听到的词语：

$\begin{cases} \text{qìchē} \\ \text{qí chē}(\checkmark) \end{cases}$ $\begin{cases} \text{láojià} \\ \text{lǎojiā}(\checkmark) \end{cases}$ $\begin{cases} \text{huàn chē}(\checkmark) \\ \text{huán chē} \end{cases}$

$\begin{cases} \text{yìfu} \\ \text{yīfu}(\checkmark) \end{cases}$ $\begin{cases} \text{huǒchē}(\checkmark) \\ \text{huòchē} \end{cases}$ $\begin{cases} \text{dàxué}(\checkmark) \\ \text{dàxuě} \end{cases}$

$\begin{cases} \text{dànshì}(\checkmark) \\ \text{dǎnshí} \end{cases}$ $\begin{cases} \text{yùxí} \\ \text{yùxǐ}(\checkmark) \end{cases}$

（2）听写（用汉语拼音写）：

① Huàjù jiùyào kāyǎn le, zánmen kuài jìnqu ba.

② Wǒ de piào shì zuì hǎo de zuòwèi, shíyī pái sì hào.

③ Nǐ qù Shànghǎi de shíhou, yídìng dào wǒ jiā lái wánr.

④ Tā xiànzài hěn máng, bù néng qù huǒchēzhàn sòng nǐ le.

⑤ Xiàzǐ huí guó yǐqián, qù Zhāng lǎoshī jiā gēn tā gàobié.

（3）朗读你写的句子。

（4）学说绕口令：

任命是任命，	Rènmìng shì rènmìng,
人名是人名，	Rénmíng shì rénmíng,
任命人名不能错，	Rènmìng rénmíng bù néng cuò,
错了人名就错下了任命。	Cuòle rénmíng jiù cuò xiàle rènmìng.

二、句重音练习：

（1）听后根据句子的重音提问：

① 那是<u>我</u>的书。　　　　（那是谁的书？）

② 那是我的<u>书</u>。　　　　（那是什么？）

③ <u>我</u>要纪念邮票。　　　（谁要纪念邮票？）

④ 我要<u>纪念</u>邮票。　　　（您要什么？）

⑤ <u>我</u>晚上看电影。　　　（谁晚上看电影？）

⑥ 我晚上看<u>电影</u>。　　　　（你晚上看电影，还是看电视？）

⑦ 我<u>晚上</u>看电影。　　　　（你什么时候看电影？）

⑧ 我喝啤酒，<u>不</u>喝咖啡。（你喝啤酒，还是喝咖啡？）

（2）听我问，你标出答句的重音：

① 他的房间是第一个吗？　　　<u>不</u>是第一个，是第<u>六</u>个。

② 第四张桌子是他的吗？　　　<u>不</u>是第四张，是第<u>五</u>张。

③ 你的座位是第二个吗？　　　<u>不</u>是第二个，是第<u>三</u>个。

④ 第十课在二十七页吗？　　　<u>不</u>在二十七页，在<u>二十九</u>页。

三、听后回答问题：

（1）话剧就要开演了。

　　问：话剧开演了吗？

（2）火车快要到了，请你们不要往前边儿走。

　　问：火车到了没有？

（3）汽车要开了，咱们快走吧。

　　问：汽车开没开？

（4）售票员小姐说：“电影开演了，您快往里走吧！”

　　问：电影开演了没有？

（5）A：您什么时候回国？

　　B：下星期四。

　　A：坐火车走吗？

　　B：对。

　　A：您走的时候，我一定来送您，跟您告别。

　　问：① 她什么时候回国？

　　　　② 她回国以前，有人来跟她告别吗？

四、听后选择正确答案：

（1）情景：A 问 B 的座位。

　　A：你有话剧票吗？

　　B：哦，是你啊，小兰。有。你呢？

　　A：我也有，是四排十四号。

　　问：小兰的座位是几排几号？

　　a．四排四号　　　b．四排十四号○　　　c．十四排四号

214

（2）情景：A 问 B 谁来北京学习。

  A：你爱人也要来北京学习，是吗？

  B：不。是我爱人的妹妹，我爱人来信告诉我，她妹妹也想来北京学习汉语。

问：① 谁来信了？

  a. 他爱人○ b. 他爱人的妹妹

  ② 谁要来北京学习？

  a. 他爱人 b. 他爱人的妹妹○

（3）情景：B 在火车站送 A，跟 A 告别。

  生词：同志　　tóngzhì　　comrade

  （火车上的广播：从北京开往上海的火车就要开了，有送亲友的同志请您下车）

  A：火车就要开了，你下车吧。

  B：好，到南京以后一定给我来信。一路平安！再见！

  A：再见！

问：A 坐火车去哪儿？

  a. 上海 b. 南京○ c. 北京

五、听录音，口头回答问题：

（1）你爱看话剧，还是爱看电影？

（2）你的座位在第几排？

（3）来中国以前，你在哪儿学习？

（4）你认识王老师家吗？

（5）你们班谁的个子最高？

（6）阿里明天走，今天晚上你去跟他告别吗？

（7）你现在忙不忙？还常常打球吗？

（8）劳驾，去北京站怎么走？

（9）今天下午我一定去看你。

第三十一课

一、语音练习：

（1）画出你听到的词语或短句：

shàng bān　　línjū　　shàngjí　　júzi

Tā qù Shǒudū Jīchǎng.

Tā gāng xǐle jiǎo.

Tā xǐhuan nà tiáo huáng qúnzi.

（2）听写：

① Wǒ zuótiān qù shuǐguǒdiàn mǎile èr jīn júzi hé sān jīn lí.

② Wǒ xià bān de shíhou, tā zhànzài ménkǒur děng māma ne.

③ Zhāng shīfu shì wǒ de línjū, měi tiān xiàle bān mǎi dōngxi, zuò fàn, xǐ yīfu, máng jí le.

④ Míngtiān nǐ qù huǒchēzhàn jiē Zhāng Zǐqiáng, shùnbiàn dào Wángfǔjǐng gěi wǒ mǎi běn shū ba.

⑤ Gāo Kāi de àiren jiào Wáng Lán, tā xiànzài shì Dì Sān Yīyuàn de dàifu.

（3）读上面的句子。

（4）学说绕口令：

家门口儿放着一垛断短扁担。

jiā ménkǒur fàngzhe yí duò duàn duǎn biǎndan.

二、句重音练习：

听问题，画出答句的重音：

（1）谁是你的邻居？

　　<u>王师傅</u>是我的邻居。

（2）你买什么了？

　　我买了几斤<u>葡萄</u>。

（3）安娜买了多少苹果？

　　安娜买了<u>四个</u>苹果。

216

(4) 约翰买的橘子怎么样？
　　约翰买的橘子<u>不错</u>。

(5) 约翰买的水果怎么样？
　　约翰买的<u>橘子</u>不错，<u>苹果</u>不好。

三、把下面的句子改成否定句：

(1) 王兰上街了。——▶王兰没上街
(2) 他去车站送朋友去了。——▶他没去车站送朋友。
(3) 我买了三斤梨。——▶我没买梨。
(4) 她吃了晚饭了。——▶她没吃晚饭呢。
(5) 张老师下了班，吃完饭，看电影去了。
　　　——▶张老师下了班，没吃饭，也没去看电影。

四、听下面的句子，选择正确的解释：

(1) 阿里刚做完练习。
　　a. 阿里在两小时以前做完了练习
　　b. 阿里在两分钟以前做完了练习○

(2) 明天上街，我要顺便寄封信。
　　a. 明天他上街去寄信
　　b. 明天他上街买东西，买完东西去寄信○

(3) 夏子买了好几本英文书。
　　a. 夏子买了几本英文书，这些英文书很好
　　b. 夏子买了七八本英文书○

(4) 那个商店的水果，梨不错。
　　a. 那个商店的水果和梨不错
　　b. 那个商店的梨不错，别的水果不太好○

(5) 我有时候去邻居家玩儿。
　　a. 他每天去邻居家玩儿
　　b. 他不常去邻居家玩儿○

五、听后回答问题：

(1) 高开下了班，回家的时候看见商店里有很多人在买苹果。他问了一下，
　　苹果很便宜。他想，爱人很爱吃苹果，就买了好几斤。
(2) 问：高开为什么买了好几斤苹果？

(2) 情景：高开和王兰谈话。

    高：你早回来了？

    王：不，刚到家。

    高：你怎么也刚回来？

    王：下了班，顺便去看了个学生。

问：① 高开和王兰现在在哪儿呢？

    ② 他们回来多长时间了？

(3) 情景：张师傅在家门口遇见了王兰。

    生词：菜　cài　vegetable

    张：王老师，您怎么刚回来？

    王：下了班，去买了点儿菜。

    张：菜贵不贵？

    王：比较贵。我没有多买。

问：① 王老师下了班上街去了吗？

    ② 王老师买没买菜？

六、听录音，快速回答问题：

(1) 王师傅是老师吗？

(2) 你刚才看见张老师的邻居了吗？

(3) 你刚到中国吗？你来了多长时间了？

(4) 你们家谁做饭？

(5) 你什么时候上街？顺便给我买一沓儿信封好吗？

(6) 下课的时候，你在门口儿看见谁了？

(7) 明天你去火车站送约翰吗？

(8) 你爱吃什么水果？

(9) 阿里有好几个中国朋友，是吗？

(10) 你爱吃葡萄还是爱吃橘子？

(11) 你的邻居是哪国人？他（她）是个不错的邻居吗？

第三十二课

一、语音练习：

（1）画出你听到的词语或短句：

pópo　　dùzi　　pízi　　túshū,

tāle yì jiān fáng

Nǐ de yīfu tuō bu tuō?

（2）边听边给下面的古诗注音：

登鹳鹊楼　　　　　　Dēng Guànquèlóu

白日依山尽，　　　　　Báirì yī shān jìn,

黄河入海流。　　　　　Huáng Hé rù hǎi liú.

欲穷千里目，　　　　　Yù qióng qiān lǐ mù,

更上一层楼。　　　　　Gèng shàng yì céng lóu.

（3）朗读上面的诗。

二、句重音练习：

（1）边听边说，注意句重音：

① 你什么时候做作业？

　我看完<u>电视</u>就做。

② 你什么时候去上海？

　我下月考完<u>试</u>就去。

③ 刘天华干什么去了？

　他吃完饭就<u>上街</u>去了。

④ 贾红春上哪儿了？

　她下了课就去琼楼<u>饭店</u>了。

（2）听我问，你选择答句，注意答句的重音：

① 你什么时候去看电影？

　a. 我吃了饭<u>就</u>去

219

b. 我吃了饭就去

c. 我吃了饭就去○

② 他干什么去了？

a. 他写完信就去买水果了

b. 他写完信就去买水果了

c. 他写完信就去买水果了○

③ 咱们什么时候爬山？

a. 雨停了，咱们就爬山

b. 雨停了，咱们就爬山○

c. 雨停了，咱们就爬山

④ 你还想去上海吗？

a. 去，我考完试就去

b. 去，我考完试就去○

c. 去，我考完试就去

三、用"真"和"多么……啊"完成句子：

先听我们说：

A：这山　高

B：这山真高！这山多么高啊！

你们做练习：

太阳　红

颜色　好看

东西　便宜

这地方　有意思

雨　大

这件衣服　合适

这个学校　大

四、听下面的句子，听后回答问题：

（1）郑教授有一个女儿、两个儿子，他们都还没有毕业。

问：① 郑教授有几个孩子？

② 郑教授的孩子是做什么的？

（2）李大年先去邮局再上街。

问：那个邮局在院内吗？

220

(3) 妈妈说对了，雨果然停了。

　　问：刚才妈妈说什么了？

(4) 我们十二点吃午饭，吃了饭我就去找你。

　　问：他下午两点钟去找朋友，对吗？

(5) 过了一会儿，天晴了。

　　问：一个小时以前，天很好，对吗？

五、听后选择正确答案：

(1) 情景：约翰请阿里去看话剧。

　　约翰：阿里，你去看话剧吗？我有两张票。

　　阿里：谢谢你，约翰。你知道，我多么想看话剧呀！

　　　　　可是，我还没做完作业呢。

　　约翰：没关系！

　　阿里：什么？没关系？不，我一定要做完作业。

　　约翰：我是说，现在有时间，你先做作业，做完作业咱们再走。

　　阿里：几点开演？

　　约翰：七点半。

　　阿里：好。听你的。

　　问：阿里去不去看话剧？

　　　　a. 去，做完作业就去○

　　　　b. 不去，还没做完作业呢

(2) 情景：早上安娜和史密斯讨论去哪儿玩。

　　生词：雨伞　yǔsǎn　umbrella

　　安　娜：雨停了，咱们走吧。

　　史密斯：不行，你看，天还没晴呢。过一会儿可能还下。下雨爬香山

　　　　　　多没意思啊。

　　安　娜：你说得真对！果然又下雨了。我们今天去哪儿玩呢？

　　史密斯：咱们去故宫，怎么样？在故宫，下雨没关系。

　　安　娜：好的。走吧。

　　史密斯：带雨伞了吗？

　　安　娜：带了。

问：① 他们今天去哪儿玩？
    a. 香山　　　　b. 故宫〇
② 他们去的时候下雨了没有？
    a. 阴天　　　　b. 下雨了〇

六、听录音，快速回答问题：

（1）今天是阴天还是晴天？

（2）昨天下雨了吗？

（3）你起床的时候，太阳出来了吗？

（4）你常常什么时候做作业？

（5）你带词典了没有？借我用一会儿可以吗？

（6）高老师的女儿叫什么名字？

（7）郑教授有儿子没有？

（8）今天下了课，你先做什么？

（9）你什么时候去吃饭？

（10）过一会儿你去打球吗？

（11）你爱爬山吗？

（12）录音停了没有？

第三十三课

一、语音练习：

（1）画出你听到的词语或语句：

mùcái　　chíxù　　shìshí　　sīrén　　zhāi huār

Tāmen dōu zuì le.

（2）听写：

① Cóng Běijīng dào Shànghǎi zuò huǒchē yào yòng èrshí ge xiǎoshí.

② Wǒ de cídiǎn méiyǒu le, wǒ zhǎole bàntiān háishi méi zhǎodào.

③ Tóngxuémen, qiúsài hěn kuài jiùyào kāishǐ le, qǐng huídào nǐ de zuòwèi shang qù ba.

④ Shāngdiàn ménkǒur de páizi shang xiězhe jiǔ diǎn kāi mén, kěshì dōu jiǔ diǎn yíkè le, mén hái bù kāi.

⑤ Tóngxuémen dǎle yí ge duō xiǎoshí qiú, yòu lèi yòu kě, dōu qù lěngyǐndiàn le.

（3）读上面的句子。

二、句重音练习：

（1）听后画出答句的重音：

① 你们上午学习几个小时？

我们上午学习四个小时。

② 坐汽车去长城要用多长时间？

要用三个多小时。

③ 小卖部几点开门？

小卖部九点半开门？

④ 我的表停了，你的表几点了？

我的表是十二点十三分。

⑤ 你渴不渴？咱们去喝汽水吧。

好吧，我又累又渴。

（2）听后给下面的句子提出问题：

  ① 电影七点一刻开演。

    电影几点开演？

  ② 从上海到北京，坐火车要用二十个小时。

    从上海到北京坐火车要用多长时间？

  ③ 现在是北京时间三点整。

    现在几点？

  ④ 我学习了两个小时了。

    你学习几个小时了？

  ⑤ 我们一节课五十分钟。

    你们一节课多少分钟？

三、听下面的句子，选择正确的解释：

（1）我八点就来了，等了你们一个小时了。

  a. 现在一点了

  b. 现在九点了〇

（2）我的钢笔忽然找不到了。

  a. 他的钢笔没有了，不知道在什么地方

  b. 他刚才还有钢笔，现在没有了，不知道在什么地方〇

（3）服装店八点半开门。

  a. 服装店的门八点半开

  b. 服装店八点半开始卖东西〇

（4）小朋友，注意，火车来了。

  a. 火车来了，小朋友不要站在前边〇

  b. 火车来了，小朋友准备上车

（5）可不是，时间过得太快了。

  a. 不能说时间过得太快

  b. 你说得对，时间过得太快〇

四、听后选择正确答案：

（1）情景：安娜和阿里在一起学习。

  安娜：现在几点了？

224

阿里：十点了。

安娜：哟，时间过得真快啊！我们已经学习了三个小时了？

问：他们几点开始学习的？

    a. 十点　　　b. 三点　　　c. 七点○

(2) 情景：约翰找钢笔。

约翰：夏子，你看见我的钢笔了吗？

夏子：没有啊，我写完信就给你了。

约翰：是啊，刚才我还写字了，可是现在忽然找不到了。

夏子：（哈哈）你手里是什么？

约翰：嘻嘻，我，我……，这真有意思。

问：约翰的钢笔在哪儿呢？

    a. 在夏子手里　　　　b. 在约翰手里○

(3) 情景：刘和李在书店门口儿。

刘：书店几点开门？

李：九点。快了，还有三分钟。

刘：哟，咱们没看见门上的牌子，星期一休息。

李：可不是，咱们走吧。

问：① 现在几点？

    a. 9：00　　　　b. 8：57○

    ② 今天是星期一吗？

    a. 是○　　　　b. 不是

五、听录音，快速回答问题：

(1) 你的表几点了？

(2) 上午你们几点开始上第三节课？

(3) 你们学校有冷饮店吗？

(4) 你们一节课有多长时间？

(5) 你一天学习多少小时？累吗？

(6) 中午食堂几点开始卖饭？

(7) 你们学校大门口儿外边儿有牌子吗？你注意上边的字是什么了吗？

(8) 冬冬和妈妈爬上香山了吗？他们爬了多长时间的山？

(9) 什么是冷饮？

(10) 现在我累了，你累吗？咱们休息一会儿吧。

第三十四课

一、语音练习：

（1）画出你听到的词语或短句：

zhīyuán　　chūbù　　zūzi　　zēng bīng wǔshí wàn

Nǐ chāi ba.

（2）边听边给下面的古诗注音：

枫桥夜泊　　　　　　　　　　　Fēngqiáo Yè Bó

月落乌啼霜满天，　　　　　　Yuè luò wū tí shuāng mǎn tiān,

江枫渔火对愁眠。　　　　　　Jiāngfēng yúhuǒ duì chóu mián.

姑苏城外寒山寺，　　　　　　Gūsūchéng wài Hánshānsì,

夜半钟声到客船。　　　　　　Yèbàn zhōngshēng dào kèchuán.

（3）朗读上面的诗。

二、句重音练习：

（1）练习"都"的重读和轻读：

听我问，你选择答句：

① 那个电影你们都看过吗？

　　a. 那个电影我们都看过

　　b. 那个电影我们都看过〇

② 那个电影你看不看？

　　a. 那个电影我都看过了，不看了

　　b. 那个电影我都看过了，不看了〇

③ 他们都走了吗？

　　a. 他们都走了〇

　　b. 他们都走了

④ 他们都坐车去吗？

　　a. 他们都坐车去〇

226

　　　　　b. 他们都<u>坐车</u>去

　　⑤ 你怎么没去看话剧？
　　　　a. 这个话剧我都看过了
　　　　b. 这个话剧我都看过了○

　　⑥ 你喜欢看什么？
　　　　a. 电影和电视我都喜欢○
　　　　b. 电影和电视我都<u>喜欢</u>

　　⑦ 小王呢？
　　　　a. 他都走了，你不知道？
　　　　b. 他都走了，你不知道？○

　　⑧ 再坐一会儿好吗？
　　　　a. 哎呀，都十二点了，该走了
　　　　b. 哎呀，都<u>十二点</u>了，该走了○

（2）练习"才"的重读和轻读：
　　听我问，你选择答句：
　　① 汽车来得很快吗？
　　　　a. 不，汽车<u>十分钟</u>才来一辆○
　　　　b. 不，汽车十分钟才来一辆

　　② 你早就买到票了吗？
　　　　a. 不，我才买到○
　　　　b. 不，我才买到

　　③ 你等了一会儿，他就来了吧？
　　　　a. 不，我等了差不多一个钟头他才来
　　　　b. 不，我等了差不多<u>一个钟头</u>他才来○

　　④ 老师讲了很长时间，他们才懂，是吧？
　　　　a. 不，老师才讲了十分钟他们就都懂了
　　　　b. 不，老师才讲了<u>十分钟</u>他们就都懂了○

三、听下面的句子，选择正确答案：

（1）我十二点就来了。
　　问：他来得早不早？
　　　　a. 早○　　　　b. 不早

（2）我等了五分钟才买上这张电影票。

    问：电影票好买不好买？

        a. 好买　　　　b. 不好买〇

（3）他怎么可能不去呢？

    问：他去不去？

        a. 可能不去　　　b. 一定去〇

（4）我一到中国就买了本《汉英词典》。

    问：他的意思是：

        a. 他来中国买了一本《汉英词典》

        b. 他到中国很快就买了一本《汉英词典》〇

（5）我们都等了半天了，还不开门。

    问：这句话的意思是：

        a. 他们等了四个小时，没开门

        b. 他们等了很长时间没开门〇

四、听后回答问题：

（1）生词：原谅　yuánliàng　to forgive

今天是星期日，张正生跟女朋友玲玲在公园有个约会。可是他到公园的时候，玲玲在那儿都等了他三四十分钟了。其实，张正生早上七点钟一起床就从家里出来了。他没想到，马路上车多，汽车开得很慢，八点半才到了公园门口儿。他看见玲玲有点儿不高兴了，就跑到冷饮店买来了汽水儿和冰淇淋，请玲玲原谅："你别生气，我以后一定提前三个小时出来。"玲玲看他的衣服都湿了，才笑了："我来的时候，坐车的人就不多。你不知道吗？今天的约会我都等了一个星期了。"

问：① 开始的时候，玲玲为什么不高兴了？

    ② 张正生在路上走了多长时间？

    ③ 玲玲为什么笑了？

（2）情景：约翰买完话剧票到了安娜的家。

    生词：骑　qí　to ride

    安娜：话剧票好买吗？

    约翰：排了半个小时的队才买到。

    安娜：给你扇子。你看，衣服都湿了，吃个冰淇淋吧。

    约翰：我真有点儿渴了，有汽水儿吗？我一买完票就骑车往回跑，才骑了二十分钟。

安娜：你骑得太快了。给你汽水儿。

问：① 买话剧票的人多不多？

② 剧场离安娜家远不远？

（3）情景：老王和小张谈爬山。

老王：小张，上星期天你上哪儿玩儿去了？

小张：和玲玲去香山了。

老王：你们爬山了吧？

小张：可不是，山不高，可是很不好爬，爬了一个钟头才爬上去。老王，您喜欢爬山吗？

老王：现在不行了。我上大学的时候，常常和同学们去爬山。

问：① 香山好爬不好爬？

② 老王喜欢不喜欢爬山？

五、听录音，快速回答问题：

（1）你们学校离哪个公园近？

（2）这个星期日他和朋友有约会吗？

（3）今天早上你几点就来了？

（4）昨天晚上你几点才睡？

（5）中午食堂吃饭排队吗？

（6）你爱吃冰淇淋还是爱喝汽水儿？

（7）现在你们可能不常用扇子了吧？

（8）你今天快八点了才到，明天提前一点儿怎么样？

（9）今天的语法你都懂了吗？

（10）你们都学完第三十五课了，是吗？

第三十五课

一、语音练习：

（1）画出你听到的词语和短句：

bàngōng　　qiézi　　xīfú　　qiáoliáng

Tā shì jíxìngzi

Tāmen zhèngzài zuò xítí.

（2）边听边给下面的谚语注音：

① 忠实的人，对人处处关心；　　Zhōngshí de rén duì rén chùchù guānxīn;

虚伪的人，对人当面奉承。　　Xūwěi de rén duì rén dāng miàn fèngcheng.

② 忠于诺言是君子，　　Zhōng yú nuòyán shì jūnzǐ,

不讲信用是小人。　　bù jiǎng xìnyòng shì xiàorén.

③ 种瓜得瓜，种豆得豆。　　Zhòng guā dé guā; zhòng dòu dé dòu.

（3）朗读上面的谚语。

二、句重音练习：

（1）听我问，你选择正确答案：

① 你是怎么去的俱乐部？

a. 我是坐无轨电车去的俱乐部

b. 我是坐无轨电车去的俱乐部○

c. 我是坐无轨电车去的俱乐部

② 你是在哪儿看的电影？

a. 我是在俱乐部看的电影

b. 我是在俱乐部看的电影

c. 我是在俱乐部看的电影○

③ 你们是什么时候看的杂技？

a. 我们是上星期三看的杂技

b. 我们是上星期三看的杂技○

c. 我们是上星期三看的杂技

④ 你们是在哪儿吃的饭？
　　a. 我们是在张文家吃的饭
　　b. 我们是在张文家吃的饭○
　　c. 我们是在张文家吃的饭

⑤ 他是跟谁一起去的音乐厅？
　　a. 他是跟他朋友一起去的音乐厅
　　b. 他是跟他朋友一起去的音乐厅
　　c. 他是跟他朋友一起去的音乐厅○

⑥ 他们是什么时候回来的？
　　a. 他们是昨天晚上回来的○
　　b. 他们是昨天晚上回来的
　　c. 他们是昨天晚上回来的

（2）听下面的句子，练习提问：
① 我是前天回来的。
　　你是什么时候回来的？

② 我是随代表团一起来的。
　　你是跟谁一起来的？

③ 我们是坐火车去的。
　　你们是怎么去的？

④ 这张照片是在敦煌照的。
　　这张照片是在哪儿照的？

⑤ 我们是从上海来的。
　　你们是从哪儿来的？

三、听下面的句子，选择正确答案：

（1）他们是前天坐火车去的。
　　这句话的意思是：
　　a. 他们前天去坐火车了（这里"去"轻读）
　　b. 他们前天坐火车走了○

（2）安娜说："张老师，我给您和玲玲照张相片儿吧。"
　　这句话的意思是：
　　a. 相片儿上的人是安娜
　　b. 相片儿上的人是张老师和玲玲○

（3）我也许明天去学校看看。

这句话的意思是：

a. 他明天可能去学校看看○

b. 他明天一定去学校看看

（4）我们后天离开广州去北京。

这句话的意思是：

a. 他们后天从北京去广州

b. 他们后天从广州去北京○

（5）那个姑娘是给他们做翻译的。

谁是翻译？

a. 那个姑娘○

b. 他们

四、听后选择正确答案：

（1）情景：安娜在公园遇见张正生。

　　　　安娜是个外国姑娘。她是前年在中国北京大学中文系毕业的。今年十月她跟一个艺术代表团一起，又来到了北京。在香山公园她看见了以前的中国老师张正生。她告诉张老师，她现在是翻译，她和代表团已经访问了广州、上海、乌鲁木齐和敦煌，后天就要离开中国了。

　　　　张正生请安娜有时间回校看看，安娜说，也许第二天去学校。

问：① 安娜以前在中国学习什么？

　　　 a. 艺术　　　b. 中文○

　　② 安娜什么时候离开中国？

　　　 a. 前天　　　b. 第二天　　　c. 后天○

　　③ 第二天安娜可能去哪儿？

　　　 a. 张老师家　　　b. 学校○　　　c. 香山公园

（2）情景：史密斯在北海公园的一个冷饮店遇见了夏子和阿里。

夏　子：哟，这不是史密斯先生吗？您前年不是回英国了吗？

史密斯：我又来了，我是跟体育代表团一起来的，我是他们的翻译。
　　　　你们毕业了吗？

阿　里：还没有呢，我们还要在音乐学院学习一年。你们是什么时候
　　　　到的中国？

史密斯：上个月。我们到中国以后访问了很多地方，前天才到北京。

夏　子：咱们都坐下说话，史密斯先生，请坐吧。您想喝点儿什么？

232

啤酒还是汽水？这儿有蛋糕，请随便吃吧。

史密斯：我爱吃北京的冰淇淋，这儿有吗？

夏　子：有，我去买。

史密斯：我也许后天晚上能去语言大学看看张老师。

阿　里：那我们也去。

问：① 史密斯先生是哪国人？

　　　　a.美国　　　b.英国〇

　② 史密斯先生什么时候到的北京？

　　　　a.上个月〇　　　b.前天

　③ 史密斯先生吃什么？

　　　　a.蛋糕　　　b.冰淇淋〇

　④ 夏子和阿里现在在哪个学校学习？

　　　　a.体育学院　　　b.语言大学　　　c.音乐学院〇

五、听录音，快速回答问题：

（1）你是什么时候开始学习汉语的？

（2）你前年在学习还是在工作？

（3）你爱吃蛋糕吗？

（4）在中国你访问了哪些地方？

（5）你能给我介绍一下你们国家的情况吗？

（6）你前天做什么了？

（7）你后天去公园吗？

（8）你什么时候离开这个学校？

（9）今天的课文你能翻译吗？

（10）你们班有几个女同学？

（11）你有妈妈的相片儿吗？你常常想她吗？

（12）上课的时候，不能随便说话，是不是？

第三十六课

一、语音练习：

（1）画出你听到的词语或短句：

chídào　　　cí zhí　　　chízi　　　bú yào zhāi xialai

yì zhāng jīpiào,

Nǐmen bié zhǎo le.

Wǒmen qù fǎngwèn yí ge gōngzhǎng.

（2）听写：

① Yuēhàn gǎnmào le.Tā tóu téng, késou, hái yǒu diǎnr fā shāo.

② Xiǎojie, wǒ sǎngzi téng, yīnggāi guà nèikē háishì wàikē?

③ Ānnà jīntiān bù shūfu, bù lái shàng kè le.

④ Wǒ měi tiān liù diǎnzhōng qǐ chuáng, qǐ chuáng yǐhòu dǎ bàn ge xiǎoshí tàijíquán, cái qù chī zǎofàn.

⑤ Tā de shǒu shì xīngqīrì qù Chángchéng pá shān de shíhou nòngpò de.

（3）读上面的句子。

二、句重音练习：

（1）听后说出句子的意思：

① 我今天头疼。

② 我今天头疼。

③ 我今天头疼。

④ 我今天头疼。

（2）听后标出答句的重音：

① 你今天怎么不舒服？

我今天头疼。

② 你今天嗓子疼吗？

不，我今天头疼。

③ 你昨天头疼吗？

    不，我今天才开始头疼。

④ 你们今天谁头疼？

    我今天头疼。

三、听下面的句子，听后填空：

(1) 冬冬的手破了，很疼，他去医院看手。

    他应该挂外科。

(2) 夏子今天头疼，咳嗽，嗓子疼，鼻子也不通。

    她的病是感冒。

(3) 常大夫给约翰试了试表，三十八度五。

    约翰试表以后知道发烧了。

(4) 这是你的药，大药片儿每天吃三次，每次吃一片儿。小药片儿每天吃
    四次，每次吃两片儿。

    大夫给了他两种药。大药片儿每天吃三片儿，小药片儿每天吃八
    片儿。

(5) 我每次来中国都要去一次长城，我已经去了四次了。

    他来四次中国了。

四、听后回答问题：

(1) 情景：史密斯在医院看病。

    大　夫：请这儿坐吧。你怎么不舒服？

    史密斯：我肚子疼。

    大　夫：哪边儿疼？

    大　夫：请你到床上去。……这儿疼吗？

    史密斯：不疼。

    大　夫：这儿疼不疼？

    史密斯：不疼。

    大　夫：这儿……

    史密斯：哎哟，疼，疼，非常疼。

    大　夫：你疼了几天了？

    史密斯：今天上午开始的。

    大　夫：我给你打一针吧。

问：① 史密斯怎么不舒服？

　　② 大夫给他开药了吗？

（2）情景：夏子在医院看病。

　　大夫：我给你开点儿药，再打两天针。

　　夏子：打针？

　　大夫：怎么？你不想打？

　　夏子：打吧。

　　大夫：白药片儿一天三次，每次一片儿。黄药片儿一天四次，每次两
　　　　　片儿。针是上午打一次，下午打一次。你要多喝水，多吃水
　　　　　果。

　　夏子：好的。谢谢你。

问：① 夏子一共要打几针？

　　② 夏子一天吃几种药？

（3）情景：张大夫给约翰看病。

　　张大夫：约翰，这儿坐。这次又怎么不舒服？

　　约　翰：嗓子疼，有点儿发烧。

　　张大夫：咳嗽不咳嗽？

　　约　翰：不咳嗽，鼻子也通，只是嗓子很疼。

　　张大夫：试试表吧。

　　　　　（过了一会儿）

　　约　翰：发烧吗？

　　张大夫：发烧，三十八度。张嘴，"啊——"。

　　约　翰：啊——

　　张大夫：嗓子非常红。这次还要打针吃药。你晚上几点睡觉？

　　约　翰：十二点。看书，学习。

　　张大夫：以后晚上不要长时间学习。星期天也应该去公园玩一玩，不
　　　　　　要只是工作，不注意休息。

　　约　翰：您说得对，我以后一定要注意休息。

问：① 约翰这次是第一次得病吗？

　　② 张大夫告诉约翰应该注意什么？

五、听录音，快速回答问题：

    （1）你手里有什么？

    （2）感冒了，去医院看病，要挂哪一科？

    （3）手破了，去医院要挂哪一科？

    （4）小孩儿病了，去医院要看哪一科？

    （5）你每天晚上几点睡觉？

    （6）每天下午你学习汉语吗？

    （7）你看电视吗？每星期看几次？

    （8）从北京坐飞机去你们国家要换飞机吗？

    （9）从外交公寓坐公共汽车去香山公园，要换几次车？

  （10）我的衣服破了，你能帮助我吗？

第三十七课

一、语音练习：

（1）画出你听到的词语或短句：

xīwàng　　qījiān　　qíshí　　shíxíng　　guā fēng le

yí bàng miànbāo　　liǎng tóu jīngyú

Tā yǒu yì kē hóngxīng.

（2）听后给下面的绕口令注音：

板凳宽，扁担长，	Bǎndèng kuān, biǎndan cháng,
扁担要绑板凳上，	biǎndan yào bǎng bǎndèng shang,
板凳不让扁担绑，	bǎndèng bú ràng biǎndan bǎng,
扁担非绑板凳上。	biǎndan fēi bǎng bǎndèng shang.

（3）读上面的绕口令。

二、听下面的句子，给"来"或"去"标上调号（注意它是读原调，还是读为轻声）：

（1）阿里来中国半年了。

（2）他拿来了一个录音机。

（3）我们去长城照相。

（4）我们带去两个篮球。

（5）上星期我从张正生那儿借来一本词典。

（6）我来借一本词典。

（7）贾红春去美国两年了。

（8）夏子的自行车我已经送去了。

三、听下面的句子，听后选择正确答案：

（1）排球比赛马上要开始了。

问：比赛开始了没有？

a. 已经开始了　b. 还没开始呢○

(2) 高老师让我告诉你们，他今天晚上不能跟咱们一起去看话剧了。

　　问：今天晚上谁去看话剧？

　　　　a. 高老师和他们　　b. 高老师　　c. 他们○

(3) 王兰看见冬冬在马路上跑，就说："别着急，注意路上的汽车。"

　　问：谁在马路上跑？

　　　　a. 王兰　　b. 冬冬○

(4) 糟糕，我的票呢？你看见了吗？

　　问：他在做什么？

　　　　a. 找人　　b. 找票○

(5) 明天中国女子排球队和日本女子排球队比赛，排队买票的人非常多，排在后面的人可能买不到票。

　　问：排队的人都能买到票吗？

　　　　a. 也许都能买到　　b. 可能有的人买不到○

四、听后选择正确答案：

(1) 昨天晚上高老师邀请我们几个学生去北京体育场看足球比赛。我们有的骑自行车去，有的坐公共汽车去。高老师从他家去体育场，在门口儿等我们。

　　　　运动员和裁判员开始进场了，可是约翰还没到。高老师让我在门口儿等他，他带同学们先进去。又过了五分钟约翰才来。其实他五点半就从学校出来了。坐汽车的人很多，他等了三十分钟才上了汽车。来体育场的路上，车又很多，公共汽车不能快开。他到了体育场已经七点四十了。我们要进去的时候，他的票又忘了带来了。您说，多糟糕！正好我还有一张票。我们上了看台，比赛已经开始十分钟了。

　　问：① 谁先进了体育场？

　　　　　a. 高老师　　b. 学生们　　c. 高老师和一些学生○

　　　　② 约翰是怎么去的体育场？

　　　　　a. 坐公共汽车○　　b. 骑自行车

　　　　③ 约翰到体育场时几点了？

　　　　　a. 五点半　　b. 七点四十○

　　　　④ 约翰为什么很晚才到体育场？

　　　　　a. 他没有提前出来　　b. 汽车不能快开○

(2) A：阿里，你怎么才回来？人多吧？

　　B：不太多。

A：东西好买吗？

B：好买。

A：蛋糕和水果呢？

B：糟糕！我忘在邮局了。

A：邮局？你怎么去邮局了？

B：我从商店买了东西，又去邮局寄了两封信，买了几套纪念邮票。

A：六点半邮局就关门了，你快去拿吧。

B：没关系，还有半个小时呢。你在宿舍等我，我马上就回来。

问：① 他买什么东西了？

    a. 蛋糕、水果

    b. 两沓信封、纪念邮票

    c. 蛋糕、水果、纪念邮票○

② 现在几点了？

    a. 六点半　b. 六点○　c. 五点半

(3) A：小王，你不是要去南京吗？

    B：我又回来了。

    A：真快呀！

    B：我刚从火车站回来。

    A：怎么？不去了？

    B：不是，该带的几件东西忘带了，现在回来拿。

    A：要晚了吧？

    B：没问题，我拿了东西，马上就走。

问：他为什么回来？

    a. 不去了　b. 回来再拿几件东西○

五、听录音，快速回答问题：

(1) 你会打篮球吗？

(2) 你们国家的姑娘们踢（tī, to play）足球吗？

(3) 你们班有运动员吗？他打什么球？

(4) 你们国家排球代表团什么时候来中国访问？

(5) 上一课的作业你带来了吗？

(6) 考试的时候，老师让看词典吗？

（7）我忘拿铅笔了，你那儿有吗？借我一枝。

（8）汤姆为什么很着急？

（9）王老师邀请我们班的同学下星期去他家玩儿，你去吗？

（10）现在马上就要下课了吗？

一、语音练习：

（1）画出你听到的词语或短句：

fēnbù　　ēnqíng　　běifāng　　mùchuán　　búxìng

fēngjǐng　　jíjù　　xúnzhǎo chǎngdì　　Wǒ kànle qī yè.

（2）听写：

① Wǒ gěi Gāo lǎoshī dǎ diànhuà de shíhou，tā zhènghǎo bú zài jiā，wǒ qǐng Wáng lǎoshī zhuǎngào tā.

② Shíyī yuè èrshíqī hào shì wǒ guó guóqìng，wǒmen dàshǐguǎn yāoqǐng zài Běijīng de liúxuéshēng qù dàshǐguǎn cānjiā qìngzhù huódòng.

③ Wǒmen dōu xǐhuan qù chāoshì mǎi dōngxi. Nàlǐ de jī、yú、ròu、cài suīrán bǐjiào guì，kěshì hěn xīnxian.

④ Jīntiān shì wǒ yéye de shēngrì，wǒ gěi tā mǎile yí ge shēngrì dàngāo hé yí jiàn pí'ǎo zuòwéi lǐwù，tā yídìng hěn gāoxìng.

（3）读上面的句子。

二、听下面的句子，给"来"或"去"标出实际的声调：

（1）你们上哪儿去？

（2）他们都去香山公园吗？

（3）我请了几位朋友来，你去做几个菜吧。

（4）客人们都来了，请您进屋去吧。

（5）妈妈刚才上街去了，她买了些牛肉来。

（6）糟糕！给妹妹的礼物我忘带来了。

三、听下面的句子，选择正确的解释：

（1）明天要是不下雨，我们和他们班比赛足球。

这句话的意思是：

a. 明天一定比赛足球

b. 明天天气好、不下雨，就比赛足球〇

(2) 我下班回家路过超市，进去买了几斤肉。

这句话的意思是：

a. 下午他没有工作，去买肉了

b. 下午他工作完了，顺便买肉了〇

(3) 这里的超市，人们可以随便拿东西，可是不是不要钱。

这句话的意思是：

a. 这个超市的东西是可以随便拿的，不要钱

b. 在这个超市可以随便拿东西，可是要交线〇

(4) 您带什么礼物！去就可以了。

这句话的意思是：

a. 您带什么礼物去？

b. 您去的时候不要带礼物〇

(5) 欢迎同学们来我家，请屋里坐吧。

这句话的意思是：

a. 他欢迎同学们，请同学们进屋去坐〇

b. 同学们欢迎他，请他进屋去坐

四、听后回答问题：

(1) 情景：晚上约翰回到宿舍看见了史密斯。

史密斯：今天的足球比赛怎么这么长时间？

约　翰：不，四点多就完了，高老师请我们去他家了。哎，你知道
　　　　吗？高老师的妈妈很会做菜。

史密斯：怎么？高老师请你们在他家吃饭了？

约　翰：是啊！他妈妈做了几个菜，都很好吃。我以前还没有吃过这
　　　　么好吃的菜呢。我想中国菜最好吃了。

史密斯：是吗？下次看足球比赛我也去。

问：① 足球比赛几点完的？

　　② 约翰在哪儿吃的晚饭？

　　③ 史密斯也爱看足球比赛吗？

（2）情景：星期日下午，安娜在院子里遇见了常大夫。

安　娜：常大夫，您休息呢？

常大夫：是啊！

安　娜：我想问您一个问题，可以吗？

常大夫：不要客气，请说吧。

安　娜：来中国以后，我胖了很多，现在差不多有八十多公斤了，您
　　　　说该怎么办？

常大夫：少吃饭，多运动。

安　娜：我很爱吃中国菜，每星期都要去几次饭馆儿。在学校食堂吃
　　　　饭，午饭晚饭都要吃两个菜。牛肉、羊肉、猪肉、鸡、鱼，
　　　　我都爱吃。

常大夫：肉可以吃，可是要少吃，应该多吃些素菜。你知道豆腐吗？
　　　　豆腐很好吃，多吃点儿，也没关系，不会长胖。

安　娜：我试试吧。别再胖了！

问：① 安娜为什么着急？

　　② 一个人要是不想太胖，应该多吃什么，少吃什么？

五、听录音，快速回答问题：

（1）你们国家有中国大使馆吗？

（2）同学们去你家玩儿，你欢迎吗？

（3）每年新年你给妈妈礼物吗？

（4）你们学校旁边儿有超市吗？

（5）从你的宿舍到教室路过哪些地方？

（6）你爱吃鱼还是爱吃鸡？

（7）你爱吃牛肉还是爱吃羊肉？

（8）你们学校每个屋子住几个学生？

（9）要是你有很多很多钱，你准备用这些钱做什么呢？

（10）阿里的家里每天晚上都有很多客人，他是一个好客的人，你也是一
　　　个好客的人吗？

第三十九课

一、语音练习：

（1）画出你听到的句子：

Ānnà yǒu cáihuá.

Zhāng Zǐqiáng mǎi yán.

Nǐ yào tāng ma?

Nà shì tā de qīzi bú shì?

Língling ài chī xiānyú.

（2）听后给下面的谚语注音：

① 生命在于运动。　　　　　Shēngmìng zàiyú yùndòng.

② 饭后百步走，活到九十九。Fàn hòu bǎi bù zǒu, huódào jiǔshíjiǔ.

③ 一懒生百病。　　　　　　Yì lǎn shēng bǎi bìng.

④ 一日三笑，不用吃药。　　Yí rì sān xiào, bú yòng chī yào.

（3）朗读上面的谚语。

二、听后给下面的句子标出句重音：

（1）五号跑得快。

（2）他骑得慢。

（3）这个队踢得不好。

（4）阿里汉语说得很好。

（5）他汉字写得怎么样？

（6）夏子乒乓球打得好，网球打得不好。

三、听下面的句子，并把它变成否定句：

（1）那个杂技团的节目很精彩。

（2）他太极拳打得真好。

（3）昨天晚上雨下得太大了。

（4）他排球、篮球、乒乓球都打得不错。

（5）阿里游泳游得非常快。

（6）琉璃厂离我们学校远得很。

四、听后回答问题：

（1）昨天晚上我们在宿舍里谈得真热闹。

　　问：昨天晚上他们在宿舍里做什么了？

（2）阿里喜欢长跑，每天早上起床以后都要跑二三十分钟。

　　问：阿里的爱好是什么？

（3）上星期我买了一辆自行车，我觉得去近的地方骑自行车比较方便。

　　问：他为什么买自行车？

（4）打球、游泳、长跑、骑自行车，这些爱好都很好。

　　问：什么爱好好？

五、听后选择正确答案：

（1）情景：同学们在教室商量星期日去哪儿玩儿，高老师进来了。

　　高老师：嗬！屋里真热闹啊！

　　安　娜：我们正商量星期日去哪儿玩儿呢。

　　高老师：昨天下午在我家已经商量好了，去香山。怎么，有人不同意吗？

　　史密斯：香山我们去了两次了。我提议星期日不去香山，换个地方。

　　约　翰：我同意。我们学校南边儿有个公园，有小山，有绿水，还有小城墙呢。

　　夏　子：是吗？离学校远不远？

　　约　翰：骑车二十多分钟。你骑得慢，三十分钟也能骑到。

　　夏　子：我同意。

　　高老师：别人也同意吗？

　　安　娜：我也同意约翰的提议。

　　问：① 星期日他们去哪儿玩儿？

　　　　　a. 香山　b. 学校南边的公园○

　　　　② 约翰的提议是什么？

　　　　　a. 去香山　b. 去学校南边的公园○

　　　　③ 学校南边的公园远不远？

　　　　　a. 不远○　b. 远

（2）听小相声《谈爱好》。

　　A：您这是做什么呢？

　　B：打太极拳呢。这是我的爱好。打太极拳是一种最好的体育运动。

246

我别的不行，可是太极拳打得最好。

A：是吗？

B：你有什么爱好？

A：我喜欢长跑。

B：长跑好，长跑是一种最好的体育运动。我别的不行，可是长跑跑得最快。

A：（对观众）您听见了没有？又一个"最"。（对 B）我还喜欢游泳。

B：游泳好。

A：（对观众）又来了。

A、B：游泳是一种最好的体育运动。我别的不好，可是游泳游得最好。

B：你也会说了。

A：跟你学的呀！

B：我的意思是各种体育运动都很好。一个人应该有多种爱好。

A：不错。

B：我告诉你，我的爱好多极了。

A：你说说。

B：我喜欢游泳、打球、爬山、长跑；我喜欢吃中国菜，喝北京啤酒；还喜欢晚上跳舞，上午睡觉……

A：什么？什么？这晚上不睡，早上不起也是爱好？

B：这个爱好差点儿。

A：这不叫爱好，叫恶习。

B：对，是饿习，饿了不学习。

A：什么呀！恶习，是一种不好的习惯。你一定要改改。

B：改，改，今天晚上就改。错了就改，这是一种好习惯。我别的不行，知错就改，我做得最好。

A：行了，行了，又来了。

问：① 两个人见面时，一个人在做什么？

    a. 游泳　b. 打太极拳○　c. 长跑

 ② 一个人应该有多种爱好，对不对？

    a. 对○　b. 不对

 ③ 什么叫恶习？

    a. 饿了不学习　b. 不好的习惯○

六、听录音，快速回答问题：

（1）你喜欢踢足球吗？

（2）你们班谁跑得最快？

（3）你喜欢体育运动吗？

（4）你喜欢什么体育运动？

（5）你的爱好是什么？

（6）你们国家谁网球打得最好？

（7）你会打太极拳吗？

（8）我提议，咱们每天早上六点起床去操场跑步，你同意吗？

（9）你们学校什么地方最热闹？

（10）你喜欢晴天还是阴天？

第 四 十 课

一、语音练习：

（1）画出你听到的短句：

Tā hěn kèqi.

Wǒ zài kàn shū.

Dōngdong cóng Shǎnxī lái.

Tā kāi yàofāng.

Yí liè huǒchē kāilai le.

（2）听后给下面的古诗注音：

悯　农	Mǐn nóng
锄禾日当午，	Chú hé rì dāng wǔ,
汗滴禾下土。	Hàn dī hé xià tǔ.
谁知盘中餐，	Shuí zhī pán zhōng cān,
粒粒皆辛苦。	Lìlì jiē xīnkǔ.

（3）朗读上面的诗。

二、听后用"一边…一边…"把两句话变为一句话：

例：他听音乐。他写汉字。——→他一边听音乐一边写汉字。

（1）他吃饭。他看报。

（2）他走。他说。

（3）我们喝咖啡。我们谈话。

（4）他在美国教汉语。他在美国学习英语。

（5）大家看课文。大家听录音。

（6）张老师吃饭。张老师回答我们的问题。

三、听下面的句子，判断句义的解释是否正确：

（1）这是我们吃饭的桌子。

意思是：我们吃饭的时候用这张桌子。（✓）

（2）那是我爱人从四川买来的酒。

　　意思是：那酒是我爱人去四川的时候在那儿买的。（√）

（3）他们一边喝酒一边谈话。

　　意思是：他们也许喝酒，也许谈话。（×）

（4）妈妈说："饭做好了。大家吃饭吧。"

　　意思是：饭做得很好，大家请吃吧。（×）

（5）这些东西好拿，你别着急，我们帮助你。

　　意思是：这些东西好，你不要着急，我们帮助你。（×）

（6）这个孩子真好玩儿。

　　意思是：这个孩子很有意思，大家都喜欢他。（√）

（7）我觉得这种汽水儿很好喝。

　　意思是：这种汽水儿好，我喜欢喝。（×）

（8）今天的练习好做。

　　意思是：今天的练习好，我可以做。（×）

（9）这种衣服很不好买。

　　意思是：这种衣服不好，我不买。（×）

（10）我们家吃饭用的桌子跟刘天华家的不一样，是圆的。

　　意思是：刘天华家的桌子是圆的，我们家的桌子不是圆的。（×）

四、听后选择正确答案：

（1）情景：郑教授请约翰、汤姆、夏子在家里吃饭。

　　生词：花篮儿　　huālánr　　　　flower basket

　　　　　真正　　　zhēngzhèng　　true, real

　　郑教授：大家别客气，随便吃。汤姆，你尝尝这个菜怎么样？是羊肉
　　　　　　做的。

　　汤　姆：真好吃。

　　约　翰：郑教授，这种很圆的东西叫肉球吗？非常好吃。

　　郑教授：不，叫丸子，是用猪肉做的。

　　夏　子：啊，那个菜真好看，红的、黄的、蓝的、白的，跟一个花篮
　　　　　　儿一样。这些菜是您爱人做的吗？

　　郑教授：不，是我女儿做的。我爱人去南京了，不在家。（向厨房）
　　　　　　玲玲，都做好了吗？你也来吧。

玲　玲：都做好了，马上就来。

夏　子：玲玲，你快来。来，请坐这儿。太好了，你的菜做得真好吃。我们一起谢谢玲玲，和玲玲干杯！

汤　姆：干杯！

约　翰：干杯！

玲　玲：大家太客气了。我做得不好，你们凑合吃吧。我哥哥做的菜才叫真正的中国菜呢。他和母亲从南京回来以后，欢迎你们再来尝尝他做的菜。

汤姆、约翰、夏子：我们一定来。谢谢你的邀请。

问：① 约翰喜欢吃的那种圆的东西叫什么菜？

　　　a. 肉球　b. 圆菜　c. 丸子○

　　② 他们在郑教授家吃的菜怎么样？

　　　a. 很好看　b. 很好吃　c. 又好看又好吃○

　　③ 郑教授家谁做菜做得最好？

　　　a. 郑教授　b. 郑教授的爱人

　　　c. 郑教授的儿子○　d. 郑教授的女儿

(2) 情景：安娜和夏子在宿舍谈话。

　　生词：说明　shuōmíng　to show

　　安娜：你怎么刚回来？

　　夏子：郑教授邀请我去他家吃饭了。他们做了很多菜，又好看又好吃。今天我吃得太饱了。

　　安娜：中国人吃饭的习惯跟日本人一样吗？

　　夏子：差不多，可能跟你们美国人很不一样。

　　安娜：是啊，我们吃饭用刀子、叉子、勺子，你们用筷子。在我们那儿，菜来了，大家分，每个人往自己盘子里盛一点儿。

　　夏子：我们那儿先分好，菜来了，不用再分，自己吃自己的。

　　安娜：中国人吃饭，菜都放在桌子中间儿，大家一起吃。哎，有一点我不懂。为什么中国人请客人吃饭做菜，常常吃不完，吃饭的时候，他们往你的盘子里放菜，让你多吃，你说吃饱了，他们还说，再吃一点儿吧。真有意思。

　　夏子：我听说，这也是中国人的一种习惯。你吃得多，说明他们做的菜好吃，他们就高兴。

　　安娜：这跟我们的习惯太不一样了。

　　夏子：哟，快十点了，我该睡觉去了。以后再谈吧。

问：① 安娜是哪国人？

    a．日本人　b．美国人○　c．中国人

② 中国人吃饭的习惯跟美国人一样吗？

    a．一样　b．差不多　c．不一样○

③ 中国人为什么让客人多吃？

    a．菜很多　b．客人吃得多，他们高兴○

五、听录音，快速回答问题：

（1）你会用筷子吃饭吗？

（2）你的桌子是长方的还是圆的？

（3）你吃饭用盘子吗？

（4）你喜欢喝什么酒？

（5）你觉得米饭好吃还是馒头好吃？

（6）我的习惯是一边吃饭一边喝汤，你呢？

（7）你会做饭吗？

（8）你会做中国菜吗？

（9）你最爱吃中国菜，还是日本菜，还是法国菜？

（10）中国人吃饭的习惯跟你们国家的人一样吗？

第四十一课

一、语音练习：

（1）边听边给下面的绕口令注音：

牛牛要吃河边柳，	Niúniu yào chī hé biān liǔ,
妞妞赶牛牛不走，	Niūniu gǎn niú niú bù zǒu,
妞妞护柳扭牛头，	Niūniu hù liǔ niǔ niútóu,
牛牛扭头瞅妞妞，	Niúniu niǔ tóu chǒu niūniu,
妞妞扭牛牛更拗，	Niūniu niǔ niú niú gèng niù,
牛牛要顶小妞妞，	Niúniu yào dǐng xiǎo niūniu,
妞妞捡起小石头，	Niūniu jiǎnqi xiǎo shítou,
吓得牛牛扭头走。	Xià de niúniu niǔ tóu zǒu.

（2）读上面的绕口令。

（3）听写：

① Tāngmǔ fāxiàn Zhōngguórén jiàn miàn dǎ zhāohu de shíhou hěn shǎo shuō "Nǐ hǎo".

② Zhè ge chāoshì lí xuéxiào jìn, dōngxi yě quán, suǒyǐ wǒ chángcháng lái zhèr mǎi dōngxi.

③ Wǒ hěn xiǎng liǎojiě xiànzài Zhōngguó de qíngkuàng, nín néng bu néng gěi wǒ jièshào jieshao?

④ Tāmen dōu shì wàiguó liúxuéshēng, duì zhèli de qìhou hái bù xíguàn, gǎnmào hé nào dùzi de rén bǐjiào buō.

⑤ Kànwán huàjù cóng jùlèbù chūlai yǐhòu, wǒ qù yóujú jìle fēng xìn, hòulái yòu dào fàndiàn kànle ge péngyou, cái zuò chē huí xuéxiào.

二、用你听到的词语说一句话：

例：从，来──➤他从日本来。

（1）从，出来	（2）从，开始	（3）从，离开
（4）对，喊	（5）对，笑	（6）对，不习惯
（7）给，打电话	（8）给，倒酒	（9）给，翻译
（10）跟，告别	（11）跟，打招呼	（12）跟，约会
（13）向，拐	（14）向，借	（15）向，走

（1）在中国，有些问话不是问问题，是打招呼，不用回答。

　　　问：什么样的问话不用回答？

　　　　　a. 问话　　b. 问题　　c. 打招呼的问话○

（2）晚饭以后，我去操场散步，正好王老师也在散步，他向我介绍了学校的情况。

　　　问：谁介绍了学校的情况？

　　　　　a. 他　　b. 他们　　c. 王老师○

（3）那两个年轻人不是爱人关系，是哥哥和妹妹的关系。

　　　问：那两个年轻人是男的还是女的？

　　　　　a. 都是男的　　b. 一个是男的，一个是女的○　　c. 都是女的

（4）在北京我有几个中国朋友，比如：刘天华、李大年、贾红春等人都是我的好朋友。

　　　问：他有几个好朋友？

　　　　　a. 有三个　　b. 可能有四五个○　　c. 可能十几个

四、听后选择正确答案：

（1）情景：史密斯吃完晚饭回到宿舍，和阿里谈话。

　　　史密斯：刘天华可能想请我吃饭。

　　　阿　里：是吗？

　　　史密斯：我今天吃完晚饭在路上遇见了刘天华，他问我："吃饭了没有？"我要是没吃饭，他会请我去吃饭吧？

　　　阿　里：不一定。

　　　史密斯：为什么？

　　　阿　里：中国人在吃饭的时间见了面说"吃饭了没有"是打招呼，不是真的想知道你吃没吃饭，或者要请你吃饭。

　　　问：刘天华想请史密斯吃饭吗？

　　　　　a. 想　　b. 不一定○

（2）情景：王老师带着儿子小华散步回来，在楼前遇见了刘师傅。

　　　王老师：刘师傅，您吃了没有？

　　　刘师傅：哟，王老师。您刚下班啊？

　　　王老师：不，我们散步去了。小华，叫刘爷爷。

　　　小　华：刘爷爷。

刘师傅：好孩子。小华，跟爸爸散步，吃冰淇淋了没有？

小　华：吃了，还喝了一瓶汽水儿呢。

王老师：小华，八点多了，回家让妈妈给洗洗，准备睡觉吧。

小　华：刘爷爷，再见。

刘师傅：再见。哎，王老师，我那孩子中学快毕业了，可是学习不好，我很着急。您能给他介绍一下学习方法吗？

王老师：可以。可是我觉得最主要的是他得喜欢学习。我发现他下课后常常和一些同学去冷饮店，跟他关系好的几个学生学习都不好。

刘师傅：是吗？我一点儿也不知道。他们一起喝酒吗？

王老师：没听说喝酒。可是他们在那儿常常要坐三四个小时，没时间学习呀！

问：① 他们说话的时候是什么时间？

　　　a. 早上　b. 中午　c. 晚上○

② 你估计王老师的儿子多大了？

　　　a. 是个大孩子，在中学学习　b. 是个小孩子，可能四五岁○

③ 刘师傅的孩子学习怎么样？

　　　a. 他喜欢学习，学习不错　b. 他不喜欢学习，学习不好○

④ 刘师傅的孩子下课以后常常做什么？

　　　a. 跟同学去散步　b. 跟同学去冷饮店○

五、听录音，快速回答问题：

(1) 你从哪儿来的？

(2) 你喜欢散步吗？

(3) 你们学校旁边的汽车站多不多？

(4) 在这个学校你的熟人多不多？

(5) 听说夏子有病回国了，你知道她现在的情况吗？

(6) 今天来学校的路上，你遇见阿里了没有？

(7) 你的衣服自己洗还是送到洗衣店去洗？

(8) 你估计今天晚上会不会下雨？

(9) 你发现中国人的习惯跟你们有什么不一样吗？

(10) 你们国家的人见了面怎么打招呼？

<h1 align="center">第四十二课</h1>

一、语音练习：

　　（1）听后给下面的谚语注音：

　　　　① 鱼好吃，腥难闻。　　　　Yú hǎochī, xīng nánwén.

　　　　② 酒是冬天的火。　　　　Jiǔ shì dōngtiān de huǒ.

　　　　③ 酒吃头杯，茶喝二盏。　　　　Jiǔ chī tóu bēi, chá hē èr zhǎn.

　　　　④ 先尝后买，才知好歹。　　　　Xiān cháng hòu mǎi, cái zhī hǎodǎi.

　　　　⑤ 一菜难合百人口味。　　　　Yí cài nán hé bǎi rén kǒuwèi.

　　（2）听写：

　　Běijīng de xiǎochī hěn yǒumíng, wǒ měi cì dào Běijīng dōu yào qù xiǎochīdiàn chī xiǎochī.

　　Wǒ juéde zuì hǎo de xiǎochīdiàn shì Huímín kāi de xiǎochīdiàn. Huímín xiǎochīdiàn de xiǎochī yòu piányi yòu hǎochī, érqiě zhǒnglèi yě hěn duō. Běijīng Wángfǔjǐng běibianr yǒu ge xiǎochīdiàn hěn yǒumíng, yǐjīng yǒu ěr bǎi duō nián de lìshǐ le. Nín xià cì guàng Wángfǔjǐng guàng lèi le, kěyǐ qù nàr chángchang xiǎochī. Nín yídìng huì mǎnyì de.

二、句重音练习：

　　听下面的句子，标出"过"是轻读还是重读，并标出句重音：

（1）他们过了马路，进了邮局。

（2）我去过那个小吃店。

（3）他还没有做完练习，过一会儿我们再去找他吧。

（4）约会的时间已经过了半个小时了，她还没到。

（5）你下车以后，往东走，过马路，就是首都剧场。

（6）那本书我看过三遍，过一会儿我洗完衣服给你讲讲。

三、听后用"次"或"遍"回答问题：

（1）阿里去过敦煌吗？

（2）约翰看过《中国菜谱》这本书吗？

（3）安娜看过中国杂技没有？

（4）他吃过四川菜没有？

（5）史密斯看过中国电影没有？

（6）昨天的课文录音汤姆听过没有？

四、听句子，听后回答问题：

（1）学校附近的超市很大，东西很多。

　　问：超市离学校远不远？

（2）今天我们去小吃店吃得很满意。

　　问：他们喜欢小吃吗？

（3）我在中国一边教英语一边学汉语，所以又是老师又是学生。

　　问：他在中国做什么？

（4）星期日我们先去颐和园游泳，然后再去香山爬山。

　　问：他们去不去爬山？

（5）玲玲离开北京到广州以后，不常给我写信，所以她的情况我不太清楚。

　　问：他知道不知道玲玲的情况？

五、听后选择正确答案：

（1）情景：汤姆跟李大年在小吃店吃饭。

　　生词：咸　　　xián　　　salty

　　　　　豆腐　dòufu　　bean-curd （老豆腐　lǎodòufu　rare bean-curd）

李大年：汤姆，今天我请客。你要点儿什么？

汤　姆：我没吃过小吃，不知道什么好吃，你要吧。

李大年：好，我去买。你先找地方坐下。

　　　　（过了一会儿，李大年买回来几盘儿小吃）

汤　姆：你买了这么多，吃得了吗？

李大年：不多，才五种。这三盘儿是甜的，另外两盘儿是咸的，你都尝尝。

汤　姆：这种圆的叫什么？真好吃。

李大年：炸糕。这种方的是油饼儿，长的是麻花儿。

汤　姆：这些是什么？

李大年：这是老豆腐，那是杏仁茶。一种是咸的，一种是甜的。怎么样？满意吗？

汤　姆：果然很好吃。这么好吃的东西一定很贵吧？

李大年：不贵，小吃都很便宜。有的几毛钱一个，贵的也只要一两块
　　　　钱，所以北京人很喜欢在小吃店吃早饭。

汤　姆：中国有学习做小吃的学校吗？

李大年：有。你想学习吗？

汤　姆：我明年不去北大学习哲学了，我要学习做小吃，把北京的小
　　　　吃介绍到美国去。美国人一定会欢迎北京小吃的。

问：① 以前汤姆来过小吃店没有？

　　　　a．来过　　b．没来过〇

　　② 李大年买了几种小吃？

　　　　a．两种　　b．五种〇　　c．三种

　　③ 北京人为什么喜欢小吃？

　　　　a．好吃　　b．便宜　　c．又便宜又好吃〇

　　④ 汤姆打算明年学习什么？

　　　　a．哲学　　b．做小吃〇

(2) 情景：史密斯和约翰在宿舍谈话。

史密斯：约翰，在北京，你最爱去什么地方？

约　翰：我最爱去公园，你呢？

史密斯：饭馆儿。北京比较有名的饭馆儿我差不多都去过。

约　翰：北京烤鸭店去过吗？

史密斯：去过，我到北京后第一次去的就是烤鸭店。

约　翰：烤鸭好吃不好吃？

史密斯：太好吃了。我吃了烤鸭才知道为什么好几个国家都开了中国
　　　　烤鸭店。

约　翰：听说北京的小吃也很有特色。

史密斯：可不是。来中国以前，我也常去中国饭馆儿吃饭，可是没看
　　　　见过卖小吃的，所以到了北京，我觉得很新鲜，小吃又便宜
　　　　又好吃。北京人最爱去小吃店吃早饭。每天早上，小吃店里
　　　　的人都很多。

约　翰：我看过一本书叫《北京的小吃》。书上说，有些小吃店已经
　　　　有一二百年的历史了。

史密斯：是啊，琉璃厂西边个地方叫菜市口，菜市口有个小吃店就
　　　　比较有名。这星期日咱们俩去逛琉璃厂，然后去吃小吃，怎

么样？

约　　翰：太好了。以后北京有名的小吃店我都要去尝尝。

问：① 史密斯最爱去什么地方？
　　　a. 公园　　b. 小吃店〇
　② 为什么好几个国家都开中国烤鸭店？
　　　a. 烤鸭又便宜又好吃　　b. 烤鸭好吃〇
　③ 约翰吃过北京小吃没有？
　　　a. 吃过　　b. 没吃过〇
　④ 星期日他们要去哪儿？
　　　a. 琉璃厂　　b. 菜市口　　c. 先去琉璃厂，然后去菜市口〇

六、听录音，快速回答问题：

（1）你吃过小吃没有？
（2）你常去饭馆儿吃饭吗？在饭馆儿吃饭是先交钱开票还是后交钱？
（3）你看过中国电影吗？看过几次？
（4）你们学校的食堂有菜谱吗？
（5）今天老师讲的语法你清楚不清楚？
（6）你们学校附近有没有小吃店？
（7）北京有哪些有名的公园？你去那些公园逛过没有？
（8）昨天的课文录音你听了几遍？
（9）你对食堂的饭菜满意不满意？
（10）你逛过琉璃厂没有？

第四十三课

一、语音练习：

1. 听后给下面的古诗注音：

秋　思	Qiū　Sī

洛阳城里见秋风，　　　　　Luòyáng chéng lǐ jiàn qiū fēng,
欲作家书意万重。　　　　　Yù zuò jiāshū yì wàn chóng.
复恐匆匆说不尽，　　　　　Fù kǒng cōngcōng shuō bú jìn,
行人临发又开封。　　　　　Xíngrén lín fā yòu kāi fēng.

（2）郎读上面的诗。

（3）听写：

　　Shǐmìsī jīntiān yào hé Mǎlì yìqǐ qù Wūlǔmùqí lǚxíng. Tāmen zuò de huǒchē shì zhōngwǔ shí'èr diǎn sìshíwǔ kāi. Xiànzài yǐjīng kuài shíyī diǎn le, kěshì tā hái tǎngzài chuáng shang chōu yān.

　　Shíyī diǎnzhōng Mǎlì lái zhǎo tā, kàndào tā hái méi zhǔbèi hǎo xíngli, hěn zháo jí. "Nǐ bú qù lǚxíng le ma?" Mǎlì wèn. "Qù, liǎng diǎn èrshí de huǒchē, bù zháo jí." "Shénme? Liǎng diǎn èrshí? bú duì, shì shí'èr diǎn sìshí!" Mǎlì hǎn le qǐlai. "Zāogāo, wǒ jìcuò shíjiān le."

　　Mǎlì yìbiān shuō："Kuài, kuài!", yìbiān bāngzhù tā zhuāng dōngxi. Shǐmìsī de dōngxi zhǔnbèi hǎole yǐhòu yǐjīng shíyī diǎn bàn le.

　　Nǐmen cāicai tāmen néng gǎnshang huǒchē ma?

二、用你听到的词语说一句话，并将"着"放在句中：

例：拿，书——＞他手里拿着两本书。

（1）装，衣服
（2）提，旅行袋
（3）吃，葡萄
（4）下，雨
（5）戴，帽子

（6）装，杂志

（7）放，鞋

（8）停，汽车

三、听下面的句子，听后回答问题：

（1）箱子里装着一条毯子和几件衣服。

问：箱子里有什么？

（2）他躺在床上一边抽着烟，一边听音乐。

问：他正在做什么呢？

（3）他的床上放着一些书和杂志。

问：他的床上有什么？

（4）你别在床上躺着了，快起来吧。

问：他现在在哪儿呢？

（5）今天晚上我得复习语法，明天就要考试了。

问：今天晚上他不复习语法，可以吗？

四、听后选择正确答案：

（1）情景：*汤姆在路上遇见了约翰。*

生词：猴子　hóuzi　monkey

故事　gùshi　story

汤姆：约翰，你去哪儿？

约翰：我去小卖部买烟。

汤姆：你这么瘦还抽烟。

约翰：不抽不行啊。我们下星期考试，今天晚上我要准备准备。我有
个习惯，一边抽烟一边看书，才能记住，另外，还想买把牙
刷、一块香皂。

汤姆：你的习惯不好。我有两张京剧票，你看不看？

约翰：京剧？我最爱看京剧。什么京剧？

汤姆：《孙悟空》，就是孙猴子的故事。

约翰：太好了！来中国以前就想看《孙悟空》，一直没看上。现在走
晚不晚？

汤姆：你不复习课文了吗？

约翰：没关系，这个星期日我不出去玩儿，在宿舍复习一天。你等我
一会儿，我还得买胶卷儿，今晚好好照几张。你先回宿舍拿照

相机好吗？

汤姆：不着急。你买完东西我们一块儿去拿吧，还有四十分钟呢。

约翰：几点开演？剧场远不远？

汤姆：七点开演。剧场就在我们宿舍东边儿。

约翰：你说的是学校的礼堂啊！

汤姆：哈哈。

问：① 你估计约翰在小卖部买什么？

　　　 a. 烟　 b. 烟、胶卷○　 c. 京剧票

② 约翰的习惯是什么？

　　　 a. 一边抽烟一边看书○　 b. 看京剧

③ 约翰今天晚上做什么？

　　　 a. 复习课文，准备考试　 b. 看京剧○

④ 他们谈话的时候是几点？

　　　 a. 六点多钟○　 b. 七点

(2) 我发现我的朋友小王这几天走路、坐车、上商店、逛公园的时候，手里都要拿着一本书，真有意思。以前他不这样，现在他爱学习了。昨天我问他，他说："我想做个爱看书的人，我先要有爱拿书的习惯。先当一个爱拿书的人，以后才能当一个爱看书的人。"

问：他发现了什么？

　 a. 他朋友小王是个有意思的人

　 b. 小王走路、坐车、上商店、逛公园都要拿本书○

　 c. 小王是个爱看书的人

(3) 今天街上的人特别多。星期天人们喜欢上街，可是今天不是星期天，为什么街上也有这么多人呢？原来今天是小学、中学开学的日子。街上的学生很多，个个都很高兴。刚上学的小孩子，穿着新衣服，拿着新书包，爸爸妈妈带着他们高兴地往学校走。

问：今天街上为什么人很多？

　 a. 今天是星期天

　 b. 人们喜欢上街

　 c. 小学、中学开学了○

五、听录音，快速回答问题：

　 (1) 北京的冬天冷不冷？去外边儿不穿大衣行不行？

（2）你喜欢旅行吗？你去过哪些国家？

（3）今天上课，你来晚了没有？几点到的？

（4）你抽烟不抽烟？

（5）你书包里装着词典没有？我想看看。

（6）你喜欢戴帽子吗？

（7）你有躺着看书的习惯吗？

（8）你一般早上几点醒？你醒了以后马上起床还是再躺一会儿才起来？

（9）来中国的时候，你带的行李多不多？

（10）谁手里拿着钢笔呢？

第四十四课

一、语音练习：

（1）边听边给下面的绕口令注音：

白石搭白塔，	Bái shí dā bái tǎ,
白塔白石搭，	Bái tǎ bái shí dā,
搭好白石塔，	Dāhǎo bái shí tà,
石塔白又大。	Shí tǎ bái yòu dà.

（2）读上面的绕口令。

（3）听写：

Shǐmìsī hé Mǎlì dàole chēzhàn, lí kāi chē de shíjiān zhǐyǒu wǔ fēnzhōng le.Tāmen cōngmáng de pǎodào yì jié chēxiāng mén qián, bǎ chēpiào jiāogěi lièchēyuán.Lièchēyuán kànle kàn, yòu bǎ piào huángěile tāmen.Yīnwèi tāmen de piào shì yìngwò chēxiāng de piào, zhè jié chēxiāng shì yìngzuò chēxiāng, tāmen shàngcuò le.

二、用你听到的词语说一句话，并将"把"放在句中：

例：车票，交，列车员——→他把车票交给了列车员。

（1）书包，递，我

（2）帽子，挂，衣帽钩

（3）箱子，放，卧铺

（4）胶卷儿，装，旅行袋

（5）书，还，图书馆

（6）牙刷和香皂，装，书包

（7）咖啡，喝

（8）脏衣服，洗

三、听下面的句子，选择与句子意思一致的解释：

（1）史密斯先生说："列车员小姐，我自己来吧。"

史密斯的意思是：

a. 他自己要到这儿来

b. 他自己做，不要列车员帮助○

（2）咱们快跑，马上要开车了。

　　这句话的意思是：

　　a. 快跑，咱们马上要开车

　　b. 我们得快跑，车马上就要开了○

（3）他把旅行袋装在书包里了。

　　这句话的意思是：

　　a. 现在旅行袋在书包里○

　　b. 现在书包在旅行袋里

（4）阿里替夏子背着旅行袋，夏子替阿里提着书包。

　　这句话的意思是：

　　a. 阿里帮助夏子

　　b. 夏子帮助阿里

　　c. 阿里和夏子互相帮助○

（5）那本书我看完以后借给了安娜，安娜看完以后还给高老师了。

　　这本书是：

　　a. 我的　　b. 安娜的　　c. 高老师的○

（6）安娜问："阿里，你把刚买回来的梨放在哪儿了？"

　　a. 在这个时候，安娜在找阿里

　　b. 在这个时候，安娜在找东西○

四、听后回答问题：

（1）情景：玲玲在北京火车站买票。

　　玲　玲：小姐，我买两张十一号去上海的硬卧车票。

　　售票员：你要哪次的？13 次还是 21 次？

　　玲　玲：13 次和 21 次都什么时候到上海？

　　售票员：13 次明天七点四十二分到上海，21 次明天下午四点五十六

　　　　　　分到上海。

　　玲　玲：我坐 21 次的吧，要下铺的。

　　售票员：好，三百四十块钱，请交钱吧。

　　问：① 玲玲坐哪次车去上海？

　　　　② 她到上海的时候是几点？

　　　　③ 去上海的硬卧车下铺票多少钱一张？

（2）情景：刘天华和玲玲刚上了火车，在放行李的时候，列车员来了。

列车员：先生，请您不要把行李放在这儿，这儿要走路的。

刘天华：我们刚上火车很匆忙，我马上就把箱子和旅行袋放到行李架上去。

列车员：箱子太重，放在卧铺下边儿吧。那个大书包是谁的？请不要挂在衣帽钩上。

玲　玲：是我的。

列车员：你把书包递给我，我替你放到行李架上去。

玲　玲：不太重，我自己来吧。

列车员：你们俩喝水吗？

玲　玲：不喝，谢谢。餐车在几号车厢？

列车员：在前面的 8 号车厢，午饭从十一点半到一点，晚饭从五点到七点半。

问：① 他们刚上车的时候，把行李放在哪儿了？

② 后来，他们把箱子放在哪儿了？旅行袋呢？

③ 谁把大书包挂在衣帽钩上了？

④ 他们准备去餐车吃饭吗？

（3）生词：亲王　qīnwáng　prince

女王　nǚwáng　queen

亲爱　qīn'ài　dear

玩具　wánjù　toy

孙儿　sūn'ér　grandson

价值　jiàzhí　value

1877 年 4 月 1 日，英国乔治亲王给他的奶奶维多利亚女王写了一封信，信中写的是：

"亲爱的奶奶：

昨天，我在商店看到一个很好看的玩具。我想买这个玩具，但是我没有钱。您能寄给我一英镑钱吗？

您的孙儿　乔治"

维多利亚女王收到乔治的信以后，写了一封回信：

"亲爱的孩子：

你自己不能随便用钱买玩具，你还不知道各种东西的价值。

你的奶奶　维多利亚"

过了几天，小乔治又给奶奶写了一封回信：

"亲爱的奶奶：

　　我非常感谢您。我把您的信卖给了一家书店，他们给了我两英镑。您看，我已经知道各种东西的价值了。

您的孙儿　乔治"

问：① 乔治为什么给奶奶写信？
　　② 维多利亚女王给乔治钱了没有？
　　③ 乔治的两英镑钱是怎么来的？

五、听录音，快速回答问题：

（1）昨天的练习你交给老师了没有？

（2）你在中国坐过火车没有？

（3）夏子病得很重，你把她背到楼下的车上去好吗？

（4）昨天的练习是你自己做的还是别人替你做的？

（5）你交给老师的本子，老师还给你了没有？

（6）请把你的书递给我看看，好吗？

（7）你们教室的墙上有衣帽钩吗？

（8）安娜和约翰他们俩今天来没来？

（9）你把词典拿来了没有？

（10）下课以后，你帮我把录音机提回去，怎么样？

第四十五课

一、语音练习：

（1）听后给下面的古诗注音：

还自广陵   Huán zì Guǎnglíng

天寒水鸟自相依，   Tiān hán shuǐniǎo zì xiāngyī,

十百为群戏落晖。   Shí bǎi wéi qún xì luòhuī.

过尽行人都不起，   Guòjìn xíngrén dōu bù qǐ,

忽闻水响一齐飞。   Hū wén shuǐ xiǎng yìqí fēi.

（2）朗读上面的诗。

（3）听写：

　　Hěn duō rén xǐhuan hē chá, dànshì hē chá de xíguàn bù yíyàng. Yǒude rén ài hē lǜchá, yǒude rén ài hē huāchá, hái yǒude rén ài hē hóngchá. Ài hē hóngchá de rén, yǒude hái xǐhuan jiā niúnǎi hé táng.

　　Yǒude rén rènwéi huāchá zuì xiāng, yǒude rén rènwéi lǜchá zuì xiāng, yě yǒude rén rènwéi hóngchá zuì xiāng. Rénmen de xíguàn bù yíyàng, xiǎngfǎ yě jiù bù yíyàng le. Yǒu méi yǒu bù xǐhuan hē chá de rén ne? Yǒu, zhè yě shì xíguàn wèntí.

二、用你听到的词语说一句话，并将"着"放在句中：

例：躺，看——→他躺着看书。

（1）坐，谈	（2）提，送
（3）喝，看	（4）吃，听
（5）笑，说	（6）听，洗
（7）抽，写	（8）骑，去

三、听下面的句子，听后选择正确答案：

（1）列车员提着壶送开水来了。

　　问：列车员干什么来了？

　　　　a. 提壶来了　　b. 送开水来了○

（2）他们俩在门口儿站着谈话。

　　问：他们俩在做什么？

　　　　a.在门口儿　　b.站在门口儿　　c.在谈话○

（3）我喜欢喝茶，红茶、绿茶、花茶都喜欢，特别是花茶，非常香。

　　问：他最喜欢喝什么茶？

　　　　a.红茶　　b.绿茶　　c.花茶○

（4）安东先生说："东方人喜欢喝茶，西方人喜欢喝咖啡。可是我不喜欢
　　　喝咖啡，我喜欢喝茶。"

　　问：安东先生是不是中国人？

　　　　a.是　　b.不是○

四、听后选择正确答案：

（1）生词：招待　　zhāodài　　to treat

　　　　　运往　　yùnwǎng　　to transport to

　　　世界上第一个发现茶的国家是中国。喝茶已经是一般中国人的一
种习惯了。客人来了，人们常常用茶来招待。中国地方大，人多，人
们喝茶的习惯也不一样。北方人爱喝花茶，南方人爱喝绿茶，还有的
地方的人爱喝奶茶。奶茶就是在茶水里放上牛奶或者羊奶。

　　　早在一千五百多年以前，中国的茶叶就开始运往国外。很多国家
语言里的"茶"，都是从汉语里的"茶"或者"茶叶"这个音翻译过
去的。日语里的"茶"字是汉字的"茶"。英语中的"茶"这个词，
是从中国厦门人"茶"的音"te"来的。

　　问：① 世界上第一个发现茶的是哪个国家？

　　　　　a.中国○　　b.日本　　c.英国

　　　　② 中国南方人一般爱喝什么茶？

　　　　　a.花茶　　b.绿茶○　　c.奶茶

　　　　③ 英语中的"茶"这个词是从哪种语言来的？

　　　　　a.日语　　b.汉语○

（2）情景：安娜在路上遇见了汤姆。

　　　生词：故事　　gùshi　　story

　　　　　　使　　shǐ　　to cause, to make

　　安娜：汤姆，你晚上去不去看话剧？

　　汤姆：什么话剧？

　　安娜：《茶馆》，写的是几十年以前，在北京一个茶馆儿里发生的各种

故事。这个话剧可以使我们知道很多旧中国的情况和那时候北京人的一些习惯。这是中国很有名的一个话剧。我在德国看过一次。可是那时候我一句汉语也不懂。现在我学了一点儿汉语，我想再去看一次。

汤姆：北京有音乐茶座儿没有？

安娜：我不知道。

汤姆：在茶座儿喝着茶、吃着点心听音乐，那才有意思呢。

安娜：那你去不去看话剧？你要是不去，我就把票送给史密斯了，我只有两张票。

汤姆：去。没有音乐茶座儿，茶馆也可以。

安娜：那你今天晚上可不能又吃点心又喝茶了。

安娜、汤姆：（笑）哈哈……

问：① 安娜晚上去做什么？

    a. 看话剧○ b. 去茶馆儿

② 安娜以前看过《茶馆》没有？

    a. 看过，在北京 b. 看过，在德国○

③ 汤姆晚上去不去看话剧？

    a. 去○ b. 不去

五、听录音，快速回答问题：

（1）你爱看小说吗？

（2）你看过中国小说吗？

（3）你家对面是不是商店？

（4）你去商店的时候，帮我买盒烟好吗？

（5）你喜欢喝什么茶？

（6）你去过茶馆儿吗？

（7）你去过音乐茶座儿吗？

（8）你觉得咖啡香还是茶香？

（9）你会下棋吗？

（10）你的桌子上摆着什么呢？

第四十六课

一、语音练习：

（1）边听边给下面的句子注音：

① 请勿吸烟　　　Qǐng wù xī yān

② 随手关门　　　Suí shǒu guān mén

③ 闲人免进　　　Xiánrén miǎn jìn

④ 小心火车　　　Xiǎoxīn huǒchē

（2）读上面的句子。

二、听写练习：

（1）写句子：

① Nǐ bǎ yīfu kòuzi kòuhǎo.

② Nín bǎ máoyī tuō xiàlai ba.

③ Nǐ bǎ chuāngliánr lākāi.

④ Tā bǎ guǒpí nákāi le.

⑤ Wǒ bǎ màozi zhāi xialai.

（2）听短文，请写下你听到的时间、地点和人名：

　　　李白是中国有名的诗人，他是唐朝人，生在碎叶，长在四川。二十五岁那年，他离开四川去中国各地旅游。他写了很多诗，他的诗，有的是描写景色的，有的是描写人民生活的。李白的诗很有特色，他是中国古代最伟大的诗人之一。

三、听下面的句子，听后回答问题：

（1）阿里给安娜的妈妈打了个电话，告诉她安娜病了。

　　问：谁打电话了？

（2）现在已经七点五分了，史密斯说不定不来了。

　　问：史密斯来不来？

（3）这件毛衣一点儿也不难看。

　　问：这件毛衣好不好？

（4）妹妹担心爸爸没有接到我的信，不来车站接我。

　　问：谁写信了？

四、听后选择正确答案：

（1）情景：一个老大爷在火车上，他快要下车了。

　　生词：收拾　shōushi　to pack up, to collect one's things

　　　　　趟　　tàng　　*a measure word*

　　列车员：老大爷，下一个停车站就是南京。您别下棋了，准备下车吧。您带了这么多东西，下车以后有人接吗？

　　老大爷：有，我已经给儿子打电话了，他和女儿来接我，说不定他们已经在站台等我了。小伙子，咱们别下了。来，把桌子上的果皮收拾一下。

　　小伙子：老大爷，您快收拾自己的东西吧。桌上的果皮我一会儿再收拾。您先把茶叶盒儿装到书包里，别忘了。南京天气暖和，您把毛衣脱了，放在箱子里吧。

　　老大爷：对，对。小伙子，到上海得几点？

　　小伙子：这趟车提前了几分钟，大概九点就能到。您以后到上海，去我家玩儿啊。

　　老大爷：好，好。这一路上没少麻烦你，太谢谢了。

　　小伙子：没什么。衣帽钩上的帽子是您的吧？您戴上吧。

　　列车员：南京到了，有在南京下车的旅客，请带好自己的东西准备下车。

　　老大爷：小伙子，再见了！

　　小伙子：老大爷，我帮您把旅行袋拿下去吧。

　　问：① 老大爷去什么地方？

　　　　　a. 南京〇　　b. 上海

　　　　② 小伙子在哪儿下车？

　　　　　a. 南京　　b. 上海〇

　　　　③ 老大爷下车后有没有人接他？

　　　　　a. 有，他给儿子打电话了〇

　　　　　b. 有，他给女儿打电话了

（2）情景：早上，妈妈叫李大年起床。

　　生词：约　yuē　to make an appointment

　　妈妈：（敲门）大年，醒了没有？大年，该起了！

　　大年：天还没亮呢，我再睡一会儿。

272

妈妈：（进门）快七点了。窗帘儿没拉开，天怎么亮呢？你还去不去
　　　　长城了？（拉开窗帘儿）

大年：（边说边起床）快七点了？糟糕！我和小华约好七点半在汽车
　　　　站见面。妈，您帮我把水果放到我的书包里，再给我装几块蛋
　　　　糕。快，快！

妈妈：带钱了吗？

大年：哟，差点儿忘了。

妈妈：看你，衣服扣子还没扣上呢。

大年：照相机呢？

妈妈：在书包里呢。

大年：好了，好了。妈妈再见！（跑出）

问：① 李大年醒的时候，天亮了没有？
　　　　a.没亮　　b.亮了○
　　② 李大年差点儿忘了带什么？
　　　　a.水果　　b.蛋糕　　c.钱○
　　③ 今天李大年和小华要去哪儿？
　　　　a.汽车站　　b.长城○

五、听录音，快速回答问题：

（1）请你把窗户打开，好吗？

（2）你的房间有窗帘儿吗？是什么颜色的？

（3）晚上你是开着窗户睡觉还是关着窗户睡觉？

（4）你来北京的时候，下了飞机有人接你吗？

（5）上星期你接到朋友给你打的电话了吗？

（6）阿里的头发是黑的还是黄的？

（7）你觉得他穿西服好看吗？

（8）你的宿舍暖和还是阿里的宿舍暖和？

（9）你的宿舍亮不亮？

（10）阿里担心明天下雨。你说会不会下呢？

第四十七课

一、语音练习：

（1）边听边给下面的诗注音：

船	Chuán
套在脚上的	Tào zài jiǎo shang de
是两只无名的小船	Shì liǎng zhī wúmíng de xiǎo chuán
因为我们向往远方	Yīnwèi wǒmen xiàngwǎng yuǎnfāng
就行走在生活的海洋上	jiù xíngzǒu zài shēnghuó de hǎiyáng shang
也许我们到不了对岸	Yěxǔ wǒmen dào bu liǎo duì'àn
但永远朝着一个方向	Dàn yǒngyuǎn cháozhe yí ge fāngxiàng

（2）朗读上面的诗。

（3）听后把下面的句子变成正反疑问句，然后用否定句回答：

① 他听得懂普通话。

② 我看得见台上的表演。

③ 我写得完这几张明信片。

④ 我找得到浴室，我知道浴室在哪儿。

⑤ 这些练习他做得完。

二、听写练习：

（1）听写句子：

① Nà ge xiǎonánháir kòu de shàng yīfu kòuzi.

② Lǎodàniáng pá de shàng nà zuò shān.

③ Wǒ zǎoshang wǔ diǎn qǐ de lái.

④ Xiànzài qù mǎi de dào wòpùpiào.

⑤ Zhèxiē jiǔ tā hē de wán.

（2）听下面的短文，边听边记下你听到的时间、地点、人名和数字：

在中国甘肃省武都县石门乡石门村，有个姑娘叫司凤英，她今年十五岁，身高一米八七，体重八十公斤，要穿四十五号的鞋。她每天能吃二三斤米饭。医生给她检查了身体，认为她身体很好，可以长到两米多。现在她正在学习打篮球。她的老师说，三五年以后，她可能成为一个很好的篮球运动员。

（1）我听不懂上海话，请你说普通话吧。

问：他听得懂听不懂汉语？

（2）广告很有意思，可是有的广告上的话不都是真的。

问：他喜欢不喜欢看广告？

（3）我听不懂上海话，可是我觉得上海话很好听。

问：他觉得上海话怎么样？

（4）这些明信片一个小时写不完。

问：明信片多不多？

（5）贸易公司在火车站旁边儿，我找得到。

问：他能找到贸易公司吗？

四、听后选择正确答案：

（1）情景：阿里和汤姆在谈一条广告。

生词：健壮　jiànzhuàng　robust

永远　yǒngyuǎn　forever，always

像　xiàng　to be like

阿里：汤姆，你看报呢？

汤姆：刚下课吗？我在看《北京晚报》。你看这条广告多有意思：小儿健美酥，小孩儿吃了以后可以长得又健壮又好看。

阿里：是吗？我要是小孩儿就好了。

汤姆：你现在也可以吃呀。这上边还说，大人吃了对身体也很好，可以永远不老。

阿里：真的吗？什么地方卖？

汤姆：大华贸易公司。你真想买吗？

阿里：不想买，我个子不矮，可是朋友们都说我长得像小孩子，要是吃了小儿健美酥，就永远不像大人了。

问：① 小儿健美酥只有小孩儿可以吃吗？

a．是的　　b．大人也可以吃○

② 阿里买不买小儿健美酥？为什么？

a．买，因为他想永远年轻

　　　　b. 不买，因为他想长得像大人〇

（2）情景：阿里和汤姆谈晚上去看戏的事。
　　　　生词：节目　jiémù　program，performance
　　　　　　　剧团　jùtuán　theatrical troupe
　　阿里：《北京晚报》上有没有杂技或者京剧的广告？
　　汤姆：有，咱们晚上去看戏怎么样？
　　阿里：太好了，我也正想去看一场呢。咱们看什么？京剧还是杂技？
　　汤姆：我看看什么节目好。……哎，这儿有上海话剧团的表演。
　　阿里：不看，他们说上海话，我听不懂。咱们看京剧吧。京剧的音乐
　　　　　很好听，服装也很好看。
　　汤姆：好吧，咱们去看京剧。不过，上海话剧团的表演说的也是普通
　　　　　话，他们来北京说上海话，别人听不懂。
　　阿里：那我也不想看。
　问：① 晚上他们去看什么？
　　　　a. 话剧　b. 京剧〇　c. 杂技
　　　② 上海话剧团在北京表演说上海话、北京话，还是普通话？
　　　　a. 上海话　b. 北京话　c. 普通话〇

（3）情景：约翰给东方旅馆九楼服务台打电话。（电话铃响）
　　约　翰：喂，你是东方旅馆九楼服务台吗？
　　服务员：是啊。您有什么事吗？
　　约　翰：我找史密斯先生。请问，他是住 9203 房间吗？我刚才给
　　　　　　9203 房间打电话没人接。
　　服务员：没错儿，可能他现在不在房间。我刚才看见他下楼了，大概
　　　　　　去餐厅了。您可以把电话打到餐厅。
　　约　翰：麻烦你了。
　　服务员：没什么。
　问：史密斯先生现在住在哪儿？
　　　a. 东方餐厅　b. 9203 房间〇　c. 9320 房间

五、听录音，快速回答问题：

　（1）你喜欢看报纸上的广告吗？
　（2）你们宿舍的浴室在不在房间里？
　（3）你常常用明信片写信吗？
　（4）你听得懂听不懂上海话？

276

（5）北京话跟普通话一样吗？

（6）你爱看杂技吗？

（7）我的耳朵不好，听不见外边的谈话声，你呢？

（8）你妈妈喜欢小男孩儿还是小女孩儿？

（9）昨天晚上你看杂技表演了吗？他们表演得太好了。

（10）下课铃响了没有？

第四十八课

一、语音练习：

（1）边听边给下面的句子注音：

① 三人同行，必有我师。　　Sān rén tóng xíng, bì yǒu wǒ shī.

② 活到老，学到老。　　　　Huódào lǎo, xuédào lǎo.

③ 经一事，长一智。　　　　Jīng yí shì, zhǎng yí zhì.

④ 只要改，不怕晚。　　　　Zhǐyào gǎi, bú pà wǎn.

（2）读上面的句子。

二、听写练习：

（1）听写句子：

① Nà ge xiǎohuǒzi pá de shàng qù.

② Nà ge háizi chū bu lái.

③ Tā wǔ diǎn yǐqián huíde lái.

④ Wǒ bān bu qǐ lái nà ge xiāngzi.

⑤ Jīntiān de lùyīn wǒ dōu tīng de dǒng.

（2）听下面的短文，边听边记下你听到的时间、地点、人名和数字：

　　　　1985 年 12 月 10 日下午北京开了一个健康老人会。参加这次老人会的有 29 人。他们中最年轻的 80 岁，最老的 102 岁。女的有 3 人，男的有 26 人。有一位老教师，叫殷寿明，今年 85 岁了。他说："我四十多岁的时候，身体不好，常常有病，工作也做不了。后来我学习打拳，天天锻炼，身体就好了。"说着，他摘下帽子又对大家说："你们看，我现在头上又长出了黑头发。"

三、听下面的句子，听后选择正确答案：

（1）老大娘进来的时候，小孙子正躺在床上看书呢。

　　问：谁看书呢？

　　　　a. 老大娘　　b. 小孙子○

（2）你应该少吃肉、多喝茶，不然就胖得上不去二层楼了。

　　　问：现在胖不胖？

　　　　　a. 很胖○　　b. 不胖

(3) 既然小伙子不需要别人的帮助，我们就走吧。

　　　问：他们愿意帮助小伙子吗？

　　　　　a. 原意○　　b. 不愿意

(4) 郑教授以前住在广州，1953年到了上海，所以他上海话也说得不错。

　　　问：郑教授现在住在哪儿？

　　　　　a. 广州　　b. 上海○

(5) 老大娘高兴地说："太感谢你了，今天要不是你爬上楼把门打开，说不定我就进不去家了。小伙子，不要客气，今天在我这儿吃饭吧。"

　　　问：老大娘为什么请小伙子吃饭？

　　　　　a. 感谢小伙子帮她把门打开了○

　　　　　b. 她今天很高兴

四、听后回答问题：

(1) 情景：一个女青年在回家的路上看到一个小姑娘正在哭，就走过去。

　　　生词：风　　　　　fēng　　　　　wind

　　　　　　危险　　　wēixiǎn　　　　dangerous

　　　　　　技术员　　jìshùyuán　　　technician

女青年：小妹妹，别哭，你怎么了？

行人甲：她的钥匙锁在屋里，进不去家了。

行人乙：小姑娘，别哭了，我们大家帮助你。你家住几层？

小姑娘：（边哭边说）五层。

行人乙：哟，这么高呢！你们哪个小伙子爬得上去？

行人甲：五层呢，多高啊！今天的风又很大，太危险了。这怎么办哪？

行人丙：没关系，我爬得上去，我是爬山运动员。

女青年：也许不需要爬楼。我去看看你家的锁，好吗？

小姑娘：我家的锁跟一层的锁一样，门一关，就锁上了。

女青年：是这种锁啊。有办法，我打得开。小妹妹，不哭了。走，我给你开门去。

行人丙：你没有钥匙也能把门开开？你行吗？

女青年：这样的事情对我是很容易的。你不相信就跟我上去看看。

甲、乙：你是……？

女青年：我是锁厂的技术员。

问：① 小姑娘为什么哭？

　　② 谁能爬上五层楼？

　　③ 谁不用爬楼也能把屋里的钥匙拿出来？

（2）生词：小偷　xiǎotōu　pick-pocket

　　　　　打鼾　dǎ hān　to snore

　　　　　沙发　shāfā　sofa

　　早上六点半，我醒了，忽然发现另一张床上没有人，毯子和枕头也不见了。哎呀，和我一起住的这个人是个小偷，真没想到。

　　我是昨天晚上住进这家旅馆的。我进房间的时候，他正在看书。他看了我一眼，没说话，只点了点头，打了个招呼。

　　我最爱逛街，吃过晚饭就去逛街了。回到房间看见他已经躺在床上睡着了。这个人的样子我也没有看清楚，他既然是小偷，就不可能只偷毯子和枕头。我打开手提包看我的东西。果然，钱包没有了。钱包里有一千多块钱呢！我着急了，马上拿起衣服，一边穿一边往外走。忽然一个东西掉在了地上，我一看是钱包。我不知道怎么办好了。这个小偷为什么只偷毯子和枕头呢？

　　正在这个时候，门外传来了服务员和一个人说话的声音。接着，一个人抱着毯子和枕头走进来。"你？你去哪儿了？""你打鼾的声音太大，我就去外边的沙发上睡了一夜。"

　　听了他的话，我一句话也说不出来了。

问：① 谁偷了旅馆的毯子和枕头？

　　② 他的钱包找到了没有？

　　③ 谁去外边睡了一夜？他为什么不在房间里睡觉？

五、听录音，快速回答问题：

（1）电视里正在演什么呢？

（2）你爱看什么节目？话剧、京剧、杂技还是电视剧？

（3）你的记忆力怎么样？学了的生词都记得住吗？

（4）你离开宿舍的时候锁门了吗？没有钥匙你开得开门吗？

（5）你想，很小的小孩儿每天哭两三次好不好？

（6）你住的楼房一共是几层？你的房间在几层？

（7）那个小朋友一定遇到了急事，不然不会哭，你说是不是？

（8）今天的语法你听得懂吗？需要不需要老师再给你讲一遍？

（9）今天下午我们一起骑自行车去公园，大家同意吗？

（10）你们上午的课几点结束？

第四十九课

一、语音练习：

（1）边听边给下面的绕口令注音：

大嫂子和大小子　　　　　　Dàsǎozi hé Dàxiǎozi

一个大嫂子，　　　　　　　　Yí ge dàsǎozi，

一个大小子，　　　　　　　　Yí ge dàxiǎozi，

大嫂子跟大小子比包饺子：　　Dàsǎozi gēn dàxiǎozi bǐ bāo jiǎozi：

不知是大嫂子包的饺子不如大小子，Bù zhī shì dàsǎozi bāo de jiǎozi

　　　　　　　　　　　　　　　bùrú dàxiǎozi，

还是大小子包的饺子不如大嫂子，　Háishì dàxiǎozi bāo de jiǎozi

　　　　　　　　　　　　　　　bùrú dàsǎozi.

（2）读上面的绕口令。

（3）听后把两句话合成比较句（一句用"比"，一句用"没有"）：

　　例：上海饭馆儿多。北京饭馆儿不太多。

　　　　——→上海饭馆儿比北京多。

　　　　　　北京饭馆儿没有上海那么多。

① 乌鲁木齐不热闹。广州很热闹。

② 北京的名胜古迹多。上海的名胜古迹不多。

③ 花茶香，很好喝。绿茶不香，不好喝。

④ 这件黄色的衣服样子好看。那件红色的衣服便宜。

⑤ 这个小房间很干净。那个大房间有点儿脏。

二、听写练习：

边听边记下数字和地点：

　　北京是一座有两千多年历史的城市，作为首都，北京也有八百多年的历史了。所以，北京的名胜古迹很多。在城里有故宫、北海、景山、天坛、地坛、日坛、月坛等十九处；在城外有颐和园、圆明园、香山、长城、十三陵等十来处。另外还有一些自然风景很优美的地方，比如八大处、樱桃沟和上房山等。

(1) 上海有一千三百多万人，天津有九百多万人，北京有一千一百多万人。

问：哪个城市的人口最少？

(2) 北京小公园不多，可是漂亮的大公园很多。

问：北京的大公园多还是小公园多？

(3) 南京的公园、名胜古迹没有北京多，公园也不如北京漂亮。

问：哪个城市的公园又多又漂亮？

(4) 史密斯说："上海的街道不如北京这么宽，公园也没有北京这么漂亮，只是饭馆儿比北京多。"

问：史密斯对上海的印象好，还是对北京的印象好？

(5) 上海的弄堂多、窄，北京的胡同也不少、也不宽嘛。我看上海和北京差不多。

问：他觉得上海好还是北京好？

四、听后选择正确答案：

(1) 情景：甲从外地来北京住在旅馆，乙在一个学校工作，今天约好，来
　　　　　陪他游览。

生词：游览　yóulǎn　　to go sightseeing

　　　打算　dǎsuan　　to plan

甲：你怎么现在才来？我都急了。

乙：刚出宿舍楼碰上个老师找我有急事，不然早到了。从学校到这儿，坐车只用了十分钟。你今天打算去哪儿逛逛？

甲：听说北海是北京城里最漂亮的公园，去北海怎么样？

乙：好啊。逛了北海还可以去景山，看完景山再去故宫。昨天你去颐和园和香山了吗？

甲：去了。爬上香山可真累啊，今天腿还有点儿疼呢。你说，我在这儿一个星期，北京的名胜古迹逛得完吗？

乙：一个星期？一个月你也不一定逛得完。我在北京三十多年了，还有许多地方没去过呢。

甲：在北京我怎么没看见大工厂啊？

乙：城里只有小工厂，大工厂都在郊区，这样城里的建筑、街道可以整洁一些。

甲：北京的街道比咱们那个城市干净。好了，咱们一边走一边谈吧。

乙：走吧。

甲：等我锁上门。

乙：别忘了把钥匙交到服务台去。

问：① 这两个说话人是北京人吗？

　　　a. 是　b. 不是○　c. 一个是，一个不是

　　② 他们都在北京工作吗？

　　　a 对了　b. 都不在北京工作

　　　c. 一个在北京工作，一个在外地工作○

　　③ 用多长时间才能逛得完北京的名胜古迹？

　　　a. 一个星期　b. 一个月

　　　c. 三十年　　d.abc 都不对○

(2)　情景：约翰刚从中国南方参观回来，李大年去看他。

　　生词：……极了　……jíle　extremely

　　　　　无锡　Wúxī　Wuxi, *a city in Jiangsu Province*

　　　　　风景　fēngjǐng　landscape

李大年：约翰，这次去南方玩得怎么样？

约　翰：有意思极了。我去了几个城市，参观了不少名胜古迹。给我印象最深的是无锡。无锡城里有许多河，河不宽，但可以走船，人们去什么地方常常坐船去，很方便。城里的商店和北京也不一样。那儿的商店一般都不大，后边是工厂，前边是商店，后边儿生产了东西，在前边儿卖。

李大年：你发现没有？南方的茶馆儿比北京多得多。很多人特别喜欢去茶馆儿喝茶。

约　翰：是的，茶馆儿多，饭馆儿多，我觉得这些地方都比北京好。另外，南方的自然风景非常美。大年，你是上海人吧？上海这几年是不是增加了不少大饭店？我看到好几座十几层高的新建筑。

李大年：是啊，有些是饭店，有些是贸易公司。

问：① 约翰觉得哪个城市最有意思？

　　　a. 北京　b. 无锡○　c. 上海

　　② 南方的什么比北京多？

　　　a. 名胜古迹　b. 茶馆儿○　c. 大饭店

　　③ 什么地方的人特别喜欢去茶馆儿喝茶？

　　　a. 无锡　b. 上海　c. 南方○

五、听录音，快速回答问题：

  （1）北京有多少人口，你知道吗？

  （2）你们住的地方有什么名胜古迹吗？

  （3）你觉得是小孩子爱穿漂亮的衣服还是大人爱穿漂亮的衣服？

  （4）你们国家的名城是哪个城市？那是个商业城市吗？

  （5）中国的黄河长还是长江长？

  （6）你知道北京郊区有哪些大学吗？

  （7）你觉得汉语比英语好学吗？

  （8）今天和昨天比，你学到的词增加了多少？

  （9）生产被子和服装的工厂叫什么工厂？

  （10）请你用汉语谈谈对中国的印象好吗？

第 五 十 课

一、语音练习：

（1）边听边给下面的谚语、格言注音：

① 白日莫闲过，青春不再来。　Báirì mò xián guò, qīngchūn bú zài lái.

② 书到用时方恨少。　　　　　Shū dào yòng shí fāng hèn shǎo.

③ 室雅何须大，花香不在多。　Shì yǎ hé xū dà, huā xiāng bú zài duō.

④ 穿衣戴帽，各人所好。　　　Chuān yī dài mào, gè rén suǒ hào.

（2）读上面的谚语、格言。

（3）边听边记，然后说出主要意思：

下面是《北京晚报》上的一条消息：

这几天北京市的市长去公共汽车、电车公司跟司机、售票员和公司的领导谈了话。市长说，北京每天坐汽车、电车的有九百万人次。这几天北京天气冷，气温低，有的时候还刮风，这你们都不怕，你们工作也很累，我感谢你们。另外，他还说，七日那天因为天气特别冷，一些汽车开不出去，给北京的人民带来了麻烦。公司的领导对低气温应该有准备。你们知道不知道天气预报？我们没做好工作，对不起人民。以后这样的情况不应该再发生。

二、把下面的句子改成比较句：

（1）今天晚上北京最低气温是零下一摄氏度，上海是五摄氏度。

（2）明天北京的最高气温是四摄氏度，广州是十二摄氏度。

（3）阿里要穿 45 号鞋，约翰要穿 42 号鞋。

（4）史密斯身高 2 米，夏子身高 1 米 65。

（5）橘子两块钱左右一斤，苹果一块多钱一斤。

三、听下面的句子，边听边填表：

（1）汽水儿一块钱一瓶，啤酒两块——一瓶。啤酒比汽水儿贵一块一毛钱。

汽水一瓶	啤酒一瓶	啤酒比汽水贵
（一块钱）	（两块一）	（一块一）

(2) 上海有一千三百万人口，北京有一千一百万人口，北京比上海少二百万。

上海人口	北京人口	北京人口比上海少
（一千三百万）	（一千一百万）	（二百万）

(3) 今天最高气温十五摄氏度，最低气温四摄氏度，风力二三级。

最高气温	最低气温	风力
（15 摄氏度）	（4 摄氏度）	（二三级）

(4) 今天晚上最低气温零下九摄氏度，明天白天最高气温一摄氏度，风力四五级。

最低气温	最高气温	风力
（零下 9 摄氏度）	（1 摄氏度）	（四五级）

(5) 中国长江长六千三百公里，黄河长五千四百六十四公里，长江比黄河长八百三十六公里。

长江长	黄河长	长江比黄河长
（6300 公里）	（5464 公里）	（836 公里）

四、听后回答问题：

(1) 情景：甲请乙介绍北京的天气。

甲：你给我介绍介绍北京的气候怎么样？

乙：北京的冬天很冷很长，还常常刮风。

甲：是吗？春天呢？

乙：春天很少下雨，差不多每天刮风，但是不像冬天那么干燥。夏天好一点儿，七八月还常常下雨，下了雨天气就凉快一些，另外也很湿润。

甲：你的意思是夏天最好，对吧？

乙：不，夏天比较热，最高气温三十多度的天气很多。最好的是秋天，不冷不热。来北京旅游还是在秋天好。

问：① 北京的冬天怎么样？

　　② 北京什么时候常常下雨？

　　③ 来北京旅游什么时候最好？

(2) 情景：天华的哥哥要去日本工作，走以前，天华和嫂子商量全家一起
　　　　去逛公园。

　　生词：转　　　zhuǎn　　　　to turn

　　　　　风向　　fēngxiàng　　wind direction

嫂子：天华，你哥哥他们银行派他到驻日本办事处工作两三年。

天华：是吗？什么时候走？

嫂子：可能下星期。

天华：嫂子，您也去吗？

嫂子：我今年公司里还有一些重要的工作没做完，明年才能去。

天华：你们走了，爸爸妈妈恐怕会天天想你们的。

嫂子：那就需要你常和爸爸妈妈多谈谈话了。

天华：其实谈也没用，反正他们会想的。

嫂子：明天是星期日，咱们全家人去香山玩儿一天，你同意吗？秋天
　　　的香山最漂亮了。

天华：那好啊。今天下了一天雨，明天天气不知道好不好？

嫂子：咱们看看天气预报吧。快七点半了，快把电视机打开。

　　　（他们看电视：今天夜间阴转晴，风向北风，风力四五级，最
　　　低气温 9 摄氏度。明天白天晴，风向北风，风力二三级转一二
　　　级，最高气温 21 摄氏度）

天华：太好了。明天咱们去吧。我去准备准备。

嫂子：别忘了多带点儿葡萄。妈妈和你哥哥最爱吃葡萄了。

问：① 谁要去日本？什么时候走？

　　② 天华的哥哥在哪儿工作？

　　③ 天华的嫂子在哪儿工作？

　　④ 明天天气怎么样？他们去不去香山公园？

　　⑤ 天华看完天气预报去做什么？

五、听录音，快速回答问题：

　　（1）昨天晚上你看天气预报了吗？

（2）这个城市的气候怎么样？

（3）你来这儿以后，给家里人打长途电话了吗？

（4）昨天刮风了吗？

（5）你估计今天最低气温有多少度？

（6）你估计今天最高气温有多少度？

（7）北京的天气干燥还是上海干燥？

（8）上海的天气湿润还是北京湿润？

（9）你估计今天的风力有几级？

（10）你喜欢冬天还是夏天？为什么？

（11）你的意见跟他的一样吗？

第五十一课

一、语音练习：

（1）边听边给下面的诗注音：

和童年留影对话	Hé Tóngnián Liúyǐng Duìhuà
"你真是我吗？"	"Nǐ zhēn shì wǒ ma?"
你用天真的笑回答了我。	Nǐ yòng tiānzhēn de xiào huídá le wǒ.
"你真是我吗？"	"Nǐ zhēn shì wǒ ma?"
回答不出。	Huídá bù chū.
因为我在寻找那颗失落	Yīnwei wǒ zài xúnzhǎo nà kē shīluò de
的童心。	tóngxīn.
明天——相信我能回答：	Míngtiān——xiāngxìn wǒ néng huídá：
"我就是你！"	"Wǒ jiù shì nǐ!"

（2）朗读上面的诗。

（3）听后把两个句子变成一个带"比"的句子：

　　例：我买了两块香皂。

　　　　他买了一块香皂。

　　　　——我比他多买了一块香皂。

① 这件羽绒服二百六十七块。

　　那件羽绒服二百七十二块。

② 山田差一刻九点到的飞机场。

　　夏子差五分九点到的飞机场。

③ 飞机平时十点起飞。

　　飞机今天十点二十起飞。

④ 阿里今天穿了一件毛衣。

　　史密斯今天没穿毛衣。

⑤ 昨天的最高温度是二摄氏度。

　　今天的最高温度是零下一摄氏度。

二、边听边记下与下面问题有关的句子：

（1）爸爸和女儿在做什么？

（2）女儿为什么哭了？

（3）爸爸看到女儿哭了，说了什么话？

十二月二十一日电视台开始播《黑猫警长》，女儿坐在椅子上看得很高兴。可是播了十分钟，忽然停了。女儿急得哭了起来。我忙说："别着急，电视台的叔叔阿姨一会儿就播。"果然，不到一分钟，又开始播《黑猫警长》了。

过了五分钟，又停了。我又用老办法对女儿说了一遍。可是过了一分钟，播出的不是《黑猫警长》，是一个公司的咖啡广告。女儿一看是广告，又哭了："爸爸，我要黑猫警长，不喝咖啡。"我没办法了，只好告诉女儿："黑猫警长找坏蛋找了半天，又累又渴，所以要喝点了咖啡了。"

三、听下面的句子，听后回答问题：

（1）我平时六点半起床，今天是星期日，多睡了一个钟头。

问：他今天几点起的？

（2）我要在中国学习四年，比阿里多学两年。

问：阿里在中国学习几年？

（3）其实绿茶比花茶更香更好喝。

问：他觉得什么茶好？

（4）飞机从东京飞北京，起飞的时候正在下大雪，降落的时候天气真好。

问：北京正在下雪吗？

（5）下雪的时候不太冷，化雪的时候才冷呢。

问：什么时候更冷？

四、听后选择正确答案：

（1）情景：山田在公共汽车上碰见了安娜。

山田：哎，安娜，你去哪儿？

安娜：我去北京饭店办点儿事。你呢？

山田：咱俩同路，我们公司驻北京的代表明天回国，我去看看他。

安娜：你们公司不是在长城饭店吗？

山田：长城饭店太贵，一个房间一个月要两万多块钱呢！

问：① 山田去哪儿？
　　　a.长城饭店　b.北京饭店〇
　　② 山田他们公司的办事处现在在哪儿？
　　　a.长城饭店　b.北京饭店〇

(2) 情景：玲玲要去飞机场接人，可是下大雨了。
　　生词：班　　　　　bān　　　　flight
　　　　　雷阵雨　léizhènyǔ　thunder shower

夏子：玲玲，你今天怎么起得这么早？

玲玲：我要去机场接哥哥嫂子，我侄子也跟他们一起来。

夏子：这班飞机几点到？

玲玲：广州起飞时间是六点，到北京大概是九点多。糟糕！昨天天气
　　　预报说今天有大雨。

夏子：你听，正下呢。你拉开窗帘看看！

玲玲：下得真大呀！飞机可能不能降落了。

夏子：下雨没关系吧。你快给飞机场打个电话问问。

玲玲：对。

　　　（玲玲打电话）
　　　喂，首都机场吗？飞机今天能降落吗？……什么？有雷阵雨？
　　　不能降落？那，那广州来的飞机什么时候能到呢？……好，麻
　　　烦您了。谢谢。

夏子：情况怎么样？

玲玲：他们说，要等雷阵雨过去，飞机才能降落。

夏子：那雷阵雨什么时候才能过去呢？

玲玲：天知道！

夏子：别着急，我估计下午就不下了。等雨一停，马上给机场打电话
　　　再问问。哎，你看，现在雨比刚才小多了。说不定一会儿就不
　　　下了。

玲玲：可是，还有雷阵雨呢。

夏子：打电话听听天气预报。

　　　（玲玲打电话听天气预报）

夏子：怎么样？

玲玲：上午雷阵雨，下午转晴。我马上打电话要出租车。
　　　吃了午饭就走。

夏子：急什么！你听，雷阵雨来了。

问：① 平时这班飞机几点到北京？
　　　a．六点多　b．九点多○
　　② 玲玲什么时候去机场？
　　　a．上午　b．下午○

五、听录音，快速回答问题：
　　（1）你们住的城市常常下雨吗？
　　（2）你觉得北京热还是你们国家的首都热？
　　（3）你觉得秋天好还是春天好？你更喜欢哪个季节？
　　（4）你坐过飞机吗？托运行李麻烦不麻烦？
　　（5）北京首都机场大厅里有小卖部吗？
　　（6）请问，去上海的飞机几点起飞？
　　（7）你觉得是大飞机飞得稳，还是小飞机飞得稳？
　　（8）今天早上你碰见张先生了吗？
　　（9）你平时常看见张先生吗？
　　（10）他是张文的叔叔，张文是他的什么人？

第五十二课

一、语音练习：

（1）边听边给下面的绕口令注音：

华华有两朵黄花儿，	Huáhua yǒu liǎng duǒ huánghuār,
红红有两朵红花儿。	Hónghong yǒu liǎng duǒ hónghuār.
华华要红花儿，	Huáhua yào hónghuār,
红红要黄花儿。	Hónghong yào huánghuār.
华华送给红红一朵黄花儿，	Huáhua sònggěi Hónghong yì duǒ huánghuār,
红红送给华华一朵红花儿，	Hónghong sònggěi Huáhua yì duǒ hóng huār,
华华有黄花儿和红花儿，	Huáhua yǒu huánghuār hé hónghuār,
红红有红花儿和黄花儿。	Hónghong yǒu hónghuār hé huánghuār.
两个笑得脸上像朵花儿。	Liǎng ge xiào de liǎn shangxiàng duǒ huār.

（2）读上面的绕口令。

（3）听后口头回答问题：

① 阿里学得比史密斯好。

问：谁学得好？

② 约翰汉语说得比安娜流利。

问：谁汉语说得流利？

③ 山田汉字写得比汤姆快得多。

问：谁汉字写得快？

④ 夏子车开得比山田稳一点儿。

问：谁车开得稳？

⑤ 约翰平时起得比阿里晚多了。

问：谁平时起得早？

二、边听边记，听后回答下面的问题：

大家都知道洗澡对身体很好，常常洗澡不容易得病。是不是越多越好呢？也不是。比如在气候干燥的地方，洗澡太多你会觉得不舒服。

另外，有些人刚吃过饭马上就去洗澡，这样也不好。这样容易得胃病。冬天很多老年人喜欢洗热水澡，但要注意，水的温度不要太高，洗澡时间不要太长。

（1）每天洗澡好不好？

（2）什么时候洗澡好？

三、听下面的句子，听后回答问题：

（1）阿里笔试得了九十一分，口试得了八十一分。史密斯笔试得了九十二分，口试得了八十二分。

问：谁的学习更好一点儿？

（2）安娜听写一分钟能写 17 个汉字，夏子一分钟能写 21 个汉字。

问：谁汉字写得更快一些？

（3）冬天最好的体育运动是滑冰和长跑，每天下午操场都有很多人在练习长跑，我想跟他们一起锻炼。

问：他想练习滑冰吗？

（4）以前，很多中国人都爱听相声，特别是侯宝林先生的相声，大人、小孩儿都喜欢听。

问：以前中国人最爱听谁说相声？

（5）现在我的胃病更厉害了，不敢总喝白酒了。

问：他现在还喝白酒吗？

四、听后选择正确答案：

（1）情景：张正生老师和同学们讨论汉语节目表演的问题。

张老师：同学们，这个学期就要结束了，考试以前，我们开个晚会怎么样？

众　　人：好！（鼓掌）

安　　娜：上次约翰和史密斯的相声说得不错。这次你们俩再来一段怎
　　　　　么样？

山　　田：这次比上次会更好。

汤　　姆：不见得。

史密斯：为什么？

汤　　姆：史密斯，这几天你的胃病比以前更厉害了，一顿饭吃不了一
　　　　　个馒头。身体这么不好，能表演好节目吗？

山　　田：可是他骑自行车、滑冰、游泳都比我们快得多啊！

众　　人：是啊，是啊。

约　　翰：汤姆，你表演什么节目？

汤　　姆：我跳舞。

夏　　子：跳舞不行。跳舞不说汉语。

汤　　姆：我一边跳舞，一边用汉语唱歌。

夏　　子：那可以。

史密斯：夏子，你表演什么节目？

夏　　子：山田，咱们俩用汉语唱两个日本歌好不好？

山　　田：我嗓子不好，你一个人唱吧。

张老师：安娜，你呢？

安　　娜：我先想想，明天告诉您。

张老师：大家回去再想想，这回的晚会一定要更好、更热闹、更有意
　　　　　思。

问：① 在他们的晚会上唱英文歌可以吗？

　　　a. 可以

　　　b. 不行，每个节目都要说汉语○

　　　c. 唱英文歌可以，别的不行

　　② 史密斯这次还能表演相声吗？

　　　a. 不能，他得了胃病

　　　b. 他身体很好，可以说相声

　　　c. 虽然他有胃病，但是还可以说相声○

　　③ 谁又能唱歌又能跳舞？

　　　a. 汤姆○　　b. 山田　　c. 夏子

（2）情景：夏子和安娜谈考试的成绩。

　　生词：困难　kùnnan　difficult

夏子：安娜，你这次考试怎么样？

安娜：笔试得了八十九分，口试得了八十四分。夏子，你呢？

夏子：我比你差，口试才得了七十九分。你平时就比我说得流利嘛！

安娜：可你的笔试比我强多了。

夏子：我是日本人，写汉字不困难。

安娜：我觉得听写特别困难。汉字总记不住。

夏子：我们日本人从小学就开始练习写汉字了，只是发音和中文不一样。哎，张老师编了一本《汉字字典》可以帮助学生练习汉字，你可以买一本。

安娜：真的？一会儿我就去买一本，放假以后好好练习练习。

问：① 夏子口试得了多少分？

　　　a. 八十九分　 b. 八十四分　 c. 七十九分○

　　② 安娜觉得写汉字怎么样？

　　　a. 不困难　 b. 比夏子强多了

　　　c. 她觉得很困难○

五、听录音，快速回答问题：

（1）你早上锻炼身体吗？

（2）你会不会滑冰？

（3）你平时一天吃两顿饭还是三顿饭？

（4）你敢不敢在长江里游泳？

（5）你喜欢读小说吗？你最喜欢读谁的小说？

（6）你喜欢听相声吗？

（7）上回考试你得了多少分？

（8）你们班谁汉语说得最流利？

（9）你们这个学期什么时候结束？

（10）他说话常常讽刺别人，你觉得好不好？

第五十三课

一、语音练习：

（1）边听边给下面的古诗注音：

杂　诗

君自故乡来，

应知故乡事。

来日绮窗前，

寒梅着花未？

Záshī

Jūn zì gùxiāng lái,

Yīng zhī gùxiāng shì.

Lái rì qǐchuāng qián,

Hánméi zhuó huā wèi?

（2）朗读上面的诗。

（3）根据问题，标出答句的重音：

① 你觉得昨天晚会上的节目怎么样？

　　——昨天的表演比上次强得<u>多</u>。

② 今天史密斯又来晚了吗？

　　——没有，他比平时早到了<u>十分钟</u>呢！

③ 广州的冬天也这么冷吗？

　　——不，比这儿暖和<u>多</u>了。

④ 你们<u>都</u>去过长城吗？

　　——不，除了<u>约翰和安娜</u>以外，我们<u>都</u>没去过。

⑤ 寒假你<u>只</u>去四川旅行吗？

　　——不，除了四川以外，我还想去<u>乌鲁木齐</u>看看。

二、听写练习：

边听边记下每个节日的名称和时间：

中国的节日很多，有传统节日，也有政治性节日。一月一号是元旦，三月八号是妇女节，五月一号是劳动节，五月四号是青年节，六月一号是儿童节，九月十号是教师节，十月一号是国庆节。农历正月初一是春节，正月十五是元宵节，五月初五是端午节，八月十五是中秋节。

三、听下面的句子，听后回答问题：

（1）李大年除了爱听相声以外，还爱听音乐。

　　　　问：李大年爱听什么？

（2）高开除了喜欢画画儿以外，别的都不喜欢。
　　　　问：高开喜欢画画儿吗？

（3）玲玲除了不吃羊肉以外，别的肉都吃。
　　　　问：玲玲吃不吃羊肉？

（4）除了阿里以外，山田和夏子也没去过长城。
　　　　问：阿里去过长城吗？

（5）那个商店除了卖点心、水果什么的以外，还卖本子、铅笔、钢笔等学
　　　习用的东西。
　　　　问：那个商店卖什么？

四、听后填空：

（1）情景：中国学生贾红春和日本学生夏子谈节日。
　　　生词：除夕　chúxī　New Year's Eve
　　　　　　亲戚　qīnqi　relative
　　　夏　子：红春，中国最重要的传统节日是什么？
　　　贾红春：是春节，在农历的正月初一。正月就是农历一月，初一就是
　　　　　　　一号。
　　　夏　子：一定很热闹吧？
　　　贾红春：可不是，人们都很重视它。为了让大家过好春节，学校都在
　　　　　　　春节以前开始放寒假。机关，工厂也要放一个星期假。每家
　　　　　　　都买很多过节吃的、用的东西。
　　　夏　子：听说过节时商店里的东西比较贵啊。
　　　贾红春：中国人过春节不怕花钱。初一早上吃过饭，人们就去亲戚和
　　　　　　　朋友家，互相祝贺春节。哎，你们日本人也过春节吗？
　　　夏　子：很早以前也有春节，现在没有了。现在我们过元旦，像你们
　　　　　　　的春节一样，也很热闹。

　　　填空：① 中国的春节在农历一月一号。
　　　　　　② 初一早上人们吃过早饭就去亲戚朋友家互相祝贺春节。
　　　　　　③ 日本人现在不过春节，只过元旦。

（2）情景：大年在书店买书的时候遇见了约翰。
　　　生词：画册　huàcè　picture album
　　　　　　毛笔　máobǐ　Chinese brush for writing Chinese Characters
　　　大年：哎，约翰，你也买书来了？

298

约翰：我刚进来。你都买什么书了？

大年：买了一本《汉英语法比较》。你有这本书吗？

约翰：没有，我能看懂吗？

大年：今年看不懂，明年看嘛。除了这本以外，你还可以买一本《古代汉语》，这本书不太好买。

约翰：在哪儿卖？我早就想买一套，可是一直没买到。

大年：就在那边儿，我跟你一块儿去。

约翰：我有一个朋友，很喜欢中国画儿。圣诞节快到了，我想买本中国画册送给他。你能给我介绍几种吗？

大年：我刚才看到一本《徐悲鸿画册》，你可以去看看。

约翰：徐悲鸿是谁？

大年：徐悲鸿是中国有名的画家。他的画儿大部分是用毛笔画的中国画儿，特别是他画的马更是有名。有一座徐悲鸿先生纪念馆，他的画儿大部分都在那儿展览。有时间你可以去参观参观。

约翰：那我就买一本《徐悲鸿画册》吧。

大年：你看那张贺年片儿上的马就是徐悲鸿画的。我要买几张送给朋友。

约翰：我也买几张。这张菊花的也不错，简直像真花儿一样。

大年：我听说外国人送菊花是道歉的意思，是吗？

约翰：那是在法国。在我们国家跟你们一样，也是高尚品格的象征。

填空：① 约翰买了三本书，一本是《汉英语法比较》，一本是《古代汉语》，一本是《徐悲鸿画册》。另外，他还买了两种贺年片儿，一种是马，一种是菊花。
　　　② 大年除了买书以外，还买了贺年片儿。

五、听录音，快速回答问题：

（1）你们国家过新年热闹吗？

（2）新年以前，你给朋友送贺年片儿吗？

（3）你们国家最重要的传统节日是什么？

（4）你们国家最重要的纪念日是什么？

（5）你知道圣诞节在哪一天吗？

（6）中国的国庆节在哪一天？

（7）中国的传统节日，除了春节以外还有哪几个？

（8）你看见过用毛笔画的中国画儿吗？你喜欢不喜欢？

（9）你们国家最有名的诗人是谁？

（10）你们国家最有名的画家是谁？你喜欢他的画儿吗？

第五十四课

一、语音练习：

（1）边听边给下面的词语注音：

①	整整齐齐	zhěngzheng qíqí
②	百花齐放	bǎi huā qí fàng
③	艺术剧院	yìshù jùyuàn
④	乘风破浪	chéng fēng pò làng
⑤	先进技术	xiānjìn jìshù
⑥	为人民服务	wèi rénmín fúwù
⑦	千奇百怪	qiānqí bǎiguài
⑧	九九八十一	jiǔ jiǔ bāshíyī

（2）听写：

① Zhōngshān Gōngyuán zhèngzài jǔxíng júhuā zhǎniǎn, měi tiān cānguān de rén duō jí le.

② Wǒmen màoyì gōngsī zhù Běijīng bànshìchù de dàibiǎo hé tā de fūren jīntiān xiàwǔ chéng fēijī huí guó, wǒ yào qù jīchǎng gěi tāmen sòngxíng.

③ Qīngdǎo de gǔjì bù duō, kěshì chéngshì hěn piàoliang, zìrán jǐngsè yě hěn měi, gěi wǒ liúxià le shēnkè de yìnxiàng.

④ Guòle yíhuìr, xuě guǒrán tíng le.Xiàwǔ tàiyang chūlai le.Wǒ zhàn zài lóudǐng shang kànzhe yuǎnchù báisè de shān hé jìnchù de shù jiù xiàng shēnghuó zài huà zhōng yíyàng.

二、听后把下面的"被"字句改成"把"字句：

例：菜被兔子吃掉了。——→兔子把菜吃掉了。

（1）我被您说糊涂了。

（2）兔子被狗咬死了。

（3）照相机被他放在旅行袋里了。

（4）那杯茶被阿里喝了。

（5）大箱子被约翰放在柜子上面了。

三、听下面的句子，听后选择正确答案：

    (1) 冬冬的爸爸被妈妈的话说糊涂了。

        问：谁糊涂了？

            a. 冬冬　　b. 爸爸○　　c. 妈妈

    (2) 约翰从图书馆借了一本书，后来又被夏子借走了，昨天才被还回图书馆。

        问：书现在在哪里？

            a. 在约翰那儿　　b. 在图书馆○　　c. 在夏子那儿

    (3) 妈妈走进屋里看了看，说："冬冬，你要的书虽然找到了，但书架上其他的书却被你摆乱了，爸爸回来一定会不高兴的。"

        问：爸爸怎么了？

            a. 找到书了　　b. 把书摆乱了　　c. 生气了　　d. abc 都不对○

    (4) 要是他先把狗带过去，菜就会被兔子吃掉，要是先把菜带过去，兔子就会被狗吃掉。

        问：应该先把什么带过去？

            a. 狗　　b. 菜　　c. 兔子○

    (5) 冬冬也跟爸爸上街了，现在，家里只有奶奶一个人。

        问：他们家有几口人？

            a. 一口　　b. 两口　　c. 三口　　d. abc 都不对○

四、听后做练习：

情景：课间，安娜向高老师问一些关于中国人过春节的问题。

生词：除夕　chúxī　　New Year's Eve

      聊天　liáo tiān　to have a chat

      拜年　bài nián　to pay a New Year visit

      庆祝　qìngzhù　to celebrate

      活动　huódòng　activity

安　娜：高老师，您说过春节是中国最重要的传统节日。您能讲讲中国人怎么过春节吗？

高老师：中国地方很大，每个地方的习惯都不太一样。北京人一般是这样的：人们在春节前一个多星期开始做过节的准备，买年货。

安　娜：什么叫年货？

高老师：年货就是过新年、过春节用的和吃的东西，比如肉、菜、酒、

点心什么的。春节前一天叫除夕，也叫年三十。这一天晚上很多
人不睡觉，全家人在一起聊天儿、看电视……人们一边玩儿，一
边包饺子。到了半夜十二点，人们互相祝贺春节好。这时候最热
闹。初一早上吃过饺子，人们就去亲戚和朋友家拜年，或者去参
加各种庆祝活动。

安　　娜：哎，高老师，我有个问题一直想问您。春节的时候，天气还很
　　　　　冷，为什么叫春天的节日呢？您过去不是说过北京的春天是从
　　　　　三月到五月吗？

高老师：你的记忆力还真不错啊。这个问题比较复杂。今天算了，快上
　　　　　课了，我以后再跟你说好吗？

安　　娜：好吧。

（1）填空：

　　① 春节前一天叫除夕，也叫年三十。到了半夜十二点，人们互相祝
　　　　贺春节好。这时候最热闹。

　　② 北京的春天是从三月到五月。

（2）选择正确答案：

　　① 中国人过春节的习惯一样不一样？为什么？
　　　　a. 一样，因为每个地方的人都过春节
　　　　b. 不一样，因为有的地方不过春节
　　　　c. 不一样，因为中国地方很大，每个地方的习惯不一样〇

　　② 人们什么时候开始准备年货？
　　　　a. 除夕晚上　　　b. 年三十
　　　　c. 春节前　　　　d. 春节前一个多星期〇

　　③ 安娜什么问题一直不清楚？
　　　　a. 什么叫年货
　　　　b. 中国的农历新年为什么叫春节〇

五、听故事，回答问题：

　　生词：斧子　fǔzi　axe

　　　下面我要给大家讲一个故事，你们听的时候，请注意两个问题。一
个问题是阿二的斧子是不是被人偷走了。另外一个问题是阿二和他爱人
谁糊涂，谁不糊涂。听完了，我让你们回答问题。好，下面我就开始讲
故事，请你们注意听。

302

　　从前有个人叫阿二。一天，他发现自己的斧子不见了。他到处找，里屋、外屋，屋里、屋外都找了，可是还没找到。他忽然想起邻居家的阿强昨天来过他家，他想，斧子会不会被阿强偷走了呢？

　　第二天，他在街上碰见了阿强。阿强没有像平时那样先跟他打招呼。他们打完招呼以后，阿强匆匆忙忙地进城了。阿二觉得阿强说话的声音比平时小，走得也比平时快得多。阿二一边想一边往家走。在门口儿遇见了阿强的爱人。阿强的爱人只向他点了点头，却没有说话。他更觉得是阿强把他的斧子偷走了。他一进屋就对爱人说："我知道斧子被谁偷走了。一定是阿强。""你怎么知道的？"他爱人笑着问："今天我在街上遇见了阿强，刚才在门口儿又看见了他爱人，他们的样子和平时都不一样，……"

　　阿二的话还没有讲完，他爱人就说："你别说了。你真是个糊涂人。上次你用完斧子放在柜子下边儿了。刚才我还用过呢。"

　　"我昨天到处找斧子，你为什么不告诉我？"

　　"你只说找斧子，却没有说找柜子下边儿的斧子呀！"

　　阿二想了想，觉得爱人说得对，忙道歉说："下次我再找东西的时候，一定告诉你我找的东西在什么地方。"

　　他爱人也客气地说："算了，不要说了。下次斧子要是真的找不到，我一定告诉你到柜子下边儿去找。我的记忆力比你强得多呀！"

问：（1）阿二想他的斧子被谁偷走了？

　　　（2）阿二的斧子是怎么找到的？

　　　（3）阿二和他爱人谁糊涂，谁不糊涂？

六、听录音，快速回答问题：

（1）你去买菜的时候，用不用带篮子？为什么？

（2）你吃过饺子没有？

（3）你会做饺子不会？

（4）你打篮球的时候，会不会抢球？

（5）你每天打扫屋子吗？

（6）你们的教室脏不脏？该不该打扫？

（7）我很喜欢听故事，你能不能给我讲一个？

（8）那本书我忘了被谁借走了，你还记得吗？

（9）你喜欢狗吗？你家有没有狗？

（10）那个小孩儿怎么哭了，是不是被狗吓的？

第五十五课

一、语音练习：

边听边给下面的词语注音：

① 玻璃制品		bōli zhìpǐn
② 长途电话		chángtú diànhuà
③ 蔬菜商店		shūcài shāngdiàn
④ 长跑运动员		chángpǎo yùndòngyuán
⑤ 糊里糊涂		húlihútū
⑥ 急急忙忙		jíjimángmáng
⑦ 精神焕发		jīngshén huànfā
⑧ 八仙过海，各显其能。		Bāxiān guò hǎi, gè xiǎn qí néng.

二、听写：

(1) Shàng jié kè lǎoshī gěi tóngxué men jiǎngle yí ge gùshi. zhè ge gùshi hěn yǒu yìsi, dàjiā dōu hěn ài tīng.

(2) Xiǎzǐ gāng cóng shūdiàn mǎi huílai yì běn shū, jiù ràng Yuēhàn jièzǒu le, zuì hòu zhè běn shū jiào Yuēhàn nòngdiū le, Xiàzǐ hěn bù gāo xìng.

(3) Jiào biéren cháoxiào, zìjǐ de xīnqíng huì bèi nòng de hěn huài, suǒyǐ wǒmen zuì hǎo yě bú yào cháoxiào biéren.

(4) Tā kāi chē sùdù tài kuài, xīn mǎi de qìchē chàdiǎnr jiào tā zhuàng huài le.

三、听下面的句子，听后选择正确解释：

(1) 他坐在地上，衣服叫水弄湿了。

这句话的意思是：

a. 他把衣服弄湿了

b. 水把地弄湿了

c. 水把他的衣服弄湿了○

（2）屋里贴的画儿让风刮下来了。

    问：什么被刮下来了？

        a. 花儿　b. 画儿〇　c. 屋子的墙

（3）刘天华被学校派到美国去学习英语了，回来后要去外国工作。

    问：刘天华去做什么了？

        a. 去美国学习英语〇

        b. 去英国学习英语

        c. 去外国工作

（4）为了记住汉字，阿里要求自己把每天学习的新字写十遍。

    从这句话里，我们可以知道：

    a. 阿里很不聪明

    b. 阿里学习很努力〇

    c. 阿里记忆力好

（5）我的朋友刚借给我一辆车，就叫我给撞坏了。

    从这句话里，我们可以知道：

    a. 我被车撞了　b. 我把朋友撞了　c. 车被撞坏了〇

四、听后做练习：

下面你听到的故事，讲的是孩子做错了事，家长应该不应该打他。

生词：家长　jiāzhǎng　parent or guardian of a child

    警察　jǐngchá　police（man）

    藏　　cáng　　hide

    文章　wénzhāng　article

    一天夜里，警察老张走到了公园。他忽然发现一把长椅上睡着一个小孩儿，脸上还盖着帽子。老张叫了好一会儿才把那个小孩儿叫醒。小孩儿一看是警察，就想跑。老张说："别跑！"老张脱下自己的大衣给他穿上，坐在他的旁边儿。

    "你为什么不回家？"老张问。

    "我不敢回家。"小孩儿小声儿地回答。

    "为什么不敢回家呢？"

    "怕爸爸打我。"

    "你爸爸为什么要打你？"

    "我，我……"

    事情是这样的。

这个小孩儿叫刘华，因为学习不好，爸爸常常打他。后来，他觉得学习没意思，就常常不去学校上课，和一些大孩子去偷东西。两天以后，他偷东西的事叫爸爸知道了，又被爸爸打了一顿，打完后又被锁在屋里，不让他出门。

昨天上午爸爸和妈妈去公司了，他就在纸条儿上写了："爸爸、妈妈，我对不起你们。再见了。"他把纸条儿贴在爸爸的屋子外边儿，就从窗户跳出来了。

以前，他和别人偷了钱，就藏在公园里。他想去公园拿一点儿钱，路上他遇见了两个大孩子。这两个大孩子听说他去拿钱，就跟他一起去了。拿出钱，大孩子只给了他十块钱，还说，要是他不同意，就打他。他用十块钱又喝汽水儿又吃冰淇淋，很快就用完了。到了晚上，他想，要是回家又得叫爸爸打一顿。他不敢回家，就在公园的椅子上睡着了。

警察老张遇到这种事情已经有好几次了。有的爸爸、妈妈因为孩子学习不好打孩子，有的因为孩子丢了东西打孩子，有的因为孩子弄脏了衣服打孩子。孩子怕爸爸、妈妈打，就不敢回家。孩子离家出走，犯了错误，或者发生了危险，他们才着急，才知道自己的办法不好。

上星期，老张给报纸写了一篇文章。他在文章里说："有些家长常常打孩子。其实这种办法很不好。我希望聪明的家长不要再做这种糊涂事了。"

（1）选择正确答案：

① 老张叫了好一会儿才把那个孩子叫醒。

  这句话的意思是：

  a. 老张叫得好，孩子醒了

  b. 老张叫了两声，孩子醒了

  c. 老张叫了很长时间，才把孩子叫醒○

② 小孩儿一看是警察，就想跑。

  这句话的意思是：

  a. 小孩儿看见是警察，想和警察一起跑

  b. 小孩儿怕警察，看见了警察就想快点儿跑开○

  c. 小孩儿看见就跑了

③ 小孩儿不敢回家，因为：

  a. 他偷了东西

  b. 他学习不好

  c. 他怕爸爸打他○

④ 警察老张遇到这种事情已经有好几次了。
   这句话的意思是：
   a. 警察老张遇到过好几个孩子，都是被家长打出来的○
   b. 警察老张多次在公园遇到这个孩子
   c. 警察老张已经遇到过这个小孩儿很多次了

（2）回答下面的问题：
   ① 故事中的小朋友叫什么名字？
   ② 这个小孩子为什么睡在公园的椅子上？
   ③ 有些家长为什么打孩子？
   ④ 孩子做错了事，家长就打他，这样的办法好不好？
   ⑤ 警察老张为什么给报纸写文章？

五、听录音，快速回答问题：

（1）那天你的鞋是被谁弄脏的？
（2）今天没有太阳又没风，你的湿衣服能干吗？
（3）你今天的心情怎么样？
（4）你会开汽车吗？你自己有没有车？
（5）你睡觉喜欢盖被子还是喜欢盖毯子？
（6）你家里有狗吗？是什么颜色的？
（7）你往你家寄一封航空信，要贴多少钱的邮票？
（8）你的朋友中最聪明的是谁？
（9）你叫人嘲笑过吗？我们应不应该嘲笑别人？
（10）你的老师要求你们每天练习汉字吗？